Half an Hour A Day
Across Massachusetts

Other Books authored or coauthored by

John J. Galluzzo

Images of America: Hull and Nantasket Beach
Then and Now: Hull and Nantasket Beach
Images of America: Scituate
Then and Now: Scituate
The Scituate Lighthouse Guidebook
Beauty, Strength, Speed: Celebrating 100 Years of
Thomas W. Lawson's Dreamwold
Images of America: Rockland
Abington in Vintage Postcards
Images of America: Squantum and South Weymouth Naval Air Stations
Rockland in Vintage Postcards
When Hull Freezes Over
The Golden Age of Hull
A Day in the Life of Hull: You Don't Have to Catch Fish to Go Fishin'
Images of America: Marshfield
Crime, Corruption and Politics in Hull
The North River: Scenic Waterway of the South Shore
Lifesavers of the South Shore
Images of America: New Jersey Coast Guard and Rumrunners
The Coast Guard
Images of America: Mass Audubon
Boston Harbor in Vintage Postcards
Images of America: Isles of Shoals
They Had to Go Out: True Stories of America's Coastal Life-Savers from the Pages
of Wreck & Rescue Journal (editor)
Images of America: Monhegan Island
Breaking 100: Valley Country Club's First Century of
Good Times and Good Friends
Half an Hour a Day on Foot: An Obsessive Exploration of the Nature
of the South Shore of Boston
Half an Hour a Day on Foot: Stepping Out of Bounds
Images of America: Camp Edwards and Otis Airbase
The A. W. Perry Company: 125 Years of Excellence
Images of America: The Coast Guard in Massachusetts
Images of America: Millville Army Air Field
Rescue: True Stories of the United States Life-Saving Service

Half an Hour a Day
Across Massachusetts

Finding Open Space in All 351 Cities in Towns of the Bay State

To Ross —
Enjoy!
John Galluzzo
2012

John J. Galluzzo

Dedicated to my sons, Anthony and Ben.
Join me on the trails when you can.

Table of Contents

Introduction

I can't quite say why I do the things I do. There's probably some underlying anger or fear or self-loathing or insecurity that drives me to push myself the way I do. I have a desire to *do* things, not just to talk about them. Life is way too short to say "wouldn't it be cool to climb Everest" and then not do it.

When I was a kid, my mother repeatedly told me I was special. Confused, I would ask the obvious question. "Why?" But she would just kiss me on the head and say, "You just are," and I would put my feet back up on the coffee table, sip my juice box and go back to watching Hulk Hogan pound the hell out of the Iron Sheik. I never carried the question beyond that initial phase.

I think, then, that as I get older, I'm reopening the inquiry. What really is it that makes me special, or at least different from others around me? And what if - heaven forbid - it's not true? What if I'm just your run-of-the-mill ordinary average John? Does that make my mother a liar? Or have I somehow failed her and her prophecy? Sure, I could recite a list of accomplishments I've made to this point in my life, but that would just be an exercise in extracurricular egocentrism.

And so, it came down to this: I needed proof. I wanted to do something I had never done before, something that, in fact, no one had ever done before. In 2009, I took a half hour nature walk in a different place every day for a full year (save for those five lost days in October when pneumonia laid me out). In 2011, I vowed to take things 351 steps further. I would walk Massachusetts. Not east to west, not north to south, but the whole damn thing, thirty minutes in each town, and I would do so in wildlife sanctuaries, state parks, even cemeteries if they were my only option.

I had to. My mother's honor had to be defended.

Then, I looked at the map.

January

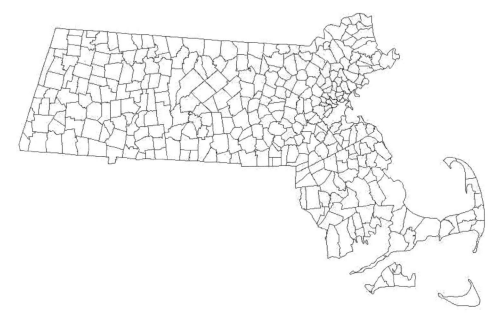

(Gulp!)

January 1

1. Dighton: Bristol County Agricultural High School

I can't say that it was my dream location for the first walk of the New Year. As the sun rose, I and six friends, some old, some brand new, found ourselves standing in a freshly manured field in Dighton.

Dighton? Manure? *Really?*

When I conceived of this project, I foresaw myself on New Year's Day standing in, oh, say Plymouth, where the Pilgrims came ashore in 1620, or better yet, on the outer Cape, where they first set foot in the New World. But the Taunton Christmas Bird Count called, and my New Year's Day walks were in the hands of the count coordinator, my friend Jim, and not mine.

He couldn't steer me wrong. Bristol Aggie is all fields and shrubs, right on the Taunton River. It abuts an extremely important archaeological site in Sweet's Knoll, a place where studies in that science have unearthed 41 features from our Native American forbears on the land, most of them hearths, not to mention a plethora of ancient tools. The place has spirit. Today it had snow. And manure. And birds.

A snow goose flew among 200 Canada geese. The manure held treasures, one flock of American pipits and another of horned larks. An out-of-season gray catbird popped up in a thicket.

Dighton? Manure? New Year's Day?

Why not?

2. Taunton: Boyden Wildlife Sanctuary

The Christmas Bird Count rolled on through thickets and fields, along streams and into the woods.

At some time during the morning - CBCs have a way of getting lost in time - we visited the home of the Taunton River Watershed Association, the Boyden Wildlife Sanctuary. As far as the count went, the place was productive. Any time you find a fox sparrow in Massachusetts in the dead of winter, it's been a good day.

Unfortunately, the trail system was currently broken. Erosion had eaten away at the path alongside the river, recently, officially and deservedly listed as "wild and scenic," limiting the walking possibilities on the sanctuary. But no worries, we found a pine forest trail to traverse.

For the most part, it was silent, and with the snow cover left over from the blizzard of December 26, 2010, it was equally as beautiful. When a bird called out, or a squirrel squawked, it sounded perfectly as nature intended, without the backdrop of a climbing airplane or a braking 18-wheeler.

I'm not religious, even in the slightest, but I could see there and then how nature can heal the soul.

3. Somerset: Broad Cove

Just over the Dighton line in Somerset is a small parking area, perfect for viewing the Taunton River. Behind that parking lot is a wide-spreading brackish cove, visible from a short walking trail that comes to an abrupt drop-off.

Hmm. Never been here before, but if I had to guess, I'd say "old railroad bed, missing bridge." And I'd be right.

The Taunton Christmas Bird Count, or at least our little section of it, rolled into its third town of the morning. We walked along the trail to find a sleeping ruddy duck, a chirping swamp sparrow, and a few other birds that would help us tally 53 species by noon on the first day of the year. It struck me that of the 300 or so species of birds I will see in Massachusetts in 2011, I saw more than one-sixth during the first twelve hours of the year. That leaves me 364 1/2 days and 348 towns to find the other 250.

Piece of cake, right?

For the second time in 2011, and I was entirely certain not the last, I found myself lost inside my own mind. My inner time machine brought me back to an age of trains and factories, when silver was king in this part of the Bay State, when the river was a highway of industry. My first inward trip took place in front of the remains of a tree at Pokanoket Park in Dighton a few hours earlier, the oak under which King Philip, or Metacomet, held council meetings in the 17th century. To say that I could see them would be stupid. I saw the representation, the interpretation my mind could produce.

I'm sure I was way off, but I'd be lying if I said I cared.

January 3

4. Abington: Ames Nowell State Park

There's nothing like the sound of an ice drill first thing in the morning.

It seems that every time I walk Ames-Nowell in the winter, the ice fishermen are here. Today there were only two. In the past it's been as many as ten. They build small campfires on the shoreline, drill their holes, set their rigs and wait. It's a cold pastime, but seemingly worth it.

As for my walk, well, do you remember Bugs Bunny's *The Rabbit of Seville*? When he has Elmer Fudd in the barber's chair, and hits him with the razor ("How about a nice close shave? Teach those whiskers to behave...")? Fudd's next lines are "Ow, ooh, ow, ooh, ooh!" That's what walking here was like today.

The snowing-melting-refreezing cycle had left deep ruts in the snow, thanks to off-road vehicles using the trails. Every step was a fight for balance, and at the very least gave me a great workout. I couldn't wait to find some flat terrain. And at that time of the day, the natural world was just waking up.

5. Whitman: Hobart Pond

Ah, flat, even pavement. Now that's what I'm talkin' 'bout.

I have no idea what purpose Hobart's Pond served, or who Hobart was, but I can guess. Whitman was a mecca of industry in the nineteenth century, split apart from Abington as its own community in a fight over town finances in 1875. The pond is formed from the pooled water from the damming of the Shumatuscacant River, which winds its way up north into Abington. Any time rivers or streams were dammed on the South Shore of Boston, it meant either industry or drinking water. The nearby shoe factories, no doubt, used the water for one or both.

As for Hobart himself, my guess is he was the first to dam the river for mill purposes. The story is the same all over New England. But don't take my word for it. Check with the Whitman Historical Society or the Historical Society of Old Abington. They'd know.

The pond was frozen today, as was much of the region, as we braced for yet another storm the coming weekend. But along the edges, where birch and cedar trees mingled, small birds dove back and forth across Colebrook Boulevard. The "boulevard" was closed at one end by a gate, the other, for the time being, by a huge mountain of plowed snow. To the south, the Colebrook Cemetery rested in quietude.

The song sparrows, white-throated sparrows and a half dozen other species, though, chattered away this morning, following me on my walk as if my pockets were full of seeds.

As if...

January 4

6. East Bridgewater: Central Street Cemetery

From the first glance at the road atlas I keep in my car, East Bridgewater was going to be a tough one. There just was not a lot of green showing up on the map. In times like this, I revert to one simple tactic. Find the nearest cemetery.

Old cemeteries - not old, *old* cemeteries - were designed as walking places for the living, and they remain some of our best public open spaces today. Ancient cemeteries - by American standards - were stark, angular, direct places. The Romantic era added hills and dells, and an explosion in the types of headstones one might choose with which to adorn his or her final resting place.

All that said, I parked near a local church and set out on a beeline for the stones. And wouldn't you know it, the very first stone I approached had a story that spoke as loudly as any marker in any burial ground. A *Titanic* victim.

Are you kidding me?

4

The snow here was packed more thickly than anywhere else I'd walked so far. Rather than posthole digging - plunging into the snow and extracting my foot with every step - I instead found myself walking, ever so tentatively, on the surface of the snow. Only under the various copses of trees did I crash through. In one of those places I found a real oddity I'd like to know more about, a man born in 1804 decorated as a veteran of the War of 1812.

So many stories, so little time...

7. Bridgewater: Carver Pond

Okay, a little back story. During the summer of 2010, while working on the Massachusetts' Breeding Bird Atlas 2 project, I offered to coordinate a "blockbust" of this section of the Bridgewaters. My boss, Joan, joined me and my coworker Matt for the day. We split up to maximize our sightings in the time allotted and she came back with stories of a great little walking area called Carver Pond. Although my road atlas did not show it as green, I took the chance today and searched for it. Sure enough, it came as advertised.

Carver Pond is one of those places where you can't imagine how, in the heart of all the noise of daily life, an oasis like this one can be so quiet. I mean, the heart of the town was *right over there*. Why couldn't I hear it?

What I could hear were the crows. American crows have a habit of ganging up on birds of prey and exposing their resting spaces. It's a pretty bold thing, to perch on a branch a few feet away from a known killer and scream in its face. I've heard hundreds of crows outing hawks and owls, though, and I've never seen the latter lash out. Usually they tune them out; sometimes they fly away as the crows dive and strike at them. I looked over my shoulder to find the source of the noise and could see everything but the targeted bird. Then, the call came...red-shouldered hawk. Figures. This place was crawling with them during the Breeding Bird Atlas safe dates in 2010.

That was a new sighting for the year, as was the hairy woodpecker that chirped loudly as I watched the show. A thicket a few feet down the trail looked so good that I had to take a pish. By mimicking the sounds of distressed chickadees, an art form known as "pishing," I drummed up nuthatches, chickadees, titmice, tree sparrows, juncos, song sparrows, goldfinches, cardinals, a Carolina wren and yet another new species for 2011, a hermit thrush.

I had no idea where I'd be in spring, but I hoped I'd get the chance to come back to this beautiful place and catch it in its glory.

8. West Bridgewater: West Bridgewater State Forest

So, so quiet. After all my walking this morning through conservation areas plugged tightly into urban surroundings, I finally found some real open space, a huge pond surrounded by dense woods. But there was no life. No birds sang, no squirrels scurried away at my approach. I walked in silence for thirty full minutes. It was almost ghostly, I tell you.

The trails were enough to give my right knee hell. I don't know what I've done to it, but it started into some serious aching, and not just at certain times of day. I hoped that like most things in life, it'd pass. I'm sure walking these trails today, deeply rutted by off road vehicles, I did it no favors.

The trails here also undulate, making for a lot of pooling, a lot of frozen puddles. Up a rise, down around a frozen puddle, up a rise, down around a frozen puddle. It made it hard to concentrate on the beauty that surrounded me. I did, though, get my first two thorn bites today, as a stalk lashed out at my left hand as I dodged some shaky-looking ice.

The sting of the piercing thorns was like a christening. Welcome to another year of walking the great state of Massachusetts.

January 6

9. Scituate: The Spit

I decided to let the South Shore fall in place as it would for this project. Let's face it. There were many destinations I'd have to travel long distances to get to, and the South Shore is my backyard. Moreover, I was scheduled to walk in many of the local towns on numerous occasions in 2011. Today was a perfect example.

I'm a SEANETter (among many, many other things). That means that twice per month I walk the same beach route and look for dead seabirds, reporting back to Tufts with any information I may turn up. In my case that means the Spit, off Third Cliff in Scituate, and to date it's meant one pair of least tern wings. That changed today.

But before I made this day's discovery, I noticed other changes. The December 26, 2010, storm continued to hang over us on the South Shore. Scituate was particularly battered. Houses burned, residents evacuated. Here on the Spit, the sea encroached upon the dunes by more than 100 feet, tossing cobble up onto the grasses. A breakthrough at the western end of the little sandy peninsula created a gully where once there was a hill. The wrack line was, well, it was sometimes so far back into the dunes I couldn't find it with the naked eye. What a mess.

Of course, it didn't mean much at that moment. The horned larks and the northern harrier seemed happy. But come spring when the piping plovers and least terns return to nest here, that would be when we'd see how these changes would affect those endangered species.

As for today, my big discovery was the remains of an American black duck, a pair of wings and a breastbone. Five walks so far as a SEANETTER, two dead birds. Well, it's all for science.

January 8

10a. Marshfield: Daniel Webster Wildlife Sanctuary

Okay, sub-goal time: I planned on walking every Mass Audubon wildlife sanctuary in 2011 as part of my project. In a few instances, that was going to cause me to double up on a town, if not double up in general.

The first one was easy. I work in Marshfield. My office is on one of the two sanctuaries in town, and I walk at the other one around 50 times per year. I hit both today.

First, Daniel Webster. Every year I lead a walk here on the first Saturday of the year (unless that Saturday is New Year's Day) called "First Birds at Daniel Webster." The hook is getting some "good" birds on the list to go with the house sparrows, starlings and pigeons we see all around our residential neighborhoods. This day didn't disappoint.

Right out of the chute we (Matt, Ellen and Allan joined me) tallied four species of woodpeckers. Sitting in a blind overlooking a frozen pond, we located a red-tailed hawk perched on a tree swallow nesting box. Within a few minutes we had northern harriers, a rough-legged hawk and a Cooper's hawk. Winter is always hawky season in New England.

Ouch.

We looped the sanctuary, walking out to Fox Hill, getting caught in a brief blast of snow on the Secret Trail and winding back along the Webster Pond side of the property. Back in the observation blind, we noticed an American crow tearing into something on the roof of the nesting box the red-tailed hawk had obviously flown away from. What was it? The crow moved off, others soared over the box, but didn't stop. We walked out into the field to check on the bloody carcass. When we got there, we could see a set of teeth dangling over one end, and an interesting tail draped over the other. Then it hit us.

Ewww! Dead muskrat.

10b. Marshfield: North River Wildlife Sanctuary

With lumbering steps I plodded on through some of my most familiar trails. And I got to thinking.

There's a spot on the Woodland Loop Trail where a massive beech tree once stood. It died a few years ago, and this past year the property manager at the sanctuary made the point that if it decided to fall, it would most likely fall on a trail, heaven forbid on a walker. Besides, he said, the tree was so big that we could make natural benches out of it. He made it happen.

Twenty years from now, will anybody remember where those benches came from? Will anybody know that the big open patch of sky that today marks the spot where the crown of the beech stood champion wowed us in 2011 as we rounded the corner after a half an hour's walk through the dense canopy of the mixed wood forest? And what about other natural landmarks? Will anybody remember that the old trail once looped closer to our neighbor's property to the east, and strolled right past two holly trees we called Big Holly and Little Holly?

Will anybody remember the day Amy, Robert and I watched as a southern red-backed vole shot out from under a salamander coverboard, the only one ever seen on this property? Will anybody even know how I used to walk through the woods with a stick, tapping at the bases of trees with holes to see if any flying squirrels would emerge?

Somebody should be writing this stuff down.

January 10

11. Weston: Weston Reservoir

I stopped wondering a long time ago why I get myself out of bed early. The rewards for pre-dawn walks are always tremendous.

As I stepped out of my car at the Weston Reservoir, I immediately knew I wasn't alone. There was a barkin' goin' on, but it didn't belong to a dog. I couldn't see it, but I knew it was a red fox, three sharp barks, the first softer than the other two. I immediately launched into memory mode. A few years ago a friend of mine was describing the wildlife he'd recently seen in his Marshfield yard. He said, "I've had red fox running through here," with a sweep of his arm. It sounded funny. Not "a red fox," but "red fox" running through his yard. All I could picture was Redd Foxx, one hand over his heart, the other one thrust in the air, yelling "Elizabeth! I'm comin' to join you, honey!" as he stumbled through Bob's vegetable garden.

I was quickly startled out of my reverie by one of nature's most stirring sights: a shooting star.

Almost as if in response to the silent rush of the meteor, a gust of wind pushed through the trees, offering up that singular, cohesive *whoosh* only white pines can make in such situations. That sound was quickly followed by one that made my heart leap out of my chest. The ice on the reservoir cracked loudly, echoing off the far trees. The red fox began barking again, marching its way along the northern edge of the pond. As two mallards dove for the sole bare patch of open water on the reservoir, I prepared to move onto my next destination.

No, I never question myself when that alarm goes off in the morning. Instead, I ask myself why I don't do it more often.

12. Wayland: Lower Snake Brook Conservation Area

I just had to find out if the Lower Snake actually exists.

I found out pretty quickly that this particular conservation area, abutting Interstate Route 90, had been claimed by the neighborhood kids. And that's not a bad thing at all.

There's been a huge disconnect between kids and nature in recent years. Thank the news. Now that there are umpty-nine (a favorite expression of my tenth grade history teacher, Mr. Hall) news channels out there competing for ratings, every child abduction story is spread heavily across the airwaves. Parents have reacted by shepherding their kids from event to class to appointment, stealing creative freedom, and part of their youthful development, from them. Years ago, only the local stories made the news. Years ago, kids like me felt perfectly safe journeying out with other kids to our favorite natural spots to build tree forts and learn by firsthand experience about thorns and rocks and dirt and poison ivy.

The kids here in Wayland were living that life. At several points on the loop trail homemade ramps formed jumps for bikes. Several trees sported perches built from scrap lumber. In the crotch of one tree, somebody had placed a bone, one that I hoped was the chew toy of a local dog.

In the end, I found the brook, but I did not find any Lower Snake. Eh, it's winter.

13. Sudbury: Piper Farm Conservation Area

Give me an old farm, an hour and a good pair of shoes, and I'll give you one happy man. Who cares if that farm is covered in snow?

Old farms just ooze history, from the stoic stonewalls that refuse to give up their *raison d'etre* to the stands of fruit trees that still push out their bounty years, decades after anyone made it part of their annual cycle to harvest them. Piper Farm, once juxtaposed with another farm, now sits beside a high-end residential development on land on which crops once grew. But just steps onto the trail, Piper Farm had that old farmy feeling.

I spooked a flock of six mourning doves from a thicket next to the main field. Blue jays screeched overhead. They felt safer when I entered the woods and pushed down the main trail. I found the old apple orchard. I stopped to chat with the occasional chickadee, and I contemplated, as I have hundreds of times in my life, who lived, worked and loved this land years ago. I'll bet the chickadees know. Their families have probably been here for decades.

Morning had broken by the time I returned to my car. I figured I had time for one more walk before I had to settle down in a meeting for the day.

14. Maynard: Summer Hill

Straight up the hill I trudged, pausing once to catch my breath. I followed the white blazes on the trees, wondering what my reward would be for reaching the summit. A red-bellied woodpecker blasted out a call, answered, though I'm sure not intentionally, by a downy woodpecker.

Then, I found it. A giant light blue water tank sat atop the hill, surrounded by high fencing and warning signs. That was the reward.

Perhaps, though, for someone history-minded like me, the reward rested just beyond the blue bubble. An older, concrete dome, also surrounded by fencing, stood nearby. Summer Hill has obviously served the town of Maynard well over the years.

If I was a wood turner, perhaps I would have considered my reward to be the huge, nasty burl hanging off an oak tree behind the concrete tank. I mean, that thing looked like Jimmy Durante's nose. Gnarly.

I gave up on all the daydreaming and turned to head down the trail marked by the yellow blazes, which would get me back to my car. But I was stopped cold. There, 50 feet ahead of me, was my reward for climbing the hill.

A red fox. Two in one morning? Are you kidding me?

15. Lincoln: Drumlin Farm Wildlife Sanctuary

Bonus.

I reached the site of my meeting exactly 35 minutes before it was scheduled to start. I had enough time to get in one more walk. I hit the trail to climb to the top of the drumlin that gave the farm its name.

The feeders around the back of the Audubon Shop were alive with cardinals, chickadees, white-throated sparrows and more. I climbed the hill and found the wind. Man, was it cold! After more than two hours into my walking for the morning, I finally reached the point when I figured it was best I moved onto other things for the day. From the apex of the hill I spied a distant mountain - Wachuset, I pondered? - and marveled at the shocking white glow given off by the bark of the birches that sporadically set the edge of the trail.

I descended the hill and headed for my meeting. Five walks in five towns, and it was then just 9:30 a.m. Not a bad morning, indeed.

January 11

16. Lexington: Willard's Woods

These past two days I had a wonderful time getting to know Jupiter. The steady ultra bright glow stood out from all around. I reached Willard's Woods at a time when it was still quite dark, when Jupiter exhibited some of the only light around. In fact, it was too dark. I almost needed a flashlight to be sure of my footing.

Ice reigned on the heavily-used trails. I only found the main path by heading for another light: a headlamp utilized by a dog walker. Slobbered on by two pups of unknown breeds, I pressed on across a small bridge and into the woods. The pre-dawn air was so still that I could plainly pick up the hooting of a great horned owl to my right. *Sweet.*

As the sun began to push its way over the horizon, the cardinals and blue jays started to chip the ice off their syrinxes and sing out, like the guy outside Joey Tribbiani's window on *Friends*. "Morning's here, the morning's here!" (sung to the tune of Chuck Mangione's "Feels So Good"). Okay, so they were monotonous chirps, rattles and squawks, but who's counting?

A single-engine plane buzzed not too distantly overhead and I thought immediately, "Oh, yeah, Hanscom." I was near the air field. At my next stop of the morning, I would be even closer.

17. Bedford: Hartwell Town Forest

The town forest in Bedford abuts Hanscom Field. At first, it didn't feel like it.

I had a decision to make. Should I take the Blue Trail, right up the heart of the property, or do I loop around the Orange Trail? I surveyed the woods and went with Orange. After all, the orangey-tan leaves of the young beech trees blended so nicely with the trail markers.

In the end, it didn't matter. Orange met Blue farther down the trail. I found a red squirrel midden, a shredded pine cone left in bits at the base of a tree. At the end of the Blue Trail I stepped over a downed log and found myself in a frozen swamp, a flooded section of woods that was now no more than a collection of stark snags poking into the sky.

Woodpecker heaven, I thought.

And soon they started up: downies, hairies, red-bellies. Despite the cold, despite the time of year, they began their drumming. Perhaps it was practice. Maybe some territoriality. Who knows.

Then, the air show began. Precisely at 7:30 the first jet engine roared from the air field. A plane took off behind the far tree line. A second powered up. I started back to my car and a third flew in just over the treetops. I felt, suddenly, like I was a grunt in Europe in World War II.

Back at my car, I tried to automatically unlock my door, but either the battery in my keyfob had frozen or gone dead. I panicked. How would I get in to my car? Was I stranded in Bedford for good? Did I leave my phone on the dash, or was it in my pocket, and for that matter, did I have my AAA card in my wallet? Then, I thought, wait a minute! Some genius had figured out that if you stuck the small metal stick-like dealie attached to the keyfob into an opening near the door handle, you could *manually* unlock the door.

Sadly, this whole episode lasted about 45 seconds.

18. Carlisle: Towle Field

Escaping the noise of Hanscom, I headed for quaint little Carlisle. But things weren't as peaceful as I might have thought they would be. Hunters were on the loose.

The first critter to catch my eye as I headed into the main grassland at Towle Field was a coyote pouncing on prey. The timing was odd. Night was long over. Perhaps this fellow understood that he wouldn't be hunting so easily the next morning, that a foot and a half of snow was on its way. Maybe he was just getting ahead, hedging his bets against the storm. With ears swung forward, focused on the ground below, he listened for scurrying voles and mice, striking downward with his paws when the moment was right.

Watching this whole scene, a red-tailed hawk pondered its own next move. The coyote, chewing on something fuzzy and dark brown, loped off into the woods. The hawk, seeing me, spooked, and flew off, flashing his vibrant red tail in my direction.

In a cedar tree in the middle of the field, a flock of American goldfinches tried to evade my sight. Nothing doing. In a thicket on one side of the field, struck by a patch of sunlight, chickadees and their usual allies greeted the day. I walked back along old stonewalls, some obviously designed to keep sheep, others littered with the tiny stones that spoke loudly of crops.

One more stop to go before my meetings were to begin for the day. And it was a doozy.

19. Concord: Walden Pond

Did you really expect anything else?

Actually, as a walking destination, Concord's got it goin' on. (Is that, like, way too archaic and expression? Am I showing too much of my '90s coming-of-age by using it? What-ever!). Had I not chosen Walden, I could have picked the Great Meadows National Wildlife Refuge, or perhaps even a walk in the town cemetery, along author's ridge. And I hear there's a famous battlefield around somewhere...

But Walden it was. I started at Mr. Thoreau's cabin, the fake. He stood outside in statue form, wondering what had gotten stuck to his hand. Down the trail to the pond I met ice fishermen with all their gear. They had claimed one end of the body of water for themselves. Skaters had claimed the far end. I would see them soon.

I set out on the trail to find the site of the real cabin, excavated on Veterans Day, 1945. Two golden-crowned kinglets flew directly up the trail at me, one veering right, one veering left at the last second. They whizzed over my shoulders and dove into a leafless shrub to find something to eat.

When I reached the skaters, I noticed that of the five of them, three of them had hockey sticks. I then deduced that they were all women (I'm good at that), and pondered how the world had changed, even in my lifetime, so much for the better. Soon I reached my destination.

So, Mr. Thoreau, we met again, and this time on your turf. I've written about you, read about you, thought about you, even walked in your footsteps, and I think we still have a long life ahead together. Our views sometimes jibe, sometimes divert wildly. I only wish you were here to defend yourself through argument. But then, I don't think you'd like Walden as much now.

As I walked away, an MBTA commuter rail train visibly and audibly roared along the back side of the pond, plainly seen from Mr. Thoreau's cabin site. No, Walden is not his Walden any more.

January 13

20. Stow: Gardner Hill

So we were buried again. It had been a whirlwind two days. First, while at work on Tuesday, the story of a very close family member having a stroke unfolded. Then, on Wednesday, the snow hit, more than a foot and a half of it in full blizzard style. I had no idea if I would be walking today, but I kept a plan in mind if the weather gods decided I could play on my way to work.

I found that by the time I reached Gardner Hill, the cross country skiers were already on the trails. The walking was difficult, but not impossible. Still, I was glad this is a half an *hour* a day and not a half a *mile*. That would have been much, much harder on this day.

I feel at times that by walking certain places in winter I'm short-changing them, not allowing them the full opportunity to impress me with what they have to offer my wide open senses. Gardner Hill gave me a crow (a crow in Stow, hmm) and a rooster. Actually, that was at the farm just near the entrance to the forest, but I heard it while standing in the woods. It gave me a mostly frozen brook, a sunrise, towering trees, and some of the most amazing natural scenery I had found in years.

No, Gardner Hill did not get the short end of the stick. It must be beautiful in spring, fantastic in fall. But I was glad I saw it in winter. Even if I never walked this way again, I would never forget my few moments here in the aftermath of the first blizzard of 2011.

21. Boxborough: Flagg Hill

The trail looked beyond walkable, so I hoofed it up the hill. I had read that there was a magnificent view from the apex.

It only took eight minutes to trek from the car to the top of Windemere Road. But so much happened along the way! First, the usual: chickadees and titmice. Everywhere. As far as the ears could hear. Then, a yellow helicopter zoomed into view, and never left the area. It continued to circle and soar the entire time I was there. And it did one more thing. It coaxed a red-tailed hawk into the sky, which gave out a classic screech as it rose ever higher.

At the top of the hill, I realized there was no view, no vista to be had...until I turned around to leave. There, in the distance, was that mountain again, the one I had seen from Drumlin Farm in Lincoln. Wachuset? Man, I needed to get a map. It turned out that the view actually was quite stunning, as advertised.

Back at the bottom of the hill (another eight minutes later), I realized that a smooth white area I believed was a field was in fact a frozen pond. I only figured it out when a great blue heron flew across it and landed about two hundred yards away from me.

With ten minutes to go, I decided to scale the mountain of snow that formed the wall of the parking lot and try the trail. Bad idea. The snow was deep, it was cold and it was wet. I trudged to a bench, from which there must be a lovely view in spring, checked my watch and called it a mission accomplished. I had one more town to tackle before the morning was out.

22. Acton: Great Hill

Why did I ever choose to walk three hills on a day with a foot of new snow on the ground?

Actually, this place made the list on this day because of its parking area. I figured that if any place would be open after the storm, it would be the town property directly behind the fire department. And I was right.

The Great Hill Recreation Area sloped up gently from that parking lot. Like in Stow, cross country skiers had opened the trails, making walking here a little bit easier than elsewhere. That said, it was still a shock to see the top of a picnic table sticking out of the snow, and a hockey net half buried on a spot that apparently hid a frozen pond.

I paused to examine some mouse tracks, just moments before being accosted by a boxer. Dog walkers had made excellent use of the trail already. I could tell by the yellow wayside markers the many pups had left behind on the sides of the trail.

I barely made it into the woods at the top of the field before I had to turn around and head for work. At the last moment, as I emerged from the woods, another cross country skier appeared. Suddenly I felt like a subhuman, as if I had not fully evolved the way she had. Limited by my lack of skis, I was left to plug my way pitifully through the snow as she glided gracefully into the distance.

January 18

23, 24, 25. Lowell, Dracut Tyngsborough: Lowell-Dracut-Tyngsborough State Forest

You just gotta love one-stop shopping.

It wasn't as easy as it sounds, but I'd be lying if I said I wasn't smiling by the end of the morning. First things first: more snow. I drove directly for Trotting Park Road, thinking Starla (my GPS) would send me to the main entrance of the park. Nope. I ended up at the Tyngsborough end of the road, which runs through the park, but is not fully open to cars. As I didn't have a map with me, I decided to just push into the sunrise in a straight line.

The problem was that the sun never really rose while I was in that section of the forest. Oh, it got lighter to the east, as my feet slipped and slid over the icy trail, but due to the blanketing snowfall, it remained nearly completely dark in the woods. I reached a lake, where the trail ran out, and turned back.

I scooted around the corner to the main entrance, in Lowell. The trail there was much wider, much more compact, much more even. And there was life: chickadees, titmice, golden-crowned and ruby-crowned kinglets. I was the first man into the woods this day, which was good. My tracks would be there on the way back.

Suddenly, my own past lurched up to say hello. I found the boundary marker between Lowell and Dracut, and noted that the Lowell side was outlined in orange spray paint. Vandalism? No. Perambulating the bounds. In days of old, the town fathers of Massachusetts towns made an annual walk around the town borders and marked the granite boundary markers as seen on this day; Lowell obviously still has the tradition, or recently revived it.

Back when I was working for the Scituate Historical Society, I helped organize a symbolic perambulation. My boss, a selectman, organized the political side. By tradition, the selectmen from the neighboring towns met with the perambulating team at the markers. I contacted the neighboring historical societies - Hingham, Cohasset, Norwell and Marshfield - and set up an exchange of gifts.

But back to the woods. I kept on the main trail until I found the Spruce Swamp. One look, and I said it. "Now that's a swamp." Although it was frozen, I could still smell it. And it's a famous swamp, too, for Massachusetts birders. There was a special woodpecker here, a red-headed woodpecker, a stray that dragged many a gawker to the edge of this particular wetland. I heard a squawk, but it was not to be. It was a red-*bellied* woodpecker. Not so rare these days.

On my way back, I followed my tracks as planned, but two problems arose. First, I ran into a snowshoer. That's typically not an issue, but he was walking directly on my footprints. They were obliterated behind him. I said hi, despite his transgressions. Second, by the time I got back to my car, my tracks were all full of snow anyway. It was as if I had never been there.

26. Chelmsford: Archer Meadowbrook Preserve

Sometimes, it's good to be the first man onto the trail. And then there was this day. In actuality, I didn't mind it, for the most part. It was just the very beginning that was a challenge.

The preserve is on the curve of East Putnam Road, and the plow guys apparently believed no one wanted to walk there in winter, so they jammed up the entrance with a large embankment of the white stuff. They probably figured that no idiot would want in. I mean, what moron walks in a foot and a half of wet snow?

I climbed over the pile, snow clinging to my jeans above my knees. I trudged down the trail to the meadow, and soon realized that the rest of the trails, well, in the snow, there were no other visible trails. The best I could do was romp around in the snow taking note of the local sights. Squirrels had run from tree to tree, climbing up in search of food, rushing back down the other sides, and heading for the next oak or maple. A hairy woodpecker chirped in the distance, the only natural sound I heard.

The snow kept falling, as it would all morning. Soon, it was blowing sideways, and striking the still-clinging leaves of the beech trees, making the sound of bacon sizzling in a frying pan. It was making me hungry...wait - where have I read those words before?

January 19

27. Franklin: Franklin State Forest

Oh, the ice! The damp! Yesterday's snow/rain storm left Massachusetts a slippery mess. It was an awful day for a walk in the woods, but hey, I had a goal.

The Franklin State Forest is accessible from a trailhead across the street from the Hockomock Area YMCA and the Forge Hill water tank on Forge Hill Road. I said accessible in the most general way on this particular. The gate was, of course, behind a wall of snow, and the trail was buried somewhere well underneath it. But somebody beat me to it.

There was one set of tracks in, and as that person had already blazed a trail, I stuck to it. When he or she turned right, I turned right; when he or she went left, I zagged that way, too. That person obviously walked the day prior, though. The prints he or she left behind were pure white. I was not so lucky. I struck slush.

I've learned there were many ways to walk in the snow: on it, through it, in it, etc. I think the worst way was what I experienced in Franklin. I plunged all the way through, as the melting snow was giving way quite easily. At the bottom, my foot inevitably slid left or right. It never seemed to land straight. My hamstrings, thighs and even my glutes got one heck of a workout.

Eh, this would all pass. I hoped.

17

28. Wrentham: Wrentham State Forest

The pinkish sunrise had given way to peeking sunshine by the time I reached the Wrentham Town Forest. I would need it, and fast. After I pulled into the parking lot, I realized that without some serious melting, I might never get out again.

But that was for thirty minutes into the future. I had an appointment to keep with nature. Yes, another one.

The first feature to catch my eye was a glacial erratic boulder, standing atop a small hill. The forest was *all* small hills, by the way, making for an interesting walk in the conditions of the day. As I walked, the never-ending rush of Route 495 roared in the background. I had to stop from time to time to be sure I was hearing the titmice, nuthatches and woodpeckers I thought I was hearing. I finally saw them, moving through the higher branches of the trees *en masse*, seeking food together.

Then I ran into Old George. Or at least the notion that he existed. I'm sure the marker that read "Old George Street" actually meant that there was a new George Street in town, and that the path into the woods here was shut down when Route 495 was laid out. I do not believe that it was named for an old man named George, though stranger things have happened. *Somebody* was named George, we know that for a fact. Washington? Well, there are hundreds, probably thousands of Washington Streets, Roads and Boulevards across the United States. Were the people of Wrentham on a first name basis with our first president?

Or is Old George the name of the erratic boulder I saw atop the little hill? Hmm, in my mind, it is now.

29. Foxboro: F. Gilbert Hills State Forest

Turkeys!

I found two flocks of wild turkeys in F. Gilbert Hills, one male and one female. They always put a smile on my face. They weren't at all scared by the skil saw buzzing loudly from the nearby road. And neither was I.

Not that that mattered. The forest is aptly-named, at least as far as the hills part goes. It rolled up and down, with interesting trail names like Wolf Meadow Road. Oh, to have been here four hundred years ago...

The most fascinating feature I found here was the water holes (although there are a ton - or tons - of glacial erratics scattered throughout the woods). The water holes bespeak history. The young men of the Civilian Conservation Corps, the CCC, dug them in the 1930s, one of the federal government's ways of creating jobs during the Depression while completing important public works projects. My guess, first and foremost, was that they

18

had to do with forest firefighting, and it was probably why the regional state forest firefighting team is headquartered here at F. Gilbert Hills.

I had one fun moment just before I turned to retrace my steps. As I was walking, I caught motion out of the side of my eye. I quickly looked left and saw a branch spring into the air, flinging the snow that was on it, indeed, that was keeping it pinned to the ground, into the distance. I often wonder how many times per day that happens in a given area, and why fate decided to allow me to witness this one little silent act.

30. Norfolk: Stony Brook Nature Center

The sun was out! It was not just peeking and poking through the clouds any more. We had full, slightly warm sunshine. It was so comparatively warm to the rest of the morning that I didn't realize until I was halfway through with my circumnavigation of the mill pond that I had never put my gloves on.

So, onto the show. Hooded mergansers, mute swans, snapping turtles, these were all things I would have expected to see here if the pond was not frozen. Instead, it was the usual gang that has been following me around from town to town: chickadees, titmice, juncos, house sparrows...

Stony Brook, also known as the Bristol-Blake State Reservation, has become deservedly well-known in recent years for its Sensory Trail. A soft rope rail runs down the main trail, marked occasionally with signs in both text and Braille. If the sign says "pine tree," there's a pine tree within arm's reach. It's a wonderful system.

But Stony Brook has always been ahead of the curve as far as nature education goes. Forty years ago, the sanctuary was synonymous with the name Alfred Bussewitz. "Buzzy," as he was known to the locals, was said to be able to make poison ivy seem friendly to anyone who wished to listen to him joyously discuss the wonders of nature.

What higher praise could there be for a nature educator?

31. Sharon: Moose Hill Wildlife Sanctuary

Wet feet, wet face. I'll explain.

By the time I reached Moose Hill Wildlife Sanctuary, my feet were soaked. The snow was still deep, despite the melting taking place. For hundreds of steps thus far, snow had reached my knees, seeping down into my boots.

So that explained the feet.

As for my face, well, that was another story altogether. I decided to take the Billings Farm Trail this day. So had a deer, but, apparently, no one else.

And that critter stayed right on the trail, all the way to the old barn. I was amazed.

I lost the trail at the barn, but only because I became distracted. I remember researching the story of Moose Hill a half decade ago when I wrote my book *Images of America: Mass Audubon*. Mrs. Billings had moved from the city, and was distraught at being separated from the social life therein. She hated the spring peepers in particular. But like many people immersed in natural settings, she grew to love the land like no one else. Walk Moose Hill and it will charm you as well.

So I got to the old Billings Farm area and approached an open shed. I had forgotten about the bat colony. There's an opening in the ceiling of the shed through which the bats fly before taking their daily siestas. And you can't help it. You have to look. I tilted my head to the proper angle, looked skyward and the melting snow caught me right between the eyes.

Wet face.

32. Stoughton: Bird Street Conservation Area

I was reaching my own melting point. By the time I finished at Bird Street, I would have been walking for three hours. That's typically not a problem, but the snow had worn me out.

So I stepped onto the trail, and immediately found out why the street and the conservation area got their names. Within minutes I had tallied fifteen species of birds, from a golden-crowned kinglet to a red-tailed hawk. I did my trick in which I stand still long enough that the birds don't realize I'm there, and just watched the show. Apparently my magic works on red squirrels as well, as I had one practically at my feet before I just finally had to move on.

The walking here was just far too difficult today, so I didn't get very far at all. There were trees down, right across the trail, that luckily I could dodge, duck, dive and dodge past. And there was a small memorial to Stoughton's veterans. Very nice.

The most obvious thing about my walk here was that this place must be a birder's paradise in spring. I had no idea where I'd be in April and May (I mean, I had a bit of a list in front of me), but I hoped I'd have time to come back and catch it again when the migrants came marching through.

January 20

33. Ashby: Willard Brook State Forest

It looked like I was going to know a lot more about the history of the Civilian Conservation Corps in Massachusetts before I was through with this little project. I crossed the big stone bridge that helps form Damon Pond (the brook has something to do with it as well) and found a sign that told the broad story.

The CCC had 51 camps in Massachusetts during the worst days of the Great Depression. It's hard for us to imagine now what those days were like. Times were so tough, families sent their young men to work - and live - in the forests. Yes, the economic climate is bad now, but we are nowhere near the most extreme depths of depression the country witnessed in the 1930s.

And so they were here, the Pine Cone Johnnies, a great nickname for the men who did so much to improve firefighting capabilities in our woods, who built roads and bridges and cabins and other buildings that today serve as headquarters for public parks.

I can't imagine what it must have been like to live out in the woods during winter days like this one. The brook was still open, but the snow was deep, crunchy on the top, soft underneath. Every step I made as I rounded the pond sounded like I was stomping on a Cocoa Puff.

Perhaps in memory of those Pine Cone Johnnies and the pseudo-military existence they led, the park's picnic tables were lined up in tight formation, standing on end, awaiting their spring call. May it come sooner than they expect.

34. Townsend: Pearl Hill State Park

I noticed as I was halfway up the hill that were it not for the sounds of my footsteps, there might be no sound at all here on this wintry day at Pearl Hill State Park. I stopped, searching for complete silence. A small plane droned sluggishly past, followed by another one a few seconds later. They never really left the range of my hearing.

To get to this point in the park, I had crossed a wide field, passed a frozen pond, and followed the tracks of a snowmobile that had compacted the snow to an easily walkable, flat path. I marveled at how different this forest was from those around my South Shore home. We just don't get the variety in evergreen trees down there like they do up here.

And is that *mountain laurel*? How cool.

On my way back down the trail, I paused again for that silence, without luck. One of the planes was barely audible, but there. Then, dueling downy woodpeckers began drumming on distant trees, one far to my right, one way to my left. Well, if I had to hear something, I could deal with that.

35. Pepperell: Heald Pond Conservation Area

Wow, almost got skunked on this one.

The seemingly never-ending onslaught of snow we faced for the past three and a half weeks closed off many walking areas. It had been more important, and rightly so, to keep schools, hospitals and other needed facilities accessible than open space trails. Heald Pond was a perfect example. There was no parking when I got there, absolutely nowhere to turn off and leave the car for even a half an hour.

But there were ice fishermen, and where there are ice fishermen, there's a way. To practice their art, they need snow shovels, among many other tools. And where there are snow shovels, there can be parking spaces.

That said, the walking was about as tough as one can imagine. The trails were mostly untouched, making for a pristinely decorated landscape. The crows seemed to be laughing at me as I wandered aimlessly, somewhat hopelessly. I couldn't blame them. It must have been quite a sight.

36. Dunstable: Larter Field

I finally did get locked out of a walking trail, as I tried to access the Spaulding-Proctor Reservation. So, thinking on my feet, I found the next viable option, Larter Field.

The sky was utterly cloudless and blue, the sun shining down on a small hill that had been recently heavily utilized by sledders. Luckily for me, a sign said "trail" and pointed me into the woods. I hoofed it in that direction.

Once again, a snowmobiler had preceded me, making for a nice, flat, straight trail. In fact, I thought to myself, it was too straight. I walked on a ridge that perfectly bisected two small valleys, one on either side. It struck me that I was most likely on an old railroad bed, and that this ridge probably represented an intrusion on what was once probably a single, peaceful valley.

A few of the usuals were there, the titmice and the nuthatches, but there was evidence of the big guy around, the pileated woodpecker. His powerful bill leaves a shredded mess of bark at the base of a tree, and an elongated hole that is pretty unmistakable. The last one is saw was at Sapsucker Woods in Ithaca, New York, and the last one in Massachusetts was at Wompatuck State Park in Hingham in the spring of 2010. A new friend from the West End of Scituate recently told me he had one at his suet feeder this winter. I hope to catch a glimpse of one in the state before the year is out.

Back at the hill, a dad and son had taken to their sled. I saw my future. My boy just turned two, so those days were ahead. I could not wait.

37. Groton: Groton Town Forest

There was only one parking space, so I took it. It was at the very beginning of the section of Town Forest Road that heads directly into the woods, as the road had not been plowed beyond that point, so I had a walk of a minute or so past the homes neighboring the forest's entryway. The sun was striking the snow so aggressively that it shot a glare up into my eyes that I had to squint to see through.

In the woods, the show began. Blue jays were harassing a red-tailed hawk, or at least screaming at it like only blue jays can. A mixed flock of chickadees, nuthatches and a golden-crowned kinglet foraged. A small group of cedar waxwings flew quickly overhead, while higher in the sky a gaggle of Canada geese pushed onto their next destination, whichever golf course that may have been.

The snow began to drift off the trees. It wasn't melting, just letting go, still frozen. Although the sky was still a clear blue, it felt like it was ever so lightly snowing.

As I moved beyond the memorial marker which dedicated the forest to the men of Groton who died in World War I in the service of their country, I realized I was Cocoa Puffing again. The recent melting had left the snow all over the region with a wet layer on top that refroze overnight. At one point, I started to reach out for a tree to brace myself after a particularly deep step, only to see the biggest, nastiest poison ivy vine I'd seen in years.

Oh, no thank you. I crunched on.

38. Littleton: Oak Hill and Tophet Chasm

A plowed road doesn't always necessarily mean an easy trail to the top. That was my lesson for today.

First, I had to wonder why the road was plowed. Well, I didn't *have* to, really. My job was just to walk it. And really my job was to pay attention to my feet. While plowed, the road was almost solid ice. And at this road's particular steepness, I was kind of wishing I had stolen the sled from the five-year-old back in Dunstable. Actually, that wouldn't have been good. According to the stickers on his dad's car, dad was a cop. Maybe "borrowed" is a better concept. Still, a slide down Oak Hill on a sled would have been a wild, potentially deadly ride on this day. What fun.

23

When I reached the top, my answer stared me in the face: a water tank. How many water tanks would I see this year? Perhaps that'd be my next challenge: *Half an Hour a Day Across Massachusetts: Finding Water Tanks in All 351 Cities and Towns of the Bay State*. This guy had ginormous icicles hanging from its edge, the type that fall off and severely injure people in hospital dramas on TV. I circled the tank and started down.

I decided I had enough time to check out Tophet Chasm. It wasn't exactly what I expected, but it was a very cool geological feature nonetheless. I was hoping for a steep canyon with a drop-off that I could then conjecture had been named for the first man to fall into it. Still, one slip could have sent me sliding and rolling down the hill in an ever-increasing snowball until I hit the canyon floor below. I left before it could be renamed Galluzzo Chasm.

39. Westford: East Boston Camps

I've discovered a story I never knew, and it's one that makes me proud to be a native of the state of Massachusetts.

Boiled down, it's this: a family with money to spare, even during the Great Depression, purchased land in the woods of Westford to open a camp for kids with tuberculosis in Boston. That land, purchased in sixteen transactions, including Burge's Pond, became a fresh air retreat for those kids. Building began and ended in 1937, with cabins made directly from wood felled on the property. The Hurricane of 1938 knocked down even more trees, which were milled on site. Campers still come today, no longer tied to the awful disease that spurred the Hyams family into their plan of action.

What a heartwarming story.

The town of Westford bought the property in 2005, and it makes for a beautiful walk. I don't think, though, I could add anything that would embellish the site's history. It was trees and birds, wetlands and ponds, and one angry squirrel that didn't want me there. After three and a half hours of walking today, I didn't feel the slightest bit tired as I left the East Boston Camps. I felt more refreshed than I had in a long time.

January 25

40. Hanover: Colby-Phillips Property

It was supposed to be a Rockland-Hanover day, but ended up being a Hanover-Duxbury day. Damn snow.

The Rockland Town Forest was my first goal for the day, but the parking lot had not been plowed. It had, in fact, been socked in by the town's plow team, a big berm of the dirty white stuff preventing all vehicular access. Looked like Rockland will have to be a spring thing. I rolled down to the next town on my route.

My trip to Colby-Phillips brought me to one of those moments I often wonder about, that strange intersection between me and one of life's little critters, which I probably would have missed altogether had I walked into the woods just sixty seconds later. Instead, because I bypassed my Rockland destination, because I chose Colby-Phillips, because I paused a minute when I stepped out of the car in the blowing snow to adjust my hat, because I took things slowly on the icy road leading onto the trails, I walked directly into a brown creeper climbing up a tree in the brief moment it decided to forage directly beside the spot where my feet would fall.

Beyond that instance, the beauty of this day's walk in Hanover rested in the wintry scenery, the snow-blasted stands of white pine, the bright orange beeches, the leafless young maples jostling for a piece of the forest canopy. The West Hanover Cemetery quietly sat at the end of the trail, never more stark than in the coldness of a winter day. I thought about how the folks interred here were likely to be among the most forgotten people in town history, permanently tucked away in the woods rather than in the large burial ground among generations of their townsmen and women just down Route 139. Their graveyard's marketing relies mainly on foot traffic and word of mouth. Without it, they'd be almost certainly perpetually alone together.

Perhaps that was the way they wanted it to be.

41. Duxbury: North Hill Marsh Wildlife Sanctuary

I reached Duxbury and almost started walking by rote. The route I marched this day was the same one I take every two weeks every spring, every two weeks every fall, for a citizen science project. My name is John, I'm 39 years old, and I count ducks.

I had been in and around Duxbury all weekend long, anyway, leading "snowy owl prowls" out on Duxbury Beach. While no snowies showed themselves on those particular excursions, a peregrine falcon did, and a northern harrier did. Duxbury is a wildlife hotspot for the South Shore, a beautiful mix of woods and ponds and marshes and shoreline that attracts species of all varieties, from horseshoe crabs to bald eagles. It's practically my second home, professionally.

So I walked up and over the rise I know so well. I took the right turn to head for the platform overlooking the pond. I turned left and headed for the

Cathedral of Trees at Insurance Point. I even stood in my favorite scoping positions, staring at the ice, subconsciously moving from duck spot to duck spot. It's a routine I've followed for three years now. It's how data sets of natural world activity are built.

But there was one other activity on the horizon for North Hill Marsh. We would soon be cleaning out the nest boxes on the marsh, checking in on the tree swallow colony's productivity, while it was down in Mexico fattening up for the big flight north in the spring. We'd even check the twenty or so wood duck nest boxes. One year we found a sleeping screech owl in one of the boxes. What would we find this year? Oo, I couldn't wait to find out. For this day, though, I had an appointment to keep, a lecture for friends at the Duxbury Senior Center.

Don't worry, North Hill Marsh. I'll be back.

February

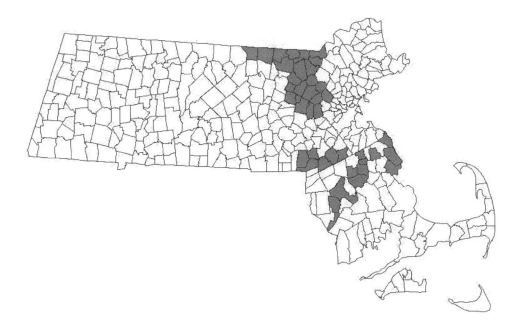

The Show So Far

Month Python had a sketch in which an announcer (Terry Jones) came on screen and a stated that he would be catching viewers up on "the show so far." When described literally - "and then a knight hit a man on the head with a rubber chicken" - the scenes you had just watched seemed even funnier, more nonsensical. He ended it, of course, by saying, "and then a man came on to tell us about the show so far." God, I love those guys.

So how's the show been so far? I started in manure, saw a red fox and a shooting star on the same morning, cocoa puffed, and then I started to write about the show so far.

At times in January, I felt like Lloyd Bridges in *Airplane!* Faced with the crisis of the pending plane crash, he inevitably reached for his vices. "Looks like I picked the wrong week to stop sniffing glue!" In my case, with all the snow that fell in January 2011, I could use the same sentence. Instead of "week," place "year." In place of "stop sniffing glue," add, "start a walking project."

Yet, even with the obvious barriers and obstructions, I still got off to a good start. If we do the math - 12 months, 351 towns - that means that I have to get to 29 towns or so per month. I jumped out of the gate fast and hit 41, putting myself slightly ahead of pace. More importantly, I didn't just hit the local communities around my hometown of Weymouth, just to put some numbers on the board. Instead I visited places I'd never been, and took out a whole chunk of Middlesex County. But Franklin, Hampden, Hampshire, Berkshire and Worcester Counties loom in the distance, ominously. There's a lot of walking to be done.

At the end of the month I spent a full day in Essex County, but never stayed in one spot long enough to rack up any towns for my list. As a participant in Mass Audubon's Superbowl of Birding VIII, I rolled with my teammates through Topsfield, Ipswich, Rowley, Newburyport and more. I saw things I never thought I would see - a common murre, for instance, at Eastern Point in Gloucester - and came out of it all with a $50 gift certificate to a birder's store. Whodathunkit.

On January 31, a day I had set aside for walking, I sat through jury duty in Dedham, a caged tiger forced to sit, except when judges entered rooms, during the daylight hours. Snow forecast for February 1 and 2 just added to my frustration.

But again, it's been a good start. To be at 12% of my goal rather than 8% after one month is a good thing. I'm still going to push it, though. We have two winters per year, and I don't want to be caught lagging on December 1.

Onto Round Two.

February 1

42. Kingston: Bay Farm Conservation Area

They'd stopped talking about inches, and now they were onto feet. The forecast I heard on this morning called for around two feet of snow. That was supposed to land on top of the several feet already covering the area. The mantra was the same everywhere: where am I supposed to put it? Mine became "where and when am I supposed to go for a walk?!"

In my desire - nay, need - to get out and walk somewhere, knowing the next two days were also going to be lost to Mother Nature's wrath, I finished delivering my lecture in Duxbury and headed south to Kingston and the blowing snow. Bay Farm is a place for tree swallows and bobolinks in summer, but when covered in snow, it's simply an open vista, a sheet of white interrupted at its edges by trees. That open vista today meant one thing: snow in my face, everywhere I turned. As soon as I could, I ducked into the cedar stand on the Kingston side.

The side trails eventually lead to a small woodland overlooking Kingston Bay, but on this day, with visibility at about thirty feet, there was nothing to see. Canada geese honked in the wintry fog, but I never saw one.

In the woods, though, where the snow was wetter than in the field, I watched with curiosity as a downy woodpecker moved through the trees. It was obvious she was no dummy. She landed on the lee, or clean side of every maple, never subjecting herself to the snow blowing in *her* face.

Well, don't I feel stupid.

February 3

43. Pembroke: Willow Brook Farm Conservation Area

With one last scrape of the ice off the car, the great two-day storm came to an end. I shoveled snow for 8 of 20 hours, and watched the piles in my yard grow to the point that I doubt I could make them grow any more. You can only throw a shovel full of snow so high.

As an escape, I visited an old favorite, Willow Brook Farm, after giving a lecture at a local retirement community. I had spoken about my walking project of two years ago, *Half an Hour a Day on Foot*, hoping to instill some inspiration in the audience to get out and walk as soon as they could. But wow, was it icy in eastern Massachusetts at that moment.

But I personally couldn't take being cooped up like a chicken any longer. With uneven steps I pushed down the main trail, knowing I wouldn't get very far in a half hour's time. In a way, this was a walk I had mentally saved for spring, when the Baltimore orioles arrived, and when the mound ants began shaking off their torpor and scurrying about again. But a hairy woodpecker chirping loudly to my left made me think another way.

I walk here in spring every year. I see those Baltimore orioles and silvery blue butterflies every year. I take pictures of those ants in the summer sunshine every year. I've *never* walked here in winter. In my never-ending quest for new experiences, I was having one, without even realizing it.

At my turnaround point, I was about to leave when a robin clucked overhead. I gave it a glance, then spun my head down and around to find the trail, when something else caught my eye, a set of coyote tracks. He or she had loped by the very spot on which I stood just a few hours prior to my arrival. It made me wish I had a motion-activated camera to mount on the robin's tree, so I could find out what else I miss when I'm not walking in places I think I know so well.

February 5

44. Norwell: Norris Reservation

It wouldn't get me this time.

The last time I walked at Norris Reservation, I made a grave error. It was a day like this one, ice-covered and gloomy, and I thought I was smarter than I was. I went right, when I should have gone left.

I've fallen into predictable patterns at my favorite walking spots. When I get to Norris, I typically take the left hand trail after crossing the mill dam and head for the open house on the North River. Last time, I went right. I didn't recognize my intersections, and I got temporarily lost. Not this time.

I went left, and I walked through the familiar trails, meeting the familiar crossings. The path was only one person wide, and as such, I stepped aside numerous times to accommodate oncoming walkers from the other direction. It meant knee-deep snow at some points, but I had good boots on. No idea how much longer they'd last, though. They'd had a worse winter than any of my other shoes.

At the house on the river, I stood and watched the bend. Small chunks of ice slid around the corner where shipbuilders at the Tilden Yard once launched their vessels. Occasionally, a small floe would meet an immovable rock - this section of the river was once known as Rocky Reach - and a slow, unyielding, *swoosh* signaled the end of that floe's slushy life. It was a sound that predates us all, and amazing to think about.

February 7

45. Braintree: Pond Meadow

Sounds delightful, doesn't it?

I may be the only person around these days who thinks about the ages of ponds on a daily basis. There are so few that are truly ancient in Massachusetts. Kettle hole ponds in Plymouth and on Cape Cod, well, for sure, they're old. The glaciers did a number on those areas during their big scouring project 11,000 years ago. But pretty much everything else in Massachusetts is manmade.

That includes the pond of Pond Meadow. Only, there's a slight difference here. Most of the other ponds in the state were millponds, meaning their outflows were dammed between 150 and 400 years ago. They powered small, single turbine or overshot wheel sawmills, and eventually larger, more industrious factories. They served their purpose and left us behind a quandary.

Dams have altered our natural order. Fish that once spawned upstream can't get to their ancestral grounds any more. Yet, we now have homes on lakes and ponds we consider to be worth a lot of money partly because of their proximity to that water. Because of our relatively short-term need for whatever it is we derive from a house on a lake, the long-term need of fish like the herring that once spawned in Massachusetts in huge numbers has gone by the wayside. We won't remove ancient dams, and because of it, the fish are dying.

Pond Meadow, though, is a new pond. It traces its existence back less than forty years, a public water supply project that has had direct benefits to the people of Braintree. Water is life, and with increasing populations, it will become more and more precious. Secondly, the pond itself, made from the damming of the Monatiquot River, is now surrounded by walking trails. I've never seen so many smiles as I do when I walk Pond Meadow.

That was the case today, as I slid on the slippery snow. Luckily, there was a sign marked "Nature" to point me to what I had come to see.

46. Randolph: Great Pond

The time had come.

I got a cool set of snowshoes for Christmas, but to this point in the winter, I'd picked my spots well. I'd walked 45 trails, most well-trammeled, others relatively close to that description. Today, I met my match. There was no way I could get far at all at Great Pond without christening the Red Feathers.

Snowshoeing was new to my arsenal. I spent my youth on skates, and my teen years on skis, but it was only last year that a friend put me on a pair of snowshoes. I was still awkward on them, but I'd get the hang of it. It's mostly the stance. You have to be sure to have a wider gait than normal, ever so slightly, to accommodate the shoes. As such, you use a slightly different set of muscles. My glutes would be ringing in the morning.

Only one fox had passed this way in recent weeks, and nothing else. Not a single person had left tracks since the last storm, and only the faintest hint of a trail existed. But the snow wasn't quite perfect for what I was doing. Softened by two days of above-freezing temperatures the snow was deceivingly mushy, to use the proper hydrology term. I sunk with every step, but knew that I did so less than I would have without the shoes on.

The snow was perfect for one thing on this day, though. All along the trail trees were being held captive. Birches, in particular, were bent to the ground and their tops encased in the snow. I freed them where I could, but finally came across a group that together were bowing in the same direction. They looked like a giant, furry-legged spider. And they were buried deeply.

I don't mind telling you I worked up quite a sweat on the walk today. I never even got to the pond.

February 10

47. Bourne: Cape Cod Canal Trail

I examined my options in Bourne and made my choice. This wasn't it.

I wanted to walk at Sacrifice Rock Woods, just for the name. I figured there had to be a story. But when I got there, I found I was too late. A developer got his hands on it last year and permanently ruined the land for open space seekers.

So I retreated to the old Bourne standby, a walk along the edge of the Cape Cod Canal. I walked west, toward the Buzzards Bay end, away from the Sagamore Bridge. The wind worked against me, and even if I couldn't, for some reason, feel it stinging my face, I could tell which way it was blowing by looking at the ducks. They face into the wind, to allow the streamlining of their feathers to keep the cold away from their skin. Their bills all pointed to the west, and I marched that way under their orders.

The access road that acts as a trail along the canal is straight, flat and wide, and on this day it was used by only a handful of us. The portion of it I walked contains a herring run, with signs strictly forbidding the taking of the small endangered creature. We used to take them by the thousands, but now they're just about gone. It's just amazing, the impact we've had on this planet.

Anyway, by walking the canal, I now had the right to use some alliteration at the end of this project. The day I visit the last town in the state, I'll write, in my best FDR voice, "From the Berkshires to Boston, from Provincetown to Pepperell to Petersham, from the Connecticut River to the Cape Cod Canal..."

Crap! I just used it. Oh well, might as well have fun with the voice. "The only thing we have to fear, is fear itself! Today, December 7, 1941, is a day which will live in infamy! Eleanor, bring me my long cigarette holder!" (That latter one is from a very obscure tape recording that doesn't exist.)

48. Sandwich: Scusset Beach State Reservation

Still alongside the canal at my next stop, I decided to get out of the wind. I ducked into the woods and headed for the Sagamore Hill Historic Site.

The return to the woods meant a return to snow and ice. The trail along the canal had been scoured clean, giving me a nice easy path to follow. Here in the woods, though, there had been no such actions. Ice ruled the walk, and as such, I spent more time staring at it and figuring out how to deal with it than truly enjoying the experience.

But I have no fear that this was the last time I would walk this trail. I walk it at least once a year during the Christmas Bird Count season. The thickets here have produced the only yellow-breasted chats I've ever seen, an occasional fox sparrow, a more-regular hermit thrush. On this day, it boasted robins, which had otherwise been among the missing this winter in Massachusetts.

The viewpoint from atop Sagamore Hill brought to mind a startling thought. In this age of GPS and other long distance tracking devices, it's kind of scary to think that just seventy years ago, in my grandfather's time, we stood atop hills and looked as far as we could onto the horizon to find our enemies. Imagine! Safety from surprise attack was dependent on a powerful pair of binoculars. Our whole coastal defense system was designed around it. Planes, blimps and soon helicopters changed all that, but until that time, we were trapped by minor extensions of the capabilities of our own bodies.

I descended the hill and got back to the ice.

49. Plymouth: Ellisville Harbor State Park

A little further up the coast, I poked into Ellisville Harbor State Park. After all, where does one go in Plymouth if he's only one trail to walk? The choices are endless. At 134 square miles, Plymouth is the largest community in Massachusetts. It looked nice on the map I was keeping of towns I'd visited, but in the end, it only counted for one out of 351.

The harbor, as it's called, is really a saltmarsh, and at the moment, it was frozen. Or at least the water was. The grasses themselves were actually exposed, uncovered by snow, and that was a good thing if you were a Canada goose. They were spread out across the marsh on this day, pecking away for food.

Not much else was interested in being exposed to the air, though, aside for a few more robins. And they were lucky, too, that they had no need to walk the trails. I found the ice an interesting challenge on the upslope; I didn't even want to think about the return trip on the downslope.

In fact, I found a separate trail, an access road, to take back, and all went well until I hit its shadier sections. There the road turned to a smoother, cleaner, slicker style of ice than I had encountered on the regular walking trail. When I could, I cut across a field studded with cedar trees and went back to the lesser of this day's two evils.

I just don't see how the Pilgrims did it. Or the Ellises.

February 14

50, 51. Newbury and Rowley: Plum Island National Wildlife Refuge

With a day off after a long weekend of work, my friend David and I decided to explore the North Shore, starting our day at the Parker River National Wildlife Refuge shortly after dawn.

It was a slow start, as the icy conditions continued to smother the northeast, but we were looking forward to a day supposed to hit 50 degrees. Fifty! Anything above 35 had been a dream for two months, yet here we were excitedly chattering about 50.

This being a birding outing, we were looking for...do I need to say it? In the cold, with a slight wind blowing, the birds were all hunkered down save for the blue jays and the Canada geese. We walked out to the Hellcat Observation Area, only to find a wide stretch of chunky ice. In the far distance, we could see that the river itself was sporting open water, but signs of life were thin.

The gate beyond Hellcat, guarding the gravel road ultimately leading to Sandy Point State Park, was closed, so our trip would be cut short this time around. We retreated back up the peninsula to find four snow buntings and an out-of-season wood duck. What it was doing there and then, we will never understand. Hunters like to say that wood ducks "don't like cold feet," and fly south at the first sign of ice forming on local ponds in the fall. They return with the earliest migrants in spring, but there is no way in hell any duck in the world would consider what we had on this day as spring. Yet there was a male wood duck, plain as could be, 50 yards offshore.

Back at the first parking lot, we walked the long boardwalk to the beach, scoping the sea and chatting with another birder. As we returned to the car, a peregrine falcon shot across the saltmarsh. I got a good view, but David didn't. We agreed to chase another one elsewhere in the region by the end of the day.

52. Newburyport: Plum Island

At the northern end of Plum Island - an island shared by four communities - sits a lighthouse and an old Coast Guard boathouse, built in the 1930s, now in sad disrepair. I say "sad" because of my side job. I work to save historic Coast Guard buildings across the country for a nonprofit organization.

From that northern point, though, is a beautiful view of the Merrimack River. We stood with our backs to the boathouse and looked to the flowing waters to find, among many other things, a thick-billed murre, a northern visitor who may be the same individual critter who spent a few weeks in Gloucester Harbor, to the south, earlier in the year. We'd never know for sure, of course.

The northern end of the peninsula, while then silent save for the sounds of a dump truck hauling away a heavy load of snow and ice, just oozed thoughts of summer, of fried clams, sandy feet, bikinis and sunblock. It's places like this one I planned on getting out of the way early in the year. I didn't want to be at seashore hotspots at the height of summer, for parking reasons alone. I'll bet Newburyport is a blast in July and August, but this year I had bigger fish to fry.

Hmm, change that. I don't eat fish. No need to kill them just for my benefit.

53. Salisbury: Salisbury Beach State Reservation

From Plum Island, we took a brief diversion northward, crossing the Newburyport Turnpike Bridge to find Salisbury. The town is as New Hampshire as Massachusetts gets. It simply feels like crossing the Merrimack River you've crossed state lines, but it isn't so. For some reason, boundaries were set to give Massachusetts just a few more miles to the north when it would seem the natural line of the river should have been used all the way to the sea.

The state reservation in Salisbury was quiet, but dozens of snow-covered picnic tables just dared us to say that in six months' time. I couldn't hear the music playing or the children laughing, but I could feel their echoes as we walked toward the boat ramp.

From that boat ramp we spotted a bald eagle sitting in the saltmarsh. We knew it was there even before we left Newburyport. I had seen a cloud of ducks - that's a technical term for "wicked lots of ducks" in Massachusetts speak - lift off together. To my experience, that means a predator is around, and nothing makes a duck, or a gull, jump like a bald eagle.

It was surprising on this day to see how many people were at the reservation, dodging the huge piles of snow and driving over the thick, intermittent ice. Perhaps the allure of the predicted 50-degree day had coaxed them out. Some sat in cars reading newspapers and smoking cigarettes, while others walked dogs on the beach. I think we were all ready, at that point, to break out of the slumber we'd been forced into.

54. Rockport: Loblolly Cove

The North Shore has always been known for its rugged scenery, as a place where the ocean meets the rocky shore. South of Boston, on the Cape and even the islands, the story has more to do with sand.

Loblolly Cove is one of those places where the romance of that never-ending collision of nature's most dynamic feature and its most immovable object reigns. Turning the corner on Penzance Road to find the cove, one's breath is taken away. Add man's engineering touch, the twin lighthouses of Thacher's Island, just out in the distance, and that swelling in the chest grows just a little bit more.

For birders, this winter, there's even more. A Barrow's goldeneye, a rare cousin of the common goldeneye (rare, at least, on the Massachusetts coast), has taken up winter residence at the cove, an easy checkmark on hundreds of lists across the state. Closer to shore, among the many ducks, an Iceland gull, another winter visitor, sat quietly wondering whether or not the season was coming to an end.

The snowmelt around mid-day told us that we had reached the 50-degree mark. For a brief moment, Valentine's Day had a brush with a Massachusetts spring.

55. Gloucester: Eastern Point Wildlife Sanctuary

David and I ended our North Shore escape in Gloucester, scanning the waters from the Elks Club on Atlantic Avenue, examining the harbor from the Jodrey Fish Pier, and watching the fishermen return to the harbor from Eastern Point.

Eastern Point is a Mass Audubon wildlife sanctuary, a next-door neighbor to the Coast Guard's property at Eastern Point Lighthouse. It's a place where, two weeks earlier, a common murre took a brief rest along the breakwater. I happened to see it while participating in a fundraiser for the local Mass Audubon sanctuary. Of course, I couldn't help myself. Although the bird had been there two weeks in the past, I immediately rushed to the spot to see if it was there. It's a malady all birders suffer from eventually. It's called historical birding.

By the early afternoon, David and I had lost our hats and gloves. The promised warmth had arrived. It made for a lot of slush on the road, but who cared? Our winter thaw, usually a late January event, had begun. Temperatures were supposed to dip back down overnight, but then rise again for Thursday and Friday. What was one more cold night at this point?

I snapped a picture of the lighthouse complex and we headed for Woodworkers Warehouse in Woburn. Onto the next project!

February 17

56. Belmont: Habitat Wildlife Sanctuary

I guess I underestimated the warming powers of the sea. While the snow has dissipated quite substantially on the South Shore, it seemed that just a bit inland, just to the west of Boston, the cold was holding firm. There was more snow in Belmont on this day than I would have guessed.

Crunch, crunch, crunch...behind me a jogger started his approach. Good thing he wasn't trying to sneak up on me. To get out of his way, I headed for a patch of birch trees, then turned onto the Red Pine Trail. Guess what kind of trees I found? Let's just say that when I found the entrance to the Red Maple Trail, I knew exactly what to expect.

Somehow I met the jogger again, despite my circuitous, wandering route. Crunch, crunch, crunch. My guess was that he knew where he was going, which made our run-ins so funny. One shooting star, one bouncing moth.

I finally found my way back toward the parking lot after passing a sugar maple with a bucket on it. Yes, even here in Massachusetts, sap runs. Climate controls how much and how fast, and what grade syrup it makes. After this winter, it'd be interesting to see what the harvest brought.

Crunch, crunch, crunch...I hopped into my car and drove off. I still think that guy was following me.

57. Waltham: Prospect Hill Park

Whoa! Crossbill!

The last time I heard a white-winged crossbill singing was at West Quoddy State Park in Lubec, Maine, in 2008. Yet here one was, right in the parking lot of Prospect Hill Park. You just never know what you're going to find when you step outdoors.

I headed up the hill on the plowed road, which made me think of one thing: water tanks. I seemed to be hot on their trail this winter. But if they were there, I'd have other guardians to pass first. Glacial erratic boulders, including one called Dinosaur Rock, mark the way up the hill. I diverted from the main trail for a brief moment to take a footpath, the Boy Scout Trail, and was stumped. I couldn't figure out what it was I was seeing. It looked like two stone shelters of some kind, with, maybe, a fire pit? I pushed on, scratching my head.

The Boy Scout Trail proved only to be a connector between sections of the roadway, Glen Road. Then, it happened. Water tanks. Two of them. But they weren't at the crest of the hill. I kept climbing.

At the top, I was stumped again. I found a structure that looked like the base of a satellite dish with antennae fixed where the dish formerly was. At least, that was the best my little pea brain could come up with. I could have been way off.

I shook my fist at Waltham with a promise to return. I'll figure this place out yet!

February 22

58. Wareham: Great Neck Wildlife Sanctuary

At first, I thought the snow would be a hindrance, but it turned out to be a savior. Considering the site's history, it was quite fitting.

Mass Audubon's Great Neck Wildlife Sanctuary is comprised of land connected to the nearby Sacred Heart retreat center. And there's a lot to be said about the connections between nature and religion, the healing power of a walk in the woods, the rejuvenating feelings that come with the sound of a singing bird, or a glimpse of a distant fox darting through the trees. In short, it's a good fit.

The new snow, although there was just about an inch of it, saved me on this day. Beneath it on the trails rested a solid layer of ice. The snow gave my poor, old, worn-out boots enough traction to keep me from slipping and sliding. I still had to watch my feet most of the time, or the ground just in front of them, meaning I probably missed a lot of the scenery.

My only companion on the trails - the Huckleberry Loop and the Old Pasture Trail - was a hairy woodpecker. It dawned on me as I listened to its chirp that I couldn't tell anyone what a huckleberry looks like, not even remotely. Blueberries, strawberries, raspberries, sure, even mulberries. My grandfather had a mulberry bush at the top of his garden and we waited until they were sweet enough to pick and eat on the spot. We'd go running through the garden like dogs on a fox hunt in England. But I guess I've just never been a huckleberry hound.

Did I go too far for that joke?

59. Carver: Myles Standish State Forest

The snow couldn't save me, though, at Myles Standish. The trails around the East Head Reservoir were just too icy. I even caught myself sliding backwards at one point. No matter how hard I tried to move forward, I could make no advancement. I felt like the Red Queen in *Alice in Wonderland*.

On the flatter surfaces, where the new snow still sat, I caught the trail of a fisher. There had been lots of talk about them around me recently, as folks seemed to be seeing them more than usual. At the sanctuary where I work, we even found drag marks, where one pulled prey through the woods to a dining spot. Another - we think - had been hanging out by a collection of feeders.

Finding one after discovering tracks is near impossible, though. They're constantly on the move, and very quickly, dashing forward looking for prey. Unless you're on an intersecting path with one, you're not likely to catch up with one. Especially if you're running the Red Queen's Race (that's an Isaac Asimov reference, for Sci Fi fans out there).

I never found it, of course, which is a shame. I'd only ever seen one, and would have loved to add another to my list.

Probably have to go for a walk outside somewhere to do that.

February 24

60. Mashpee: Mashpee River Reservation

I had heard about places like this one, in legend and song, sung by bards throwing their melodic words to the four winds. I had read about it in books, in dusty old tomes that told tales of the way life used to be. Finally, I had found my Nirvana.

I realized when I stepped onto the trail that as far as my eyes could see, there was absolutely, positively, not even the slightest hint of snow!

For the first time in 2011, I walked on bare ground. In ways, it was a truly strange sensation, knowing that there was no chance of slipping and sliding on the trail, that I could plant my foot with that old confidence that brought me through 360 days of trail walking in 2009. Then I hit the mud.

Still, I didn't care. I slid, stretched out an inner leg muscle I didn't even know I had, but stayed on my feet. And I was glad I did, for there was plenty to see. Ospreys nest on a power line pole crossbar here, and their nest awaited their return in a month or so. There was a tree that grew a limb that decided to hug the ground for a while and take a 90-degree turn into the sky. The trail went right between it and the main trunk. There was a big holly tree at the river's edge. While standing there examining it, I realized I was hearing something I've only heard one other time this year: nothing.

I stood as still as possible, watching the water roll past. I thought back to a visit to Townsend earlier in the year, and how close I had come to complete silence. This spot was almost there. If not for the tiniest drone, the smallest hum of traffic on Route 28, I might have found it, but no luck.

Still, standing there, no hats, no gloves and no snow, I was in heaven.

61a. Barnstable: Skunknett River Wildlife Sanctuary

I ran into my own best laid plans today. I promised myself that I would walk every publicly-accessible Mass Audubon wildlife sanctuary in 2011, even if it meant walking in two places in one town. For the second time so far, I came across that situation.

Barnstable, though, is an odd duck, as far as towns in Massachusetts go. It's actually seven communities that are better known on their own than as individuals. Take Hyannis, for instance. It's as recognizable a village as any in Massachusetts, and probably more well-known than some towns. Yet, when you look at a map of Cape Cod, Barnstable is the town, and Hyannis, West Barnstable, Centerville and all the rest are swallowed up by the whole.

So here, in Osterville, I walked the Skunknett River Wildlife Sanctuary. The river is not the main feature of the sanctuary, at least to the trail walker. Nope, it's the pond, West Pond, to be precise. And on this day, the main feature on that pond was an odd duck, a northern pintail. The pond was being used as a feeding ground by several dabblers, including green-winged teals, American black ducks, hooded mergansers and a mallard. I saw them from every angle as I circumnavigated the pond, without even breaking out my sextant.

In all, I counted 11 species of birds on my walk, which wasn't bad for a cold, windy day in February. It's always good to have company on the trails.

61b. Barnstable: Long Pasture Wildlife Sanctuary

Elsewhere in Barnstable, within full view of Sandy Neck Lighthouse, I started on the Long Pasture Trail. I had heard a rumor that a rehabilitated barred owl had been released recently and was being seen around the property, specifically in a grove of cedar trees. I just had to check.

Instead, I found turkeys. Not the reintroduced wild turkeys that we see walking up to cars and pecking at their own reflections, thinking they're their evil twins, but white, domesticated turkeys. They were sharing space with guinea fowl, goats and sheep. It was one big, happy farmyard family, the kind that I read to my son about in his board books.

The thickets surrounding the pens were alive with chattering birds, white-throated sparrows, northern cardinals and even a gray catbird. That bird was supposed to be down south, staying warm until migration. Either it jumped the gun or it spent the winter on the Cape. Occasionally that happens. I saw one in Dighton on New Year's Day, so why not Barnstable on February 24?

I searched the cedars, unsuccessfully, and came out the other side, beyond the Button Bush Swamp and near the Butterfly Mosaic Garden. Then I heard something I hadn't heard for months. It was the slithering of a snake. I peeked and peered into the thickets but couldn't come up with anything. It seemed impossible that it was a snake, but weirder things had happened in 2011 already in regard to the animal world, from northern invaders like redpolls overwhelming Massachusetts feeders to southern birds like black vultures soaring over Cape Cod in the middle of winter.

As I walked back into the trees, I saw a gray squirrel with a mouthful of dry leaves, scurrying up a tree. It was a mom, building a nest.

Hallefreakinlujah.

62. Yarmouth: Old Yarmouth Historical Society Nature Trail

Now we're talking.

One of the biggest problems facing the preservation world today is specialization. Land conservancies buy land that include historic buildings, but aren't interested in saving them, as it doesn't fit their mission. Historical societies have opportunities to purchase lands, but don't because there are no extant buildings on them to interpret local history. It's time the two came together.

Yarmouth has it right. The two can coexist. And there's a whole layer of interpretation that a historical society can give to a piece of land that many land conservancies never even think about. Let's face it - is there any square foot of Massachusetts land left untrammeled by man (or, by the end of this year, by me)? If white Europeans haven't been there, there's a damn good chance that the land's first inhabitants, the Native Americans who lived here for thousands of years, have.

I often think in human terms when I walk a trail. Sure, I bring it all in, the full natural picture of the woods, the wildlife, the flora, the way weather affects and changes it all. But what, for instance, do the rhododendrons on the main trail here in Yarmouth say about the land? Since they're ornamental, transplanted from elsewhere, they speak of prior land usage. Today, with their big flower buds just aching to burst and their leaves only partially rolled up, they also spoke of a pending spring.

It was obvious, too, that the historical society had created a walking brochure for the trails. Either that or I had mistakenly stumbled onto a coincidentally perfectly arranged number of numerically-marked stones. I'm sure they were waymarkers that told bits of local history.

I watched a brown creeper slink its way up a tree, and wondered how many of the land's "owners" over time had the same experience.

63. Brewster: Nickerson State Park

To misquote a character from one of my favorite movies of all-time, *Johnny Dangerously*, I will say this: I once saw two yellow-bellied woodpeckers on the same tree at Nickerson State Park in Brewster.

Once.

On this day I was not so lucky, but a dearth of birdlife does not make for a bad day. I had already walked for two full hours on Cape Cod by the time that I reached Brewster, had given a lecture in Duxbury in the morning and had another one ready for the Cape Cod Postcard Collectors' Club in Dennis later that night. It was already an exhilarating day, and there was more to come.

So my wandering at Nickerson took me past a frozen pond and out onto pine-needle laden trails. I found a giant glacial erratic boulder that when viewed three-dimensionally looked like a big stony catcher's mitt. I had the urge to sit on it, where the giant rock baseball would sit, and set my camera up to take a picture. Then I thought of a new blog, MeOnARock.com. I could go all over the planet and have my picture taken on the famous rocks of the world.

Did I mention that I had already been walking for two hours?

64. Dennis: Indian Lands

At first, I was starting to get upset. Very upset. It just didn't seem fair.

I set off down the trail for Indian Lands, accessible from the town hall in Dennis, and found that even after five or six minutes I was walking on a utility line trail. Next to me were railroad tracks, grown over and unused for years. Indian Lands? Really?

I guess when I set off down the trail, I was hoping for something more than overhead phone lines and rusty rails. I thought that if we were going to memorialize this land's first inhabitants, that perhaps we could have done it in some better way.

Then, I realized I was simply on a feeder trail. A second set of signs - second *set* because the state and town each had their own signs, despite the fact they both celebrated it as a joint project - led to the entrance to the Indian Lands. Once inside, on the Ladyslipper Trail, the magic began. Indian Lands is a stunningly beautiful place, my thoughts apparently shared by a great blue heron in the marsh alongside the Bass River. I'm no anthropologist, but I could see in my mind's eye the warm days of summer when the local tribes would move to the water's edges to find food. It felt like a Native American place.

But my imagination should not stereotype the place or the people. Either way, it is still a piece of property in a heavily developed part of the country that is almost exactly as the early Natives saw it. I thank Dennis and the state of Massachusetts for it, but have to admit that I'm still not sold on the name, if for only one question: weren't they all?

February 28

65. Westwood: Lowell Woods

Sigh...back to the snow.

It had been funny over the past few days. We had several inches of snow in the Boston area, but we were at the point where unless it was eight inches or more, we didn't only skip the snowblower, we didn't even shovel the snow. We'd become resigned to walking on it and in it, knowing that collectively we fought the good fight in January, and that the major thawing was already underway.

The trail at Lowell Woods was well-packed, obviously heavily used in recent days. I could see why and by whom about halfway down the trail. I was accosted by a pair of black labs, one a puppy. Is there anything more excitable in life than a young dog trying to make new friends? The owner kept apologizing for the attack, but I loved it.

The woods here were just that, thick woods. Lots of pine, lots of beech, lots of oak and lots of noise from Route 128. The regular woodland dwellers were around, the nuthatches and the chickadees, and they had one surprise guest, a brown creeper. I was on a creeper hot streak, having just seen one down the Cape. But this one had a bonus: it was singing. Of all the songbirds in the eastern half of the United States, the creeper has one of the shortest seasonal song windows. It could be missed very easily. Glad I got mine in for the year on this day.

66. Dedham: Wilson Mountain Conservation Area

The trail at Wilson Mountain, well, as far as I could see there was no trail. No one had ventured here in recent days but the wildlife, and the deer had made quite a show of themselves. Their tracks cris-crossed the path - or at least what I figured had to be the path - even intersecting at times with mouse tracks.

I decided to add my own. There would be no doubting that I, or at least a human with a size 11 1/2 boot, had been there. I plunged. I plunged with about every fifth step on average, about eight inches in depth. I never knew which leg was going down when, but they did.

Despite this obstacle, I decided to head upwards, to find out what the allure of Wilson Mountain really was. I should have known. Water tank! My unwitting quest continues.

As I plunged my way back down, I realized that my left foot was getting cold. When I could, I extracted my foot from the snow and looked. The upper on my left L.L. Bean boot - only two years old - had torn at a seam and the snow was getting through. Nothing I could do but walk on.

At one point, I decided to test something I had read about in *The Book of General Ignorance*. Urban legend says that water has no color, that it's clear. But that's not true. It has a faint blue tint, and one of the best ways to tell is to look deeply into a hole in the snow. My plunge-prints proved to be plenty deep to see the truth.

And there it was.

67. Needham: Ridge Hill Conservation Area

By the time I hit Needham, the rain had started to fall. I ducked into the woods to dodge most of it, and was pleasantly surprised to find a Fit Trail.

There are dozens of ways to walk a trail. A straight ahead beeline walk is, of course, very pleasurable. Just ask Henry David Thoreau. A stop-and-smell-the-roses meandering does a soul fine, too. Then there's the Story Walk, the pages of a book being posted on the trail at different intervals. There's questing, or letterboxing. There's one of my favorites, time travel. Picture yourself walking the same woods in 1900, 1800, 1700. Do you see anything different?

Then there's the Fit Trail. Twenty-seven stretches and exercises were spread out along the path on this particular trail, with instructions even on how to travel between them, walking, jogging or running. I found them all, but some components have obviously been taken away for the winter, so I couldn't compete every exercise, even if I wanted to, which I did not. Not on this day, not in the rain.

I walked back towards what I thought was the trail on which I had walked into the woods, and was surprised to run into my second, third and fourth brown creepers of the morning. Wow! I'm usually happy with one or two per year, and here they were in a bunch, a total of five in the week.

Perhaps I was punch drunk, or creeper happy, when I left the woods, because I missed. I came out into a field, near my goal, but definitely not on it. I plunged. This time around, it wasn't just once, or once every few steps. It was every step, and it was over my knee. With every step, to extract myself, I had to bring my knee almost to my chest. After 70 steps or so in the heavy rain, I finally reached the pavement. Now that's how you get fit.

There was also a good lesson to be learned in an exercise like this one, about making sure your pockets on your jacket are zipped so you don't have to retreat through the deep snow to find your cellphone.

Like I did.

March

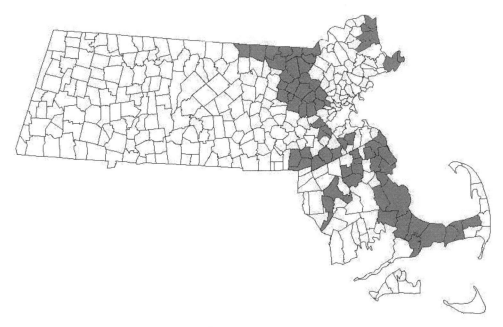

By the Letters

There are numerous ways to break down the state of Massachusetts into little categorical and manageable chunks. One of the stupidest ways is alphabetically. So naturally, I'd like to start there.

Well, after all, I need benchmarks. I needed to know, especially in these early days, that I was making progress. While Massachusetts is a small state, taken one community at a time it can be daunting. There's the new slogan: *Massachusetts: The Daunting State*. I'll call the office of travel and tourism right now.

So, taking Massachusetts by the letters, we find that, by far, there are more towns that start with the letter "W" than any other letter. Forty-six of them! That's almost one-fifth of the state, from Wakefield to Wrentham, that starts with the letter that Bert used to sing about on Sesame Street (*"Oh, what is the letter we love? What sound are we extra fond of? Without any trouble you know it's a "W" when you hear wu wu wu wu!"*).

What is it about the English language that at the time most of these towns were named, the letter "W" reigned? They run from Weymouth in 1635 to Wellesley in 1881, so it's a pretty large swath of Massachusetts history. Yet, while it might be fun to ponder what about Massachusetts and its landscape evoked "W's," there's one fact we have to keep in mind. More than 200 Bay State towns were named for counterpart British communities. Less than half, then, are of definite local origin. Norwell, for instance, was named for Henry Norwell, a businessman from Boston who summered in the town in the latter half of the nineteenth century, when South Scituate decided to rename itself (its mail was being sent to South Scituate, Rhode Island). When Old Abington broke up in 1874, the people of one ward, East Abington, voted to rename themselves Rockland - although someone did cast a vote to become Commotion, Massachusetts. How cool would that have been?

Going down the list, we have 35 towns that start with the letter "S," 31 with "M," 29 with "B," 27 with "H." That's 122 towns, or more than one-third, that start with those four letters. There's no "J," no "V," no "X," no "Z." There's one "I" (Ipswich), one "K" (Kingston), one "Q" (Quincy) and one "Y" (Yarmouth).

So what does this all mean in regard to my positioning on March 1? It means that I can take heart, perhaps a little solace, in the fact that I've made alphabetical progress. With four of the 26 letters in the alphabet being unrepresented, that means that fifteen percent of the alphabet is already accounted for. I picked off the "K" and the "Y," bring me up to 23 per cent. But that's where it ends. I'm not even halfway done with any other letter.

See? I told you it was stupid.

March 2

68. Newton: Cold Spring Park

Needham, I see your Fit Trail, and raise you the Exer Trail.

What were the chances that two walks in a row, in two separate towns, I would find a dedicated exercise trail set-up? Well, the chances were better than you might think.

Two years ago while walking every day for a half an hour, I made some discoveries about the hows and whys of trail walking. The one that stuck with me most was the notion of the inverse proportionality between walker friendliness and the proximity to Boston. The farther someone was into the sticks - sometimes literally - the nicer they were. Walk the parks surrounded by the streets of the city, and eye contact is at a premium, hellos unavailable for love or money.

Walking in places like Waltham, Needham, Dedham - you know, the ham towns - I've found that the small sections of open space that are kept for the populace have to be all things to all. Walkers, joggers, birders, dog-walkers, they all have very limited access to open space in the heart of an urban center. So they share. I was, in fact, the only person walking the trail at Cold Spring today that did *not* have a dog.

All that said, I got what I needed, 30 minutes of trees, shrubs, white-throated sparrows, the old Cochituate Aqueduct, a cold little brook, freedom to think and freedom to roam. And I met a few canines along the way. I'll take that kind of experience any day.

69. Wellesley: Longfellow Pond

With ice still on the ground and a bite in the air, I set off for another walk in an unfamiliar place. It's amazing, though, if one knows a little New England history, how a stranger can feel at home in a place he's never visited.

Take the wildlife, for instance. Well, on this day, there was barely any of which to speak, besides a few red-winged blackbirds in a tree at the far end of the trail, but just take it anyway. Even without knowing specifics, the average trail walker in Massachusetts recognizes basic sounds: robins, chickadees, cardinals.

Then, take the name of the pond: Longfellow. That's a good, historical, New England-y name. If it wasn't named for that bit of history, it would have a Native American name or something flatly descriptive: long, west, halfway, mill. We, New Englanders, rarely strayed from those tenets when naming our bodies of water.

As if to corroborate my thoughts, the supports for an old ice house popped out of the water at the far end of the pond, just past the bridge over Rosemary's Brook, which I will forever remember as the turnaround point of my walk at Longfellow. Ice ponds were all the rage even just a century ago. Their crews were most productive in winter, cutting and storing ice, for summer revelers along the coast. This particular ice house was run by an outfit called the Metropolitan Ice Company, which went under only when automated home heating and cooling systems came into widespread use in the 1920s.

The story expands outwards. I've visited ice ponds in Abington, Duxbury, Hingham and more. The Wenham Ice Company provided Queen Victoria's favorite ice. The story told in Wellesley is the same one told in small towns all over Massachusetts, all over New England.

In some ways, my visit to Longfellow was an all new adventure; in other ways, I felt right at home.

70. Rockland: Rockland Town Forest

I love walking here. Love, love, love it.

I used to live in Rockland, attended my freshman year of high school here, and within the past decade have had the privilege of coauthoring two books on the history of the community with my talented and absurdly knowledgeable friend Don. And this spot is one of those great crossovers of history and nature, with a little bit of both in every step.

Not only that, I get to pretend I'm someone else entirely when I set foot on the trail. To quote Inigo Montoya in *The Princess Bride*, "Let me 'splain. No, is too much. Let me sum up."

The Rockland Town Forest, or at least the first few hundred yards of it, was a nursery. When it closed up shop several years ago, the plants were just left where they were, free to grow and be wild. The main plant to take advantage of that fact was the spreading yew, you know, the kind we all have next to our doorways at home, the kind we trim every year to keep in check.

Well nobody's keeping these babies in check. They've grown to towering heights and even formed cavernous passages between their rows. All I can imagine when I walk through them is that I'm some small impish creature, as it's the only way this place makes sense. I've often wondered if I should paint my skin blue and call myself Big Johnny Smurf. Probably wouldn't be a good look for me, topless with a floppy white hat and footy pajama bottoms.

Beyond this fantasy land, the town forest extends into a system of trails that are becoming ever more accessible due to the pride and commitment of several local individuals. Bird boxes now peek out along the trail where they didn't even two years ago. It's a work in progress, but something of which every Rockland resident should be proud. *Go Bulldogs!*

71. Hanson: Burrage Wildlife Management Area

I think it hit 50 degrees. And when I set off on the trail at Burrage, the bright sun was so powerful I had to shut my eyes for a few moments. We just hadn't had this kind of sunshine for a while. I wasn't complaining.

I wasn't alone on the trails at Burrage, which are mostly the ridge-like dividers between the retired cranberry bogs that make up the hundreds of acres of open space here. There were dog walkers, of course, and even one other guy with binoculars. The biggest surprise was two hunters walking with their rifles casually tossed over their shoulders. It's just not a sight you see very often these days.

It was as if "All of Rome was at the Baths," which included the wildlife. While the whipping wind kept much from happening sky-wise, there was a flock of about 150 snow buntings feeding on one of the bogs, and I watched a muskrat swimming beneath the surface of one of the old channels. It ducked into its lodge, and when it did, it released a few bubbles of air that popped to the top. A great blue heron flew low over the bogs until it found a good spot from which to look for food.

I walked toward an opening in the woods that led to my next destination, and oddly, as I did so, the clouds overtook the sun.

72. Halifax: Stump Brook Wildlife Sanctuary

So I stepped from Burrage to Stumpy. Mass Audubon's Stump Brook Wildlife Sanctuary is landlocked, with no dedicated access point of its own, but luckily one of those landlockers is Burrage. If you know where to go, you can trek from one to the other and vice versa with ease.

I had one of the most amazing natural experiences of my life at Stump Brook in the spring of 2010. While there with my colleague Robert, preparing to conduct a breeding bird study, I caught something from the corner of my eye. "Look!" I whisper-shouted. Several - five? six? - gray fox pups had spotted us, tilted their ears forward and cocked their heads to investigate. "Exhilarating" doesn't even come close to describing the moment.

On this day, though, the woods were quiet. I found my rock, the one that helps me relocate the bird study spot, and set still for a few moments. I could hear nothing but the wind, and started to focus on the sights. I never realized how heavy this particular area was with holly trees, or how densely the ground was covered with princess pines.

When I emerged from the woods and went back out to Burrage, the sun slid from behind the clouds again. Weird. But what did I care, it was 50 degrees!

73. Middleborough: Pratt Farm

Fresh out of the driver's seat, BAM! I ran into Bill, an old friend.

Bill used to join our regular Friday morning birding group, but dropped off in recent years, part of the typical ebb and flow of program participation. We chatted about common friends, how so-and-so was doing, when I last saw what's-his-face. It was wonderful catching up with him. I'll always remember the day that he handed me a copy of *The Day the World Came to Gander, Newfoundland*, one of the best books I've ever read. Thoughtful guy.

He told me I had two options: straight ahead down a long trail or to the left, to a pond. I chose the pond, despite the fact I knew it would still mostly be frozen. Unfortunately, it was the trail itself that was the icy hazard. Every walker I met coming from the other direction was just off the edge of the trail, where the ice had melted. I shared their strategy.

As I crossed a dam that held the pond, after weaving through fields and orchards and thickets, I thought to myself that at one time, this all made sense. The farmer - I'm assuming it was a Pratt - who laid it out had a method to his design madness. The pond was where it was for a reason, and the field nearby was probably located based on the positioning of that pond.

Today, of course, it makes no sense, because it doesn't have to. It's open space, with many varied habitats, offering homes to innumerable species of birds, butterflies, salamanders, ants and whatever might want to make Pratt Farm its home.

Bill was gone when I got back, but I'm sure I'll run into him again someday. And I can't wait until I do.

74. Plympton: Land Behind the Dennett School

Sigh...I think Plympton beat me. From everything I can see, Plympton does have a town forest, but trying to find that town forest is like looking for a chicken at the bottom of the ocean. And I don't mean tuna, the chicken of the sea. I mean the feathery, clucking kind.

I chanced that the land behind the Dennett School might be it. I went for a walk around the edges of the schoolyard - on a Saturday, of course, to steer clear of the important work of the teachers and students - and found that I could not get into the woods. There is a large wooded parcel behind the school, so the open space does exist, but the best I could do was tiptoe around its perimeter.

Oh well, I got my half an hour in, which was the key. And Plympton should have plenty of open space in the future, if American trends away from farms continue. It certainly is a beautiful community.

March 19

75, 76. Rochester and Marion: East Over Reservation

I gave myself almost two weeks off between walks, to let the snow melt and the mud dissipate, but the itch finally overwhelmed me. I guess sitting still is not something I should be putting on a resume, as I'm not very good at it.

Oh, I'd been busy in between, with board meetings, work, book publishing projects, turning 40, raising my son...you get the picture. And I even managed to do a few of my regularly scheduled walks on the South Shore, but did not get out and forge any new personal trails. That stalemate ended on this day.

East Over is a two-for, but not in one leg. I had to find both of the separate entrances to the tracts of the Trustees of Reservations' reservation, both of which were quite well marked. In Rochester, the trails wound back and forth through fields and woods and more fields and more woods, a system which kept me happily guessing as I went. All the signs of the old farm were there, from stone walls to wooden fences strung with barbed wire, perfect for keeping sheep or cattle in place and view. In some instances, the barbed wire had bitten into the trees, which consumed them and kept on growing right over it.

There were bluebird boxes and owl pellets, but the wind made sure I saw neither the user of the former nor the producer of the latter.

In Marion, the trails were woodsier and muddier. Long boardwalks led across wet patches and deeper into the woods. No trail map had yet been printed for use on the paths, and that was my downfall on this day. I ended up spending nearly twice as much time here as I planned, as I got lost. Normally, I don't care, but I did have an afternoon appointment and wanted to be sure I was there on time. But had I not taken the wrong turn, crossed the dirt road and emerged on the far side I would never have seen the log cabin somebody was trying to build, nor the beautiful swampland from which the American black ducks emerged at my what-I-thought-was-silent approach.

I found my way out in the end. and made my appointment. I can also honestly say now that I've seen all of the Hale's Brook Tract of East Over, whether I planned to do so or not.

77. Mattapoisett: Tinkham Forest

There are some things you just wish you didn't see when tackling a project like this one, but there's no hiding the facts when you do.

The Tinkham Forest came as a gift to the people of Mattapoisett in 1968, and in recent years has become quote a controversial piece of real estate. The problem mainly stems from the fact that the selectmen in Mattapoisett see the land as just that: real estate. A developer asked, the selectmen determined a price, and were ready to sell before a cry arose.

In my humble opinion, the notion of selling land given as a gift to a community with the intention that it would be open forever is incorrigible.

But there are deeper problems with the forest. The first I saw was the dirt bike that blasted out of it past me. I will say, though, that whether or not that is a problem for the people of Mattapoisett depends on the community's definition of the space; if they choose to allow ORVs (off-road vehicles) in their open spaces, as long as they fall within state and federal laws, that is their choice. I can tell you, though, that if the intention is to let nature be nature, off-road vehicles have no place in the woods. Against exhaust fumes and the destructive trampling of tires, woodland creatures just don't stand a chance.

Second, there's the trash. Mattapoisett is not the only place in Massachusetts with these concerns, of course. Somebody, most likely several somebodys, is using the entry road to the forest as his or her personal dump. Old televisions, computer monitors, mattresses, toilet seats and other scattered junk sit in huge piles off to the sides of the road. It was disheartening to see, to say the least.

What was heartening was the call of the wood frogs I heard clucking from a small wet area just inside the woods, the first I'd heard in 2011. Nature was persevering, for the moment.

78. Fairhaven: West Island State Reservation

Back to the good stuff.

I reached Fairhaven and West Island not knowing exactly what to expect. Typically a Massachusetts state reservation on the ocean means huge parking lots and beach access. I was nonplussed (not that I've ever been plussed, to my knowledge) when reaching the end of Causeway Road and finding myself facing dense woods. Nevertheless, I dove in.

The wide trails made for excellent walking, and probably help keep down Lyme disease in the area, if in a small way. Signs warned of deer ticks when I walked in. Staying far from the vegetation on the sides of the trails helps to keep them somewhat, if not entirely, at bay.

At one point, though, I had to pull myself over and do some inspection. I found two trees, side-by-side, surrounded by piles of freshly stripped wood. Porcupine damage! The only other thought I had was woodpeckers, but none operate like this, and there were no drill holes anywhere on the trees. If it wasn't porcupines, I'll eat my hat, and pick my teeth clean with a porcupine quill.

Eventually, if you have a nose for the ocean like me, the trail will emerge onto a sandy shore. From where I stood, I could see the Cape Cod Canal Railroad Bridge, and therefore Bourne, where I'd already been in 2011. I surmised then, though, that I could also see Falmouth. *Grrrr...*that was one that was still on my list.

But I couldn't summon the negative energy to shake a fist across the bay. It was just so beautiful.

79. Acushnet: New Bedford Reservoir

I've gotten used to the "No Trespassing" signs on the South Coast of Massachusetts. It's almost epidemic in the region. But I was disappointed when I followed the directions to the one piece of open space I could find in Acushnet and found just such a sign at the trailhead. So I headed for the nearest body of water.

The ponds of the New Bedford Reservoir are now polluted, according to a sign in the parking lot that divides the three bodies of water. Specifically, the sign outlaws swimming and wading. These ponds once supplied New Bedford with an emergency water supply, but that's no longer the case. New Bedford turned the ponds over to Acushnet, and the town has begun studies to determine the extent of the system's health and/or lack of same. A concrete slab platform that once apparently held a small building, probably connected with the waterworks sits surrounded by volunteer trees that have shot up around its edges.

Yet something was going right here on this day. Canada geese and mute swans swam on the water's surface, the latter dipping their heads low to tug on the vegetation below. Spring peepers - my first of the year - sounded off, heralding the season for which they are named. Aesthetically, these ponds were holding their own, and nature had not yet given up on them. Here's to hoping the good people of Acushnet can tackle the pollution problem and fully restore the beauty of this wonderfully natural place.

March 22

80. Holbrook: Holbrook Town Forest

Holbrook Town Forest, where have you been all my life?!

Actually, we go back two years, the forest and me. I walked a portion of it during my first grand year-long walking experiment in 2009. The difference was that I entered it from a different access point the first time around. This day's adventure was all new.

This place had everything! A cellar hole, stonewalls, little brooks that interrupt the path, smooth-barked beech trees with fading leaves, exorcised tufted titmice ranting in a witch hazel grove, and some nice, freestanding boulders. I dig glacial erratics.

If there was one drawback, it was the constant hum of the nearby electric behemoth run by NSTAR. Its presence, though, creates a powerline scrub-shrub habitat, which is actually quite beneficial to local wildlife. It's a habitat that's vanishing almost as quickly as farmland in Massachusetts, and powerline corridors are almost the only things keeping birds like prairie warblers coming back to Massachusetts to breed.

I stood at the edge of that corridor and took it all in, the grackles, the cardinals, the flickers, the blue jays, the edge of one habitat giving way to another, on the edge of one season giving way to the next.

Beautiful!

81, 82. Avon and Brockton: D.W. Field Park

It's really incredible, when one sits down to think about it (or does so while walking, which is usually what I do; sitting down in the woods during a muddy spring is no fun), how much of our open space has to do with water. I've met more town water towers this year than I ever thought I would. I'm assuming that they're on the tops of hills for their gravitational advantages, and not just because communities can paint their towns' names on them as a "you are here" indicator.

But it's also the old municipal water supplies that make up many parks today. In some instances, those places are retired, as towns have found alternative sources, or have found the need for larger sources of drinking water. In other instances, park infrastructure has been simply built around those active water supplies with stern warnings to stay out of the water itself. The northern half of D.W. Field Park, in Avon, is dominated by just such a body of water, called the Brockton Reservoir.

The rest of the park, extending into Brockton to the south, is defined by Waldo Lake (the donor of the land was Daniel Waldo Field, a captain of the shoe industry in Brockton), Upper and Lower Porter Ponds, Thirty-Acre Pond and Ellis Brett Pond. Field donated the land in 1925, feeling that a town needed both industry and open space to be considered a success to its inhabitants. His gift remains the crown jewel of the city today.

It's been a long time since I've seen as many dedicated walkers on the paths as I did this day. There were no dogs to be seen; these folks were just out for the exercise and enjoyment of a good, solid, healthy walk. They were treated to sunshine, spring peepers, numerous species of ducks on the ponds and a snow goose, which, unfortunately, looked a little bit too much on the domesticated side, but we'd see whether or not it would stick around for the summer or fly north to breed.

I chalked this one up to "pleasant surprise." I knew Brockton for its excellent high school football program, Rocky Marciano, Marvelous Marvin

Hagler and its fantastic late Victorian era architecture, that being the height of the shoe industry in southeastern Massachusetts. D.W. Field Park will now pop instantly to mind when someone asks me what I like most about Brockton.

83. Canton: Mildred Morse Allen Wildlife Sanctuary

Ha! Another trail I could walk in my sleep.

I've gotten to know Mass Audubon's Mildred Morse Allen Wildlife Sanctuary trails well over the past decade or so. You might know the property as the Visual Arts Center. By any name, it's a wonderful place.

I first met this land when working on a pictorial history of New England's largest environmental organization, *Images of America: Mass Audubon*. I learned about the amazing life of Ms. Allen, a woman I'm sad I never met, through her artwork, her photography, her films, and, ultimately her donation of land and funds to create this special entity we have today. At about 180 acres of open space with indoor facilities dedicated to art education, it's the perfect place to study art and its connections to the natural world.

But, like all natural places, it has its potential for moments of true individual discovery. I wasn't on the Main Loop Trail for more than five minutes when I ran into my moment. "What in the name of Mildred Morse Allen happened here?" was all I could think. There, before me, in the heart of the trail, was a classic woodlands forensics scene. Thick tufts of gray fur, some hairs pure white, the gray tipped in orangey-brown, covered a ten-foot by four-foot patch. And it was thick, and long. There had obviously been a confrontation of some kind. And it wasn't a squirrel, lest today that squirrel is today wandering around the sanctuary completely naked. My first thought was gray foxes or coyotes.

I looked for clues of a getaway, for there was no carcass, no obvious loser left on site. There was more fur snagged in the brush on both edges of the trail. This fight didn't stay on the path by any means. But I could find no more clues. I guess I'll never know. If two coyotes fight to the death in the woods and no one's around to hear it, do they make any noise?

The whole experience was one that focused my senses. I realized that rather than just ambling down a trail, I was hyper-alert, eyes darting around, mind racing. I wanted to figure the scene out.

And I wanted to thank Mildred Morse Allen for leaving this gift for all to enjoy.

84. Milton: Great Blue Hill

I finished my morning of walking with another old familiar trail, the hike to the top of Great Blue Hill.

It's one of the most vertical trails I've ever walked. And me, being gravitationally challenged (for those of you in the Boston area, that's fancy talk for "wicked fat"), well, I felt every foot in elevation. It's incredible how just that change in incline from a normal flatlander's path to a hillside works a completely different set of muscles, and tires one out so much quicker.

Beyond that fact, there's the trail itself. It's heavily rocky, and that's the way it should be. The hill is studded with chunks of blue rock, hence the name of the range, the Blue Hills, and if there had been an attempt in the past to clear the trail of it, it didn't take. And that's not surprising, considering that gravity thing I mentioned earlier. I'm sure the footing on the trail is constantly changing as rocks tumble and fall, pushed and pulled by the whims of rain, snow and mud. It's as nature intended.

The goal for me on this trail is always the Eliot observation tower, named for the man whose vision shaped the Massachusetts state park system. A short walk around the corner brings one to the Rotch observatory, from which come all the weather updates we hear on the radio in the Boston area.

The views are worth the walk, from the Boston city skyline to the harbor islands and beyond. A little sweat and heavy breathing? Eh, another day at the office for me.

March 28

85. Provincetown: Beech Forest

Imagine if the world's political boundaries were laid out by dominating habitat types. Cape Cod would be practically a world unto itself, which, of course, you may argue that it is already. It would lead to an interesting arrangement; all the pine barrens, the glacier-scoured lands, of southeastern Massachusetts, the eastern end of Long Island, and into New Jersey, would have one governor, one Schwarzenegger, one Ventura.

That governor would need to be an expert in, for instance, pitch pine, its exportability, its uses, how to maximize its commercial potential. Locals would be experts in pitch pine soup, pitch pine soap, pitch pine construction methods, because they'd have to be. Everything else non-pine barrens related would have to be imported: dolls, bananas, baseball cards, everything.

Instead, we're proud as Massachusetts residents to include the pine barrens as one of a wide array of habitat types, one that many people have to travel long, long distances to see and still claim it as part of their state's natural heritage. With sand underfoot, I started my Outer Cape adventure for the year.

I wasn't planning on wind, but then, I was at the tip of the Cape. Chalk that up as a "well, duh" moment. The birds didn't seem to mind, at least not that early in the morning, as they were chattering away, even in the subzero wind chill. One sound caught my attention and I zeroed in on it. It sounded like a cuckoo, but it was way too early for a cuckoo. I remembered what my friend and colleague Wayne once said. If you're thinking you're hearing cuckoo in March in Massachusetts, think chipmunk.

He was so right.

86. Truro: Pilgrim Heights

Now, this is where I thought I would begin my walking project this year. But, as I said, Dighton got in the way.

I was thinking that I would find myself somewhere historically significant, even as wavering and dubious a connection as this one might be, at least geographically speaking. Let me explain.

We know the Pilgrims came ashore in what would become the northern Truro area before they touched down permanently in Plymouth. We know that they reported seeing deer and finding a water source, and from that water source they drank their first draughts of New World goodliness.

What we don't know is *exactly* where these events happened.

We know generally where, and that is good enough for you, me and the National Park Service. We need just a little suspension of disbelief when we stand before the marker declaring the story. We have to understand that it took place somewhere in the area. There is no giant tree, no huge rock, no homestead built on the site. And that's just fine. Instead we have a forest full of bear oaks and highbush blueberries, which, oddly, might not even be as historically significant themselves as one might think. More on that later.

87. Wellfleet: Wellfleet Bay Wildlife Sanctuary

There are few places in Massachusetts you can go and expect to see whale vertebrae as lawn ornaments: several Cape Cod towns, Nantucket, Martha's Vineyard and the communities around New Bedford. After that, they're hit and miss.

Mass Audubon's Wellfleet Bay Wildlife Sanctuary has a good one, on the left hand side of the trail as one enters, opposite the solar array. Past, meet future.

My walk here on this day, on the way to Try Island, was punctuated with a huge, cold exclamation point. The wind had not relented one mile per hour in my travels from P-Town to Wellfleet. It didn't bother the belted kingfisher much, nor did it dissuade the dozen or so species assaulting the bird feeders near the nature center. But there were no early herons or egrets stalking the marshes, no hawks or kestrels or ospreys in the sky. It was just too darned cold.

I reached the point where I had a decision to make - do I go for Try Island, or do I turn back? The decision was partially made for me, as the trail suddenly became overwhelmed with saltmarsh hay, right in the place I typically try to sneak up on the resident fiddler crabs and watch them scurry into their muddy holes. Faced with that fact, the deep cold, the need to stick to my schedule and, I fear, a growing internal wimpiness, I turned to retreat farther south along the old Grand Army of the Republic Highway.

88. Eastham: Doane Rock Area

Eastham, near the Salt Pond Visitor Center, the public home base of the Cape Cod National Seashore, was where a significant piece of the Cape Cod natural picture came together for me. Walking the Doane Rock area, one finds numerous interpretive signs on the trails, all well done, some more intriguing than others. That, of course, is based on subjectivity. Do you believe in the power of history or the lure of nature? How about both?

Looking through the trees to understand the story of the forest, one is struck by one particular fact. This was not what the pilgrims saw. There's more oak here now than there was pine then.

Shade tolerance is the key. The oaks growing in these woods are capable of growing in a relative dearth of sunlight; the same cannot be said of the pines. So, as those young oaks mature and grow into bigger trees, they create even more shade, making it ever more difficult for those pines to thrive. Over the course of a few years, it might not be noticeable. After a lifetime of walking in the woods, you probably would notice a few changes. Give it a few centuries, maybe a millennium, and you have a different set of trees.

And then, there's that rock. Wow. The Doanes knew what they were doing when they picked that out as their genealogical landmark.

89. Orleans: John Kendrick Woods

Finally, I found a way to get myself out of the wind. It was still there, attacking the forest ceiling, and, in fact, it helped me with a revelation, but it wasn't assaulting me personally any more. Hearing the branches rattling above, I glanced directly upward and was startled by the rich, luxuriant blue that unrelentingly covered the sky.

The cold, though, had done its duty for the day. Wildlife had hunkered down as I entered the John Kendrick Woods. By the time I reached a bench overlooking a ravine, I had only heard two species - a chickadee and a crow - and that would be 67% of the total I would tally there for the day. A passing goldfinch would buff out the stats as I left.

Along the trail I found a box for doggie treats, yet no doggies were to be found on this day. I walked so far that I came out the other end of the property, which I did not know was possible. I think in loops. I turned and headed back, only to be almost run over by a guy on a mountain bike. He apologized - not necessary, as I'm always happy to share a nature trail - and seconds later his wife or girlfriend or some mysteriously coincidental female version of him did exactly the same thing. I dodged to the left, without feinting, as I figured that would be too dangerous at her speed, and survived to walk another trail.

Good thing, too, as there was still more Cape to go.

89. Chatham: Conservation Land

I couldn't find a name for this conservation parcel on any nearby signs, but I certainly found a story.

I now know it's called the Triangle, and that I have walked it in its entirety. But it was the first few steps that were of true significance. I stumbled onto a burial ground - not, of course, unprecedented in suburban Massachusetts. Family plots dot the landscape in southeastern Mass, and I'm sure in other parts of the state as well. I'd be finding out for sure later in 2011.

So I wasn't surprised to see headstones, and old ones, at that. What I was surprised at was the words "small pox" being inscribed into every one of them.

It must have been quite a scare the first time small pox ran through the area. It's a horrible disease, highly contagious and quickly deadly. Scituate, for instance, went as far as banning all outsiders from spending the night in their town by law to prevent the spread of the disease into the community. If you entered that town from anywhere else, the locals shunned you, for at least the years in which the disease was sadly prevalent, cold shoulders and downcast eyes reigned.

That distrust spread into death. Small pox victims often ended up buried far from the normal places, the spots where they figured they'd spend eternity alongside their loved ones and other townsfolk. What a sad ending to a cut-short life. It's hard not to think about those poor lost souls when you walk the rest of the loop.

91. Harwich: Hawksnest State Forest

What? Another cemetery? Go figure.

I'd been reading online about Hawksnest, the standard case of neglect by the state's Department of Conservation and Recreation, erosion issues and difficulty in parking in the area. So I was very content to park near the cemetery and walk down to the pond, even if it meant lengthening my journey for the day, and not contributing to the ongoing issues.

Trails were a bit difficult to find, tougher to follow once I found them, and I think at one point I walked off the state property. I was serenaded by a particularly melodic American crow. They offer a range of calls, from grotty, nasal squawks to songbird-like trills. Even so, I can pretty safely say this was the most pleasant sounding crow I'd ever heard.

At one point I found myself pinned in between two ponds on a thin little wooded isthmus. The trail eventually and unceremoniously petered out, leaving me stranded halfway. It was the isthmus of no return.

By the time I noticed a brown creeper climbing a nearby oak, watching it dive headlong towards the ground before hopping its way up again - singing occasionally, picking at food sources constantly - I realized I was done for the day. I had been heavily breathing in bitingly cold air for 3 1/2 hours, and my lungs were burning. But to paraphrase the cowboy in the famous *Far Side* cartoon said, "Sure it hurt. But it was a good kind of hurt."

March 30

92, 93. Stoneham and Medford: Middlesex Fells Reservation

After a day immersed in pine needles, sand and ocean breezes, I found myself somewhere between utterly lost and feeling right at home in the Middlesex Fells.

Living now as I do in Weymouth, this land was much more what I am accustomed to experiencing when I walk out my front door. Life just isn't the same without protruding bedrock, glacial erratic boulders and oak-pine-maple woods.

The Fells have a bit of the Blue Hills in them (for those of you who live locally, the Blue Hills have a bit of the Fells in them). Paths walk directly up the sides of rocks, using their natural breaks as stairways. There are ups and downs and hills and dells and the occasional wide exposed section of rock that leaves a hole in the forest canopy. When you see one, you can't help it; you have to run for it. Something that instinctual has to go back through time. It's at those moments that you wonder if you're standing in the footsteps of the local natives from centuries ago.

Rocks with recognizable profiles reveal themselves. I found one that looked like a polar bear. Old paved roadways appear here and there, leading to further brow-furrowing mysteries. A jumbled pile of rocks, once, probably, a single entity that crashed to earth from the slippery slope of a retreating glacier, lurch into view. And then Spot Pond emerges, covered with common mergansers, powerfully relaying the sounds of the nearby roadways. If only those roads had been pushed even a half mile farther away when the park was designed...but I dream.

Yes, after a day on the Cape, it was good to be "home" again.

April

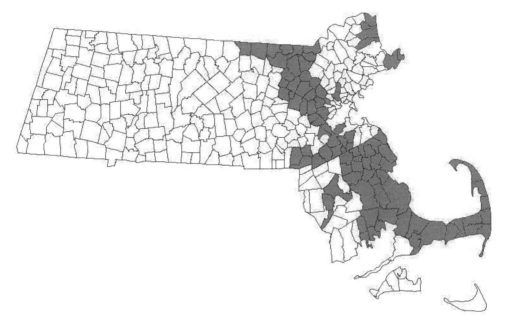

County Lines

After three months, I glanced at the map, and noticed that if I wanted to, I could retrace my own footsteps from Provincetown at the tip of Cape Cod to Ashby, on the New Hampshire border, and do so without stepping out of the bounds of communities I had already walked. The problem, of course, was that it was 171 miles from point to point. Might need to do some training before I set out on that little excursion.

In my never-ending search for progress against benchmarks in this project, I had decided to check myself against the fourteen Massachusetts counties. After three months - three snowy, cold, rainy months - during which, by design, I had attempted to conquer the east, I had done pretty well.

That said, I hadn't completed a single county yet. But I was close.

Let's take Barnstable County, for instance. Of the 15 towns in Barnstable County, or "the Cape," I was down to just one, Falmouth. Piece of cake. I would probably eat that cake, though, when I dealt with the oddball of Dukes County, Gosnold. Gosnold is the governmental name for the Elizabeth Island chain, off Falmouth, the seat of which is Cuttyhunk. In short, I needed a boat. Luckily, I lead trips to Cuttyhunk and Penikese for Mass Audubon. I would get out there in August. To finish Dukes, I'd need to hit the six towns of Martha's Vineyard.

Plymouth County was the next closest to being finished. I needed just three more towns - Hull, Hingham and Lakeville - to put a huge checkmark next to that 27-town unit. Norfolk was looking good, 15 of 28 down, and I was more than halfway through Middlesex County, 28 of 54. I'd done six in Bristol County and six in Essex, but the rest were goose eggs.

I needed Nantucket, a county of one. Suffolk, Boston and vicinity, equals four towns. Then, it was time to listen to Horace Greeley and go west. Worcester, Franklin, Hampden and Hampshire Counties were just taunting me at this point. *When are you gonna come for us, walker boy? Waiting for 70 degrees? Well, that's just fine. We'll have the mosquitoes ready for you.*

And therein was the trade-off. I had worked hard to finish off the towns that would soon be overwhelmed by summer beach goers. I did not want to try to cross the Sagamore Bridge to Cape Cod in July. I mean, I'm not stupid. But by reserving the warmer days for the interior, I was subjecting myself to more mosquitoes and ticks and God knows what else. But I'd take it, in exchange for gridlock and exhaust fumes.

April 1 was about to arrive, and snow was forecast yet again. Still, at 93 towns down, that was 26 percent of the state gone, or just more than one-quarter. I was not well ahead of the pace, but instead right on it after a lot of tough weather in which to walk.

I was feeling good! Bring on the snow.

April 11

94. Southborough: Breakneck Hill Conservation Area

Over the previous few years, I'd come to know pneumonia almost as soon as it hits me. Around the first of April, that tickle started at the back of my throat. By the 5th, I knew I was seriously sick; by the 6th, I knew it was pneumonia. It was a rough couple of weeks.

I've also figured out that it's the fifth day after the fever breaks that I can get back in the game full time. By that time, too, I'm itching to exercise my lungs. So on Monday, April 11, the time had come. I hit the trail.

And when I did, I struck apple.

I started to understand that as I continued my westward expansion across the state I'd start to realize just how much farming was and is a major facet of Massachusetts life. Breakneck Hill is part orchard, part field, all rolling hills. Where bedrock pokes through the earth, trees grow in the field. The hint of fresh manure wafted on the breeze with the sounds of Route 9. Hawks soared overhead, robins foraged on the ground, blackbirds squawked in the trees. I even heard a chipping sparrow, a recent returnee from southern wintering grounds.

With temps predicted to hit 80 degrees, the feeling of spring - even early summer - was everywhere. Now if only the cloud cover would break overhead...

95. Westborough: Walkup and Robinson Memorial

Could this place be any cuter?

First, the main trail is an old trolley line: Victorian days, people ridiculously overdressed to be outdoors, picnics, politeness (or so the Victorians would have us believe). Open-air trolley cars brought revelers to places like this one, with little stone stairways that were at once stoically utilitarian and natural-looking, on bright, cheery summer days.

Then, there's the Cattlepass Bridge. Are you kidding me? Farmers using fields nearby, the remnants of which survive, could safely shuttle their cows beneath the trolley bridge to keep them free from fear of collision with passing streetcars. On one side of the bridge there's an old pasture tree, on the other, an old well. Under the bridge itself, a pair of eastern phoebes were building a nest.

Did I just see a bunny? *Oh my god.*

I spooked a chipmunk on the way back to the parking area, then did the same to a red-shouldered hawk a few feet later. Regarding the former, I've often thought I'd love to write a book called *Chasing Chipmunks*, about traveling the United States to find all the different species. So far I can score eastern, least and cliff, but I think that's it. Maybe when my son's a bit older he and his dad will take a road trip.

When I got back to the car, I noticed that the temps had actually dropped. Whatever happened to the 80s, as my hairstyle, wardrobe, taste in music and choice of re-runs on TV Land often ask?

96, 97. Northborough and Berlin: Mt. Pisgah Conservation Area

I think I found my second favorite natural place in Massachusetts.

Mt. Pisgah (not to be confused with New Hampshire's Pisgah State Park) straddles the town boundaries of Berlin, to the north, and Northborough to the south. The park is somewhat evenly split across the two communities, making for a nice exploration.

Starting from the south on the Mentzer Trail, I found a patch of snow, having to do a double take to be sure I was seeing what I thought I was seeing. I guess there still is some hanging around in Massachusetts. A moment later, at 9:32 a.m., the sun broke through the clouds, before quickly retreating. It was going to be that kind of day.

Before turning onto the Berlin Road trail I ran across a flock of six wood ducks deep in an upland section of woods, which was odd, but not unprecedented. I've seen them standing in trees before (hence their name), so I wasn't really surprised. The last time was at Sapsucker Woods in Ithaca, New York.

Crossing the Berlin line I took to the North Gorge Trail, and found my runner-up paradise. The trail hugs the ridgeline pretty closely, and with the trees not yet fully leafed out (but starting!) I could see all the way down to the bottom of the gorge, where the little stream that, I'm guessing, cut it flows. Even there, stonewalls run straight and corner sharply, dividing the land up for the ghosts of the farmers who once tended the land. A blue jay grabbed a twig and flew off to build a nest while pine siskins sounded in the trees above it all.

My favorite spot in Massachusetts? I'll let you know when I get there later this year.

98. Bolton: Bolton Flats Wildlife Management Area

As the morning rolled on, I finally came to a familiar place. Birders from across Massachusetts know Bolton Flats as one of those, "well, I should get there at least once a year" kind of places. The last time I was here a hunter walked up with two dead American woodcocks in his hand, telling my friend David and I how he planned to clean and cook them.

There's an irrigation canal that runs through the property, which is enormous, by the way. I barely scratched the surface of it today, which is what a tractor had recently done in preparation for this year's crops. Despite the fact that the morning was wearing on, the birdlife was staying busy. I started to realize, too, that perhaps the fact that it was 65 and cool was going to be more advantageous in the long run than 80 and directly sunny. For both me and the birds.

I found more wood ducks. This time, they made much more sense to me, riding the waters of the canal, spooking with their unmistakable flight call as I approached. Mud on the trails made for some hard walking in places, and at one point I broke a hastily made bridge, a 2 x 6 stretched across a puddle. My bad, folks.

From about twenty feet I noticed something shiny on the ground in the heart of the trail. Hmm, fish. I guess it's not just the hunters who take advantage of nature's bounty here.

What a beautiful place.

99. Harvard: Oxbow National Wildlife Refuge

Rack up another "I've always known about it but have never been there" sanctuary for the list. As The Rock used to say to professional wrestling crowds around the United States whether he'd been to their venues before or not, "Finally, the walker has come back to Oxbow!"

I have to say I wasn't nearly disappointed. My three quick issues: 1) a train had a problem near the parking area and sat idling the entire time I was there; 2) hunters were blasting the hell out of something across the Nashua River; 3) the government's no trespassing signs. It just seems so odd and out of place. We're on government land when we walk the trails, yet across the river - which none of us are really planning to ford when we start walking - there are numerous and repetitive signs stating in bold letters that it's government land, keep off.

Now to the good stuff. Beavers! I found beaver damage on trees up and down the Riverside Trail. More on them when I get to Lenox later this year. Frogs! Repeated splashes along the bank told me they were seeing me coming and diving for cover (as if I could ever hurt a frog). I stopped and watched a pod of bubbles rushing to the surface, and waited to see if it would repeat itself. Sure enough, it did, every eight seconds or so. But I freaked myself out, thinking about the periodic bubbles of oil that have been escaping from the *USS Arizona* at Pearl Harbor on a rigid schedule since 1941 and the scores of sailors who lost their lives entombed in the sunken ship.

Spring peepers, peeping in the woods! A swamp sparrow, throwing me for an identification loop! A singing brown creeper!

Yup, I fell for Oxbow. It probably won't be 'til 2012, but I'd be back.

100. Ayer: Mirror Lake

The magic number! It meant nothing, of course.

I chose Mirror Lake because of my past visits to the place. It's a recreation area in the heart of Fort Devens, and the ghosts here just speak to me.

I coauthored a book in 2010 with a good friend on Camp Edwards and the Massachusetts Military Reservation. One of our research visits took us to the Fort Devens museum, as, since Devens was the forerunner to Edwards, on Cape Cod, there was a collection of photographs we needed to see. We visited the small military graveyard, which holds the remains of some German U-boat officers, among many American fallen, and stopped by Mirror Lake.

The lake has a sandy waterfront, a little knoll with a platform for picnickers and more. It has the feel of the 1940s and 1950s for me, when physically fit and mentally tough young men brought their young families here during downtimes, knowing that at any moment their peaceful little lives could be harshly and forever altered by the fickleness of war. I feel that tension when I walk the trails at Mirror Lake.

But I also feel peace. The waters here are calming, the evergreen trees across the way spread out just enough from each other to allow viewing to the road rimming the water. If another person was walking the trail on this day, I'd be able to see him no matter where he was. But I was alone. And at 12:27, it became just me and the sun, as it burst into the sky, signaling the end of my day's adventures.

April 12

101. Winthrop: Deer Island

If I'm not careful, I might go on forever.

I grew up on the other side of Boston Harbor, in Hull, looking out at the "eggs" of the Deer Island Wastewater Treatment Facility for what seems like forever. As luck would have it, my college roommate was from Winthrop, spending his youth looking south toward Hull.

Without pretending to be a wildlife sanctuary because of its location and immediate surroundings, Deer Island nevertheless attracts nature. Yes, planes from Logan International Airport soar overhead, and tankers and other huge ships glide slowly out of the harbor proper for anchorage in President Roads. The city dominates the skyline in one direction, the treatment plant in another. But the brants, the northern mockingbirds, the red-winged blackbirds and on this day, the hermit thrushes, don't care.

The ocean is everywhere one looks, and growing up in Hull, it's the most peaceful of existences for me. I never take for granted my continental edge existence. There's an odd thrill in looking eastward and saying to yourself, "if I started swimming from here, the next land I would touch would be Portugal." Deer Island, with its prominent hills, begs such pondering.

I'll stop now. Gotta save something for the movie version of this story.

102. Revere: Revere Beach

I came seeking dead birds, and man, did I find them.

They'd been planted, of course. The folks at SEANET, for whom I volunteer as a dead bird finder on the Spit in Scituate twice a month, had asked me to join them in a training session for local college students. Hence my trip to Winthrop and Revere. When in Rome, take a walk and make it count for your silly little year-long walking project. As least, that's what I always say.

We escorted the students through the process, as unsuspecting passersby gawked at the dead gannets, scoters and shearwaters strewn across the beach. In a real surprise, seven Manx shearwaters, live ones, flew up and down the beach a few times, right atop the breakers. They should have bene far to sea, but for the past few years had adopted Revere Beach as their home. Go figure.

By the time we were done, on this gorgeous early spring evening, the sun was about to set, and the Red Sox were ready to take on the Tampa Bay Rays at Fenway. Rain was predicted for the evening and into the next day, and two dozen college students had a better appreciation of the world of citizen science, a world in which I live just about every day.

April 13

103. Hull: Nantasket Beach

When you walk Revere Beach, you are legally bound to walk Nantasket Beach within 24 hours, according to the *Book of the Legendary Battle Between Boston's North Shore and South Shore*. I followed the law to the letter, but got a raw deal.

The predicted rain arrived, with violence. The wind blowing off the water formed the drops into stinging needles, and were it not for my raincoat, I would not have walked. My legs did get soaked, but they expected discomfort to be the least of their issues when I told them what they'd be doing this year.

I learned a long time ago to never bow my head when it rains. I walk upright, letting the water hit me as it may. I'm a true believer in the notion that if you hunch your shoulders and act like the rain is getting the better of you, it will. Take nature in for all it's worth. Watch what it can do. Feel its power. Listen to its effects. Revel in it.

I also hearken back - here I go historifying again - to the days of the storm warriors of yore, the men of the United States Life-Saving Service who walked these storms, on this very beach, at their worst because they had to as sworn protectors of the people who worked upon the sea. I walk with them in mind, and with our Coast Guardsmen of today, who risk their lives to save others in peril upon the ocean.

So I got wet. Who cares? I'd walk on plenty of sunny days in 2011, and for the rest of my life. I'll take a rainy day once in a while.

May

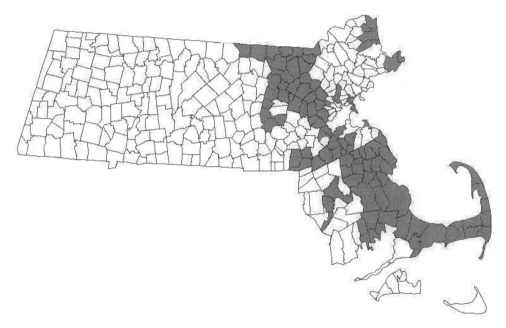

Out of Bounds

The pneumonia had struck me at the worst possible time. One can argue, of course, that there is no good time for it, but in all my planning for walking in 2011, the one thing I had not scheduled was sickness. Hitting 351 towns in 365 days was going to be tight enough, especially when I looked at my out-of-state travel calendar. I didn't need pneumonia.

Not that I was complaining. It began in April, when I left for eight days in Colorado, co-leading a trip for Mass Audubon with my friend Charlie. My father had been there twice when I was a kid, a hockey coaching savant called to the home of the Olympic team to share his stuff, and came home raving about it. "If you ever get the chance, you have to go," he said. So I went. I designed a program with Charlie, got participants excited about it, and we went.

We went to the Garden of the Gods, where we found juniper titmice against the backdrop of Pike's Peak. We went to mountainside leks in the pre-dawn to watch greater sage-grouses perform their mating rituals. We visited the Chico Basin Ranch, where we found a horned lizard, or what Yosemite Sam would have called the "Great Horny Toad!" We traversed the mountain passes in blinding snow, and walked the lowlands in 75-degree, dry, dusty heat - on the same day. We saw a kit fox. We stayed in a hotel in a town so small that the proprietor told us not to go outside after dark, as there would be no employees on site overnight, and if we got locked out, well, it might get cold.

And the whole time, I was thinking, "Crap, when am I going to walk in Mendon?"

As if that wasn't bad enough, I returned home just to jump on a plane a few days later and head for Santa Barbara. I was scheduled to take part in a maritime history conference, and take part I did. I landed in L.A. and drove up the coast, just for the experience. The conference had two on-the-water components, one by whale watch boat to see the offshore oil rigs (and the natural seeps that no one caps) and a second on a multi-million dollar catamaran to see the house on the cliff that Beanie Babies built.

And, all I could think was, "When the hell am I going to get to Russell?"

There would be more throughout the year, southern New Jersey at the end of the month, Downeast Maine in July, Montana in August, Block Island and Mt. Desert Island in October, but I would just have to suffer through them and know that Alford would be there when I was ready.

But come May 1, I was hurting. I was at 103 towns, when technically I should have been at 117. I took solace in the fact that the sunlight hours were outcompeting the hours of darkness, and I would be able to walk longer days. June, in particular, would be an ace up my sleeve.

I had catching up to do.

May 7

104a. Falmouth: Crane Wildlife Management Area

With a walk through Falmouth, I finished off Barnstable County.

It was a sad one, though I was with friends. I led a group from Mass Audubon in search of a certain species of bird that is all but gone from Massachusetts, the northern bobwhite, and, unfortunately, the walk went as expected: completely devoid of bobwhites.

We're quickly killing off the planet's wild critters, and bobwhites are a perfect example. Massachusetts hunters killed them in such great numbers over the past century that the state had to begin stocking them on state wildlife lands, so the hunters could continue to hunt them. That strategy backfired, though, as the birds they chose were from the south, and could not survive Massachusetts winters. I guess that after the winter of 2010-2011, especially, it should have been no surprise that there were no bobwhites to be found at Crane this spring.

If you haven't seen a bobwhite in the wild in Massachusetts to this point, you may never see one. The same goes for ring-necked pheasants (which have a side story, being an introduced species). And soon, we'll be saying the same for American kestrels, for reasons other than hunting, more to do with development, global climate change and, perhaps, poisons in the environment. And they're just the tip of the iceberg. All around the world our excesses - hunting, dining, collecting - are causing the sixth great extinction of wildlife on earth. Bobwhites are just one, small, local example.

Yup, there was lots on my mind as I walked on this day.

104b. Falmouth: Ashumet Holly Wildlife Sanctuary

In order to keep my promise to myself to walk every Mass Audubon property in 2011, I had to take on another two-walk combo in one town. And I'm glad I did, as it was a mood-lifter for sure.

Ashumet Holly is a fun and a funny place. One of the first sights one finds when entering is a barn swallow barn, built specifically for the little guys. These little daredevils love living in buildings and feel no compunction to slow down when diving through an open window into a one. I once had one circle around outside an observation blind in which I was sitting until I moved my head; when it saw I had cleared out it blasted through the open window and circled the interior twice before deciding it wasn't for him, or, more likely, her. I'll bet she was looking for a nesting site.

Tree swallows were nearby, not so brave as their cousins, living in a series of small boxes spread across a field. Still, though, their frantic flights, in search of yummy bugs, made for quite a show.

There's a pond at Ashumet, called Grassy Pond. There's a vernal pool, a franklinia tree, and, of course, holly trees. The previous owner collected them, first the varieties that appeared naturally on Cape Cod, then others that grew around the world.

It's a happy place, there's no denying that fact.

May 9

105. Quincy: Squantum Point Park

It's hard to describe how it feels to research the history for the writing of a book, and then to walk the land on which that history happened.

The best analogy I can offer is family discovery. Imagine you're touring an old house, and someone drops the bomb on you: your great-great-grandfather was the man who built the house. You get an instant sense of awe. The place suddenly feels different. It's no longer just another old building. Perhaps that corner of the living room is where he had his favorite chair and an old radio that entertained him after dinner. And dinner! Perhaps the worn spot in the floor in front of the stove was carved out by great-great-grandma herself.

I coauthored a history of the Squantum Naval Air Station with a friend a few years ago, and I never tire of visiting Squantum Point Park. The main portion of the park, the large grassy field, once served as Runway 3 for the old airfield. It's no stretch for me to see the pilots of the '20s, '30s and '40s taking off in their small fighter and observation planes, looking for German U-boats approaching Boston Harbor.

The place has not been quiet for three quarters of a century, and probably won't be for a long, long time, at least until we perfect teleportation. Planes approaching Logan International Airport cross the field, roaring over every minute or so. It's an entirely different sound from the prop planes of World War II, but it's something.

Places like this one pull at my heartstrings. I feel like I've been here before - not last week or month, but in another lifetime. Such is the life of a historian, I guess.

106. Weymouth: Webb Memorial State Park

Raw days have their value, and so far in the spring of 2011, eastern Massachusetts had certainly had a raw deal.

It was cold when I walked the trail at Webb, one that I'd walked dozens of times. It never gets old. That's the power of the sea.

The site has family ties of which I only have vague notions. My uncle served in the region in the Army in the late 1950s, at the very height of the Cold War. Webb Park was, in its most recent previous lifetime, a NIKE missile launching site. Ugh. The thought is enough to make one's skin crawl.

I wasn't alive for the worst of it, but I do have certain strong memories of the Cold War. I remember being in a friend's house in Hull walking through the living room - probably with an armload of GI Joe action figures - and catching a glimpse on the television of the expected blast zone of a nuclear bomb hitting Boston. Yup, there was Hull. Obliterated. In a way, it's sickening to think that we bring children into a world in which they, too, may be obliterated before they're even cognizant there are other countries, other agendas.

Uncle Billy was a young man when it all started, and came from Kentucky to work at sites such as this one, Turkey Hill in Hingham, and Hog Island in Hull. He came back a few years ago and couldn't believe the changes. His memories of this place will forever be different from mine. And mine will be different from my son's. I hope he's as interested to ask me about it someday as I am to ask my Uncle Billy.

May 10

107. Hingham: Wompatuck State Park

There are some paths that are just old friends. You don't walk them. They walk you.

I don't know how many times I've walked Pleasant Street in Wompatuck State Park in Hingham, and I don't care to know. I've been walking it since I was in my teens, and I'll probably walk it for another forty years.

It's a straight shot, from the outside world to the heart of the park. There's a little stream that runs under the road, and small, dense concentrations of pine trees that harbor odd little birds like worm-eating warblers. There used to be a star bird here. I'll be able to look back on this brief little period in my walking life on Pleasant Street and say "Forty years ago, for five years, a hooded warbler used to sing from *that tree* right there!"

Despite the wind and the clouds and the mist, the birds were singing up a storm. And well they should have been. It was May and they had all just returned in migration. Whether or not they'd reached their mating grounds, they had to sing. Mates had to be attracted. Nests had to be built. The next generation had to hatch.

Yup, I could do this walk for another forty years.

May 11

108. Cohasset: Whitney/Thayer Woods

If you haven't heard by now, I'm into boulders. I'm into the whole glacial erratic thing. I dig big rocks.

Cohasset is strewn with them. There are three major conservation lands - Wompatuck State Park, Wheelwright Park and Whitney/Thayer Woods - that are hotbeds for geologists. The evidence of the last ice age is just spread all throughout the town.

The best part about it is that most of the boulders are named. That's a dangerous things with animals that aren't pets, like the turkey that walks in and out of your yard during the winter. It's one thing if the turkey eventually gets hit by a car, but it's another if it's Charlie and gets hit by a car. Anthropomorphization is an awful thing for conservationists to deal with.

Big rocks in wildlife sanctuaries, though, they're not going anywhere, and they're as much landmarks as buildings are on our city streets. They can hold names in perpetuity. I could send you a letter to give to your great-great-granddaughter with GPS coordinates to Ode's Den or Rooster Rock with instructions not to open it 'til 2095, and she'd still find them. They might, by that time, be surrounded by an overflow parking lot for the new Galactic Stop & Shop, but they should still be there.

It's a handshake across time. Staring at Bigelow Boulder on this day I could honestly say I was standing in the footsteps of the man for whom it was named, E. Victor Bigelow, author of the first history of Cohasset. He wrote that book more than a century ago, and he probably knew he was looking at something the local Native Americans had gazed upon for centuries.

Big rocks rock!

May 17

109. Worcester: Broad Meadow Brook Wildlife Sanctuary

Add another hash mark in my quest to walk all Mass Audubon wildlife sanctuaries in 2011.

We were still socked in with wet weather, sometimes under siege from downpours, most of the time mistily pushing through fog...or foggily moving through the mist. At this point, it was all personal perspectives. I decided, with a 1 p.m. meeting in Boston, to get on the Mass Pike and head west until the spirit moved me to take the next exit. That led me to Worcester, and Broad Meadow Brook.

And into the rain, of course. The trails that leave the nature center drop back in switchback fashion into low wetlands, and then back up into a power line, if you want them to. It's your choice. I followed the all-persons access trail, a snaky monster that is slowly and happily growing across all Mass Audubon sanctuaries, mostly to avoid the mud that was deeply accumulating elsewhere. I reached the end of the boardwalk to find a sign saying that there was more to come, but then ran headlong into a recently downed tree, most likely from overnight, that blocked anybody from using the trail beyond it at all. It was time to turn around anyway.

It was a wet start to the day, but a fun one. I busted open the atlas I bought at the gas station on the Pike and thumbed my way through the pages to the local towns of the Blackstone River Valley. Hmm, where to go next...

110. Millbury: Deering Wildlife Management Area

The map looked intriguing. A single road ran into the sanctuary, looped around and came back out. What was the destination? Only one way to find out, of course. As Bill Cosby quipped, in his famous bit about Stepin Fetchit, "Feet, do your duty!"

Despite the rain, it was a birdy morning in Worcester County, or, as it's pronounced locally, "Wista." The woodland birds - red-eyed vireos, scarlet tanagers, black-throated green warblers, ovenbirds, eastern towhees - kept up their chatter as I walked the trail. That trail wound up to the right, and soon I came to the island on the map. It all came together.

First, signs of human life revealed themselves. Straight lines in the woods can't lie. Just like nothing is perfectly round in nature, nothing is perfectly straight, either. And neither was the stonewall I was looking at, but then, it was probably more than a hundred years old. I'll be damned if I'll be standing up straight the day I become a centenarian.

I could see a clearing behind the trees, in the center of the island. I looped around the right side, and made the discovery - old house site! Good old Martha Deering. She probably loved her life here.

The site, though, brought to mind a query. How many historic chimneys, devoid of the rest of their historic homes, now stand across Massachusetts, as the final sentinels of the history of their owners? How many in the United States? Did I just find my new blog, www.abandonedchimneys.com? Or does that one already exist?

111. Grafton: Marsters Preserve

The rain doesn't really bother me that much, as I'm a Pisces. It's only when my feet get wet that I get uncomfortable. That's also a part of being a Pisces. But enough astrology.

The walk down the old farm road to the Marsters Preserve was wet with morning dew and mist, and the grass was tall. I knew the second I set foot on the path I was done for. Oh well. It was a nice walk anyway, with a grand old farm field to one side. The signs for the preserve marked the entrance to the woods, into which I dove.

Had it not been for the birdsong, I might have been disappointed with this site. It had nothing to do with the land trust that has so lovingly cared for this place; nay, it was our need for speed. The sounds of the highway roaring in the background take away an important element of peace that should come with our natural places. Sadly, this place will always be tainted by the stain of progress.

But you couldn't tell that to the black-and-white warbler that was singing up his own storm this morning. Perhaps he was putting extra oomph into his call, knowing he needed to drown out the passing big rigs, or maybe his volume knob broke and he got stuck on "high." Either way, he was blasting out his song as loudly as possible, making it nearly impossible for me to consider focusing on any other natural sounds. If I was a female black and white warbler, I guess I would be more than impressed. 'Tis the season, after all.

112. Sutton: Purgatory Chasm State Park

Like I had any other choice?

I think I would have done well in the 1920s. The automobile was finally coming into full vogue, and becoming more useful than ever. No longer did one need a partial degree in engineering to get from Boston to Worcester, nor did he need driving gloves, goggles and scarves, although that is, admittedly, a good look for me. Tourism, at least automobile tourism, was in its infancy, and the wonders of the natural world still held the imagination of many people in the palms of their hands.

Purgatory Chasm was surely one of the places that brought people from far and wide. Its formation had even by that time long been debated. Did an ancient sea run through here, or an ancient river? Even today, the story is somewhat unclear.

But I can tell you one thing. This place was cool.

I wanted to walk the chasm, but was met with a pre-emptive rebuff from a state Department of Conservation and Recreation employee. "Have fun in the park," she said, "but whatever you do, don't walk through the chasm." It sounded, at first, like a script from a horror movie, but then she added, "It's wicked slippery." Ah, Boston.

So I walked up and over and around the chasm, knowing I would someday have to return to walk through it. Maybe I would do so in a 1920s roadster, with a big picnic basket and a red and white checkerboard blanket. And maybe my wife.

113, 114. Uxbridge and Northbridge: Blackstone River Valley National Heritage Corridor

I moved from south to north along the river, starting in Uxbridge and ending in Northbridge.

I started, in fact, at River Bend Farm. That choice put me in direct contact with the waterway, as I walked right along its edge, greeting other walkers taking advantage of the wide open trail.

The fact that it was a farm was made even more obvious (there was a huge restored barn, after all) by the system of tubes running through the woods at waist height. Sugar maples here had been tapped, and in a complex way, with sap flowing from numerous trees down into a central feeding tube, which ran to the barn. I craved pancakes.

After salivating like a chump, I moved down the trail to an old crossing of the river where a bench sat. Turning around there, I moved to Northbridge.

Much like I was a slave to the name Purgatory Chasm, so, too, was I held captive by the name Lookout Rock. I walked up the trail, found a rock, and thought to myself that it was the same old story: there used to be a great view from here, but the trees had grown up and swallowed it. I moped away from the rocks and up another trail. That's when I discovered the real Lookout Rock.

Problem: fog. Only after peering deeply into the distance could I see a hint of the Blackstone River. The one thing I could see clearly was that I would be coming back here again someday, probably the same day I walked Purgatory Chasm from end to end.

Was that an eastern wood-pewee? What do you know, my first of the year.

115, 116. Dover and Sherborn: Broadmoor Wildlife Sanctuary

So, in one day, I wiped out both of the Mass Audubon sanctuaries with "Broad" in their names.

A few years ago, when I wrote *Images of America: Mass Audubon*, I studied more than a dozen sanctuaries in depth, this one being the most confusing. It took numerous land purchases to puzzle-piece together what is now the sanctuary. I remember the first time I tried to figure it out.

I looked at the deeds. I got a headache. I took an aspirin and laid down to rest my eyes for ten minutes. When I woke up an hour later, I looked at the deeds again. My eyes started to water, so I went outside for a walk. I vowed never to look at the deeds again, then went inside and gave it one more shot. I still don't think, if my feet were held to the fire, that I could successfully and adequately describe how they came together without the help of my book.

But, the beauty of this story, is that every piece of the sanctuary has its own story, rather than just one old family homestead for the whole place. There were mills, and farmhouses, praying Indians, ancient arrowheads and even a George Washington reference. That's all on top of the plain old natural beauty of Broadmoor.

With so much land, and an hour to walk it, I expected a surprise - and got it. My first blue-winged warbler of the year sang near the tree swallow boxes where I unsuccessfully tried repeatedly to photograph a swallow in flight. Fast little buggers, they are.

May 24

117. Cambridge: Mt. Auburn Cemetery

There are certain rites of spring for birders in Massachusetts. Ok, there's only one universal one: Mt. Auburn.

Honestly, the month of May is the biggest conundrum faced by birders at this particular latitude. While many tell themselves that they'd like to be at Point Pelee, or wouldn't it be nice to be in Colorado or perhaps in Oregon along the Pacific flyway, the fact is that while the warblers are running, it's nearly impossible to tear yourself away from your own stomping grounds.

Birders have a particular superstition that makes them stay put. It's spotting spot fidelity. If in 1975 a Tennessee warbler appeared in a patch of trees in Marshfield, then every time that birder passes that spot for the next forty years, he has to look to see if there's another Tennessee warbler there. He can't *not* look. It's weird. Maybe it's why we show allegiance to sports teams. The players change, sometimes on a yearly basis, but we can't pull ourselves away from watching the games because somebody did something good in those clothes four years ago.

Back to Mt. Auburn. On this particular day, we walked for more than three hours. It was at the end of a ten-day stretch of rain, and, as such, the lawnmowers were out in force. Not a good thing if you're trying to listen for tiny little birds singing from hidden perches in trees and shrubs. We did luck into one rarity, a mourning warbler - perfect for a cemetery - and were able to get all of our program participants "on it," as we say.

And you can bet that for the next 35 years I'll be walking by that bush every spring on my annual trip to Mt. Auburn and saying, "I saw a mourning warbler in there once."

May 27

118. Douglas: Douglas State Forest

Oh, the mosquitoes were back, chillins. I started this day in the Douglas State Forest with a particular mission. I was on my way to New Jersey to sign books at the Millville Army Air Field air show and was taking the six-hour drive in sections. Part one: beat the Boston traffic by getting through early. Part two: pause to allow the New York City traffic to ease somewhat. Part three: shoot through New York to the Philly area.

But the bugs stopped me in my tracks. Actually, it was quite the opposite. I had to keep moving because every time I did stop I was swarmed. My bug spray hadn't made the trek from the house to the car yet, so I was stuck. My arms and shoulders got quite a workout as I swatted away. The humidity was up, even very early in the morning, so it looked like every half hour walk would end up feeling like much longer.

I did make one screeching halt, when I noticed a wood frog hopping in the trail. I steadied the camera, captured him or her for all eternity, then ran like hell. Ahhhh!

119. Webster: Mt. Zion Cemetery

I really wanted to do something different in Webster, preferably along the shores of Lake Chaubunagungamaug, but, unfortunately, I couldn't find any open space alongside Lake Chaubunagungamaug. I must have missed a turn, and by the time I found the local cemetery, I decided I had to take that path to stay on task for the day. Too bad, as I really wanted to dip my toes into Lake Chaubunagungamaug, just to say I did. Of course, if I said that, I'd actually have to *say* Lake Chaubunagungamaug.

But, as fate often does, it played me like a volleyball on this morning. It was a beautiful small town cemetery, with plenty of old stones and stories attached no doubt. As usual, I "knew" one person interred here. Not personally, of course, but historically. I was obviously meant to be here today.

The proud veterans section of the cemetery held a small gathering, and I was immediately drawn to the white Civil War era stones. There, on the end, was Private Charles F. Reed, 54th Massachusetts Volunteer Infantry. Significance, you say? The Fighting 54th! The all-African-American regiment raised by Governor John Andrew and led by Colonel Robert Gould Shaw to war in the south. The assault on Fort Wagner. Still not ringing a bell? Try the movie *Glory!*, Denzel Washington, Morgan Freeman, Matthew Broderick. I'd been making a specialty of stumbling into the graves of the men of the 54th for the past few years. Perhaps that's another book I have to write: *Finding the 54th*. Well, it's alliterative, anyway.

Onward I pushed. If I lingered too long in Webster, I'd miss the boat on the rest of my plans, which is not a good thing when you're near Lake Chaubunagungamaug.

120. Dudley: Pierpont Meadow Wildlife Sanctuary

Scratch another Mass Audubon sanctuary off the list.

The first thing I noticed about Pierpont Meadow was the butterflies. With all the recent rain, there hadn't been much activity. Suddenly, though, in the gorgeous sunshine, the butterflies had emerged. As I walked the descending path towards the heart of the sanctuary, I was joined primarily by two species, spring azures and cabbage whites. It was like seeing old friends who'd been gone for a year.

The singing birds, too, had returned, and by this point in the season, from what I could figure, the breeders ruled, and the migrants were gone. I counted 16 species in the short window through which I walked, and here they are in their entirety, in the order in which I heard them: gray catbird, red-winged blackbird, veery, house wren, blue jay, American crow, American robin (Americans tend to stick together), blue-gray gnatcatcher, ovenbird, cedar waxwing, song sparrow, black-capped chickadee, tree swallow, pine warbler, common yellowthroat and scarlet tanager. That's quite a varied list, from forest to field to marsh. But then, Pierpont Meadow is much more than a meadow.

Perhaps my favorite sound of the morning was the twang of a green frog emanating from that marsh. Among my many citizen scientist hats is my amphibian sounds survey beret (seems like a froggy sort of chapeau). If I hear an amphibian on any Mass Audubon sanctuary, I have to reach into my pocket for my official amphibian sounds survey data form and fill out the species, temperature, sky conditions, the number I think I heard, and the exact location. Yes, I keep it in my pocket, right next to my osprey monitoring data form and my salamander coverboard survey form.

By the time I got back to my car, after walking the entire stretch from the parking lot to the rental cabin and back, I felt like a frog. The morning dew had soaked my boots straight through. The shade had felt nice on my otherwise quickly roasting flesh, but it also meant wet grass. Eww.

121. Charlton: Buffumville Dam

From the moment I saw it, I wanted to be on top of it. It happens when I see mountains, and towers, too. I wanted to walk atop the dam, if just to see what was on the other side.

But I had to dodge the Frisbees first. The Army Corps of Engineers, in the federal government's ongoing search to please all people at all places, had designed a frolf course through the dam property, which includes some abutting woods. Some of these guys were good. They were hitting their targets with the old underhand flip we all try as kids. Pretty impressive.

So, too, was the dam. I quickly found the access point and climbed to the top only to see that the water on the lake side was actually quite low. But then, I figured, that was the point. The dam was there for those outlandish moments when the water rose to unexpected heights. Kind of a disappointment, but what the heck. The view was still beautiful.

I walked the length of the dam and found a few crows struggling with the heat. Absorbing everything being thrown at them with their black feathers, all three were keeping their bills open to allow inner heat to escape. As my friend Ellen says, why not come back as a crow in the next life, as basic black looks good on everybody? Summer, that's why not.

Duh, Ellen.

122, 123. Southbridge and Sturbridge: McKimsey Brook Wildlife Management Area

So, even at this point in the day, as it was pushing noon, I was obviously the first one into the woods. I can always tell by the number of cobwebs that decide to wrap around my face as I walk. And today I was slowly being mummified.

The walk through the woods here ran right alongside the brook for which the sanctuary is named, although it's certainly held at a safe distance from the trail. A buffer zone's a good thing, although it would have been nice to stride up to the water's edge at some point to take it in.

But there was plenty to see otherwise, as usual with any Massachusetts open space parcel. I found a toad. I found jack-in-the-pulpit in bloom. And I found numerous tiger swallowtail butterflies cris-crossing the path.

I walked deeper and deeper into the woods, until my only friends were the eastern wood-pewees and the veeries. With a full hour with which to play, I wandered to side trails and back again, eventually finding my way back to the place I started.

From there, the next time I set foot on bare ground would be in Millville, New Jersey, to get ready for the Pilot Party on the eve of the air show. I felt good after three hours of walking, prepared to stand in one spot signing books for the entirety of the next day. But boy, did I need a shower.

June

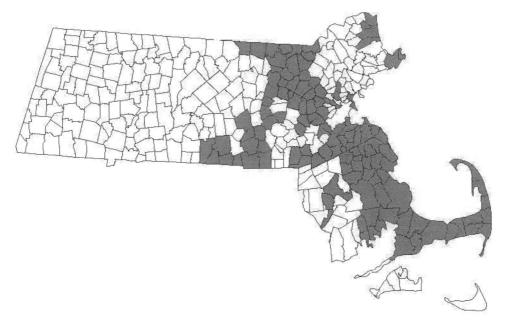

BBA2

With May gone, I was still well behind. I should have been at 146, but was 23 towns behind. I had doubts about my prospects, but the Breeding Bird Atlas 2 project was on my side.

I was excited about participating in the project from its inception. It probably goes back to all my collecting instincts, but I think there's more. I love statistics. As a kid, I memorized the serial numbers on the bottom of mu matchbox cars. Later, I recited baseball statistics like they were poetry. Hell, friends and I developed our own dice-based strat-o-matic baseball and professional wrestling games. I even developed my own hockey game on paper.

Then, in year two of the atlas project, I became a made man. I was asked to be the regional coordinator for Plymouth County. I said yes, even though I was way over my head. In year three, at that point treading water pretty successfully, I took on the regional coordination of Bristol County. 2011 would be year five. I would atlas my ass off, from Adams to Plymouth. My walking throughout the next few months would hold double, sometimes triple meaning. Each bird sighting was a point of data. I had to start thinking of the state in ten square mile blocks, being very careful to know where I was when a common grackle fed a fledgling, or a white-eyed vireo was caught carrying a stick.

But Atlas or not, it was put-up-or-shut-up time. If I was going to finish the full state, and do so before the winter snows bogged me down, I had to make hay in the summer sunshine. Halfway through the year, at the end of June, I needed to be at about 175 towns. I needed to walk 52 communities in June, almost two per day. And I couldn't get sick.

I had a pair of boats in reserve.

I had extra water in the back of my SUV.

I had my maps.

It was dark, fifty miles to Chicago, I had a half a tank of gas and I was wearing sunglasses.

I hit it.

June 5

124a and b. Attleboro: Attleboro Springs and Oak Knoll Wildlife Sanctuaries

I have a love affair going with Attleboro that I'm afraid to even tell my wife about. I think it's because I can't explain it, even to myself.

I was pulled into the Attleboro fold by friends at work. A new sanctuary was being designed, one that had deep human history attached to it. I listened to stories of what I would find as I walked the property, the extant landmarks in the woods, the pond shaped like a hockey rink, the old cart paths. Could I help with the research? I itched. I couldn't wait to go and see it. I befriended a local historian, and we walked the property together, finding that we spoke the same language.

After the history research was done - at least, temporarily - I moved onto the nature side, taking on the breeding bird circle studies on the property. Stand still for ten minutes, listen, record. Lather, rinse, repeat two more times in June. Do it again the next year. And the next.

Then came the fun of naming trails. I'm proud to say that I left my personal stamp on one of them, with my history buddy Larry. I won't gloat by pointing out which one, but I'll always smile whenever I look at a sanctuary map and know that if nothing else, I left my mark on the trails at Attleboro Springs.

I walked here on this day for the breeding bird circle study, more than an hour deep in the woods on a cool late spring morning. Heaven.

I left there for Oak Knoll and Lake Talaquega, for a singing northern waterthrush, and for the Breeding Bird Atlas project. Yup, I double-dipped: two Mass Audubon sanctuaries, two citizen science studies, one more town to add to the list for the year.

125. North Attleboro: World War I Memorial Park

I carried my Breeding Bird Atlasing act north into a topographical block known as Attleboro 01, hitting the jackpot with the beautiful World War I Memorial Park. I entered from the western portion of the park, and was immediately hit with an unsuspected song. Luckily, the singer was not at all worried about being seen: an indigo bunting, one of the most stunning little critters to visit Massachusetts.

I thought, at first, that I was solely in a wildlife sanctuary, but I soon learned that the park encompassed many more things. I walked across a field where a brown thrasher sought food in the bordering bushes. I found pavement, in circular form, and swore I heard roosters. An overlook marked an old ski area, where I answered the inevitable "so, whatcha doin' with the clipboard and binoculars?" question from a local citizen. I found emus in a pen marked "eums." And I walked a powerline trail in time to catch a red-tailed hawk being harassed by blue jays, Baltimore orioles, eastern kingbirds and a northern mockingbird. They all obviously were defending breeding territories. It all went in my report.

In all, I spent four hours in the park, taking note of the ascending notes of prairie warblers, of a bluebird nest, of a gray catbird carrying nesting material, of a tufted titmouse beating the hell out of a fat green worm in order to make it easier to carry to its young.

When I finished, the indigo bunting was still there, singing away.

126. Plainville: John Bowmar Memorial Trail

I plunged into Plainville, not sure where I would end up, until I saw the sign on the side of the road. The trailhead lined up with the local baseball fields, where young girls were practicing softball with their coaches. I found a yellow softball in the woods and tossed it back towards the field.

I only found a few spur trails, but decided to walk straight ahead as far as I could, to see what I could find. The woods got quieter and quieter, which wasn't a bad thing. I retreated to the entrance, wondering what I would do for a photograph for the blog. Nothing had truly stood out, though all around me was beautiful.

Enter the volleyball of fate, once again.

As I stood and badly photographed a brook, a flash of blue caught my eye. Three flashes, in fact. Three butterflies, known as red-spotted purples, arose from the earth together and danced in what had to be a mating ritual. I froze and waited, and finally one returned to a sunny patch on a rock. I zoomed in and fired. I crept closer and fired again. I eventually had to walk that way anyway, so I inched closer, finally nudging it to fly from my presence.

127. Medway: Choate Park

I didn't have the heart to tell the fishermen on the other bank what I had seen. A number of fish had created their own circular territories in shallow water about a foot from shore. Catching them by dropping bait in each of the circles would have been like shooting fish...well, you know what I mean.

The park was alive with typical Sunday summer traffic. One man walked his dog, and then walked him again when he realized that he had lost his glasses and had to retrace his steps in entirety. One couple posed for a photographer in a tight, smiling embrace, most likely an engagement announcement picture. Two firemen with fishing poles talked about how they'd each been called to respond to the terrifying tornadoes that had swept through Springfield and its surrounding towns earlier in the week.

Out on the pond, tree swallows had moved into a metal pipe sticking from the water. In the background, a mama mallard shepherded her numerous babes to the shore, then back to deep water. The cycle of life began anew, right there for all to see.

128. Millis: Prospect Hill Cemetery

Hmm, this was my second Prospect Hill of the year. I wondered how many more there would be.

After several hours of walking, my legs were pretty stretched out. That wasn't the problem, though. It was how much strength my legs had left in them, specifically to walk inclines and declines. As fate would have it, I chose a particularly hilly section of a particularly hilly cemetery.

But laughter can do wondrous things, although looking back now I wonder if laughing in a cemetery - at the dead, no less - didn't earn me a one-way ticket to that big comedy club down below.

But, seriously? Abigail just had to marry Amos Abbe, to become Abbie Abbe? Really? *Really??*

Well, at least as it goes with any cemetery, I met someone new I wanted to know more about, and that was besides Abbie Abbe, who reminded me of the serial killer on *Cheers* who was haunting Diane, Andy Andy. No, it was the Reverend Nathan Bucknam, "man of God, citizen, patriot, soldier during the French and Indian War and American Revolution." Whew! What a resume.

I waved bye to Abbie Abbe and thanked her for making me forget how tired I really was.

129. Medfield: Noon Hill Reservation

One final push would do it, one last walk for the day and I would be done.

I reached Noon Hill just after noon and was immediately hit with one of those serendipitous moments for which nature lovers live. As soon as I set foot on the trail, a song rang out, a high-pitched, three-note call: an olive-sided flycatcher. It could possibly be the only one I would encounter in 2011 in Massachusetts, definitely in eastern Mass.

Nature was slowing down for the day, as the morning rush to feed young birds had dissipated, and only the most determined of potential breeders had continued to sing. And, of course, the red-eyed vireo continued unabated, repeating its song over and over, as it had and would for hours.

A sign told me that I was on the Bay Circuit Trail, the brain child of Charles Eliot II, a loop of interconnected open space just west of Boston that would bring one from Duxbury and Plymouth, out around the city of Boston and back to the water of the North Shore. Someday, I'd like to walk it all in succession, and watch how the state's nature changes from sanctuary to sanctuary.

At one point near the top of the hill I noticed that all the leaves on the trail had been washed away to one side, as if by torrents of rushing water. It took me just seconds to think back to the previous Wednesday, and the thunderstorms that accompanied the killer tornadoes that touched down just west of this part of the state. It was an eerie reminder of a horrible day in Massachusetts history.

And then, it all made sense. The olive-sided flycatcher - was it blown east by the storms?

June 6

130. Lakeville: Betty's Neck

Not to be confused with Betty's Spleen, Betty's Kneecaps, or Betty's Medula Oblongata.

91

In actuality, Marilyn, my trusty Breeding Bird Atlas sidekick and I walked many places in Lakeville on this day, in search of the birds that...were...breeding. Hmm, could have used a little help thinking that sentence through.

And we had luck! Catbirds with worms, a robin on a nest, a fish crow being mobbed by songbirds. A yellow warbler sang through a bill clenched on a chubby green worm. A cedar waxwing tore at fibers from a tree branch, carrying them off toward a nesting site. Grackles darted back and forth with food. The activity was tremendous, but mostly reflective of how hard the natural world works to perpetuate itself each spring. By the end of summer, it's always easy to tell the new birds from the old, as the moms and dads are haggard and beaten from the process of pushing their youngsters into a position of survival against the odds: predators, weather, starvation, etc.

After several hours around Great Quittacas Pond, Pocksha Pond, at Betty's Neck, at Tamarack Park and more, we packed it in, tallying exactly forty species of birds in some type of breeding activity. Not bad for a day's "work," if I do say so myself.

Oh, and by the way - bye bye, Plymouth County, you're done for 2011.

June 9

131. New Bedford: Buttonwood Park

I left another session of Breeding Bird Atlas work in Freetown to find my way down to Buttonwood Park. I'm very ashamed to say that despite my long life here in Massachusetts, I've barely stepped foot in New Bedford. It was something I intended to change in the coming months and years. It has so much to offer. And that's beyond where I've already been, like the New Bedford Whaling Museum and the national park.

So this was my first visit to Buttonwood Park, which blows even my own mind, as I've known of it for so many years. Just add "Zoo" to the end of it, and you'll see what I mean. But I never got that far.

Walkers were out in huge numbers, and from what I could see were as cosmopolitan as New Bedford is advertised. It's times like this I wish I knew more Spanish, and more Portuguese. Not that I like to eavesdrop. That would just be wrong, *amigos*. (For those of you counting, that's "friends" in not one, but both languages).

I was amazed to see so much natural life concentrated in this one small area of an otherwise heavily developed city. Canada geese, well, they were to be expected, especially at this time of year with their young unable to fly just yet. The regular city birds were here - house sparrows, starlings, pigeons, ring-billed gulls - but some of the nicer, nature-sanctuary loving birds were here, too, like cedar waxwings, yellow warblers, common yellowthroats and a Baltimore oriole.

With the weather threatening to douse me for a third time that morning (I'd been drenched in two separate thunderstorms while walking a rail line in Freetown a few hours earlier) I decided to keep moving to the next town, but vowed to return to New Bedford to continue this new personal exploration.

132. Dartmouth: Allen's Pond Wildlife Sanctuary

It had gotten to the point where I had to question my decision. I stated early on that I wanted to avoid the beach in summer, and as such, I tackled Cape Cod and the entirety of Barnstable County in the first months of the year. I left Nantucket and Martha's Vineyard for the fall. Had to wait for those ferry fares to drop.

But here I was in summer, and the woods awaited, all across Massachusetts. And within those woods were poison ivy and mosquitoes and who the hell knows what else. The trade-off was that I don't have to wait in traffic to get where I need to go.

(Sigh). Nobody ever said obsession would be easy.

I entered the Allens Pond Wildlife Sanctuary woodland loop planning, once again, on re-emerging with wet feet. I had assured myself of once again going through a set of boots in a season. There's only so much moisture that any piece of leather can take. With the morning rains and the lingering humidity the plants were dripping with wetness - and good for them. We can go through some uncomfortable droughts from time to time, and it was good to see them satiated. The ferns, in their glory, particularly looked happy.

Sadly, not all was well in this bucolic little glade. First, I came across a deceased shrew. This is not unusual for me. I tend to attract small dead mammals for some reason. Some shrews are toxic to their predators. A hawk or an owl will catch one, take a bite, and spit it right back out, leaving it where it is. Many times, that's in the middle of a trail.

Today, though, there was a frog, and a ridiculously dramatic one at that. Shakespeare would have been so proud. This little guy had his head thrown back in his death throes, as if delivering one last plea to the amphibian gods for justice, "Avenge me, oh Slimy One!" If all works out, the creature that took this character's life will be swallowed whole by a giant toad, like the ones that populate the great fantasy game realms online.

133. Westport: Gooseberry Neck

Ah, another Neck. Who knew that Massachusetts was a many-headed thing?

I have a slight connection to this area, one that starts just before the neck, on the shoulders of Horseneck Beach. For several years the Westport Fishermens' Association worked to save an historic Humane Society of the Commonwealth of Massachusetts boathouse right there. I jumped in early when requested, giving a talk on the general history of "the Humane" and the U.S. Life-Saving Service, consulting on historical themes, connecting the fishermen to the people who could help them with artifact collection and exhibiting, and so on. In the end, I was there for the unveiling of the whole shebang, the glorious day it was.

On that cold, wintry day, I walked Gooseberry Neck for the first time. Then it was windy, drab and weather beaten. It made the old coast artillery spotting tower look even worse than it does on a regular day, which is a pretty amazing feat. It's been neglected and abused to no end.

Today, though, the subject was sunshine and rebirth. A group of ospreys, seven I could see at one time, were fishing high above the surf. And the *rosa rugosa* was in full bloom, bright splashes of pink hiding a dense thorniness beneath.

Another glorious day.

June 15

134. Seekonk. Carotunk Wildlife Sanctuary

I had to check the map. Was I even in Massachusetts anymore? I thought I was in Seekonk, but the sign clearly said "Audubon Society of Rhode Island." I checked my bearings, dotted my tees and crossed my eyes, but yes, it was true: a Rhode Island sanctuary in Massachusetts.

Grrrr...

In all honesty, while it seems unusual, it's not really that uncommon. Mass Audubon's overnight camp, Wildwood, is in New Hampshire. And the important fact is not who owns the land, but rather that it got saved and is being actively protected. Judging by the neatness of the nature center grounds, the busy feeders, the predator guards built onto the mouths of the bird boxes spread throughout the fields and the two guys I saw walking the well-maintained trails with loppers in hand, I'd say excellent care was being taken of this beautiful place.

Old farms just hold so much charm. They needed it all: woods for firewood and building construction, fields for crops or grazing, and water to supply both of those processes. They make wonderful wildlife sanctuaries, as their habitat variation leads to species diversity, from plants to mammals to birds to bugs.

This place also had two other natural things that caught my attention. First, Monument Rock - after all, you know me and rocks - led me on an at first exhilarating and then frustratingly disappointing journey. The anticipation was the enjoyable part; seeing the rock covered in graffiti by some moron with enough manual dexterity to operate a spray can trigger and not much else deflated my balloon. Second, I found a rock ridge that got a whole line of *Blazing Saddles* jokes going in my head. Rock Ridge was the town that welcomed their new sheriff with a laurel, and hardy handshake.

So, yes, Carotunk is a place I would visit again. Not bad for a bunch of Rhode Islanders.

135. Swansea: Swansea Village Park

It seemed rocks would be a central theme as I walked in Seekonk, Swansea and Rehoboth. As I sought my Swansea destination on the fly I consulted a map that pinpointed Abrams Rock in Swansea Village Park, and I decided that was to be the place to be. Seein' as there was no other place around the place, I reckon, I reckon, to misquote the Three Stooges.

I was hit initially with the fragrance of the flowers as I stepped from the parking lot behind the library, past the cemetery and into the woods. Almost immediately I happened upon some fascinating conglomerate rocks, but nothing like the purplish Roxbury puddingstone I'm so used to seeing on the South Shore, my little home corner of the state. I sensed that there'd be more.

But my geology lesson was quickly interrupted. A flock of chipping sparrows spirited into the area, a quartet of chattering little voices, three smaller than the one: a mama and babies! As mama moved through the trees finding food, the little ones clung right to her side, begging the whole way. I noted it for the Breeding Bird Atlas project and jokingly told myself that for the next half hour I didn't have to pay any attention whatsoever to chipping sparrows. They were officially *avifauna non grata*.

I turned the corner on the trail where I figured Abrams Rock was supposed to be. Was that it, seriously, that distant erratic with no discernible accessibility? I walked away slightly disappointed, then bumped right into the real thing. I felt like Frank Barone on *Everybody Loves Raymond*.

Holy crap!

My first reaction is always the same - I have to climb that bad boy. The pathway up was pretty simple, so I scaled it to the apex and took in the treetop view.

Ahh, that's the stuff.

136. Rehoboth: Rehoboth State Park

For the first time this year, I came across something that made me retreat for more research. And I think I'm still stumped, but I'm not sure. And that's not a tree joke.

As I walked through the Rehoboth State Forest, among the towhees and ovenbirds and veeries, not to mention the completely out-of-control chipmunks, I found a sight I had never seen before. Witch hazel trees - among my favorites in New England - were sporting horrible-looking - and that last word is important - blisters of some kinds. I took photos, finished my half hour and went home to investigate.

It looks to me that what I was seeing was the result of aphids that regularly attach themselves to witch hazel leaves. The stem mother locates a plant, injects enzymes or hormones into the leaf and a gall builds around her. She then lays her eggs and releases her first brood, all females, upon the world, who sprout wings and disperse to increase their population. The process is not life-threatening to the plant. But man does it look ugly.

The oddity is the comparison to the plant itself. The witch hazel tree holds its seeds in tightly-packed cases in fall that build up so much pressure that they literally pop, and shoot the seeds across the neighboring forest floor, spreading out their own population.

Either way, I learned something new on this day. Even if it did make my skin crawl.

June 22

137 and 138. Mansfield and Easton: Borderland State Park

My buddy Taylor had been telling me about Borderland for years, but my schedule had just never swung me through the area. Strangely, I did get married about three miles away, or at least partied the night away after the ceremony, in Sharon. Would have looked weird, though, walking through the woods in a tuxedo. In the rain. At night. Might have been a first for Borderland, who knows.

But with this project, it was inevitable that I should find Borderland. I strolled down the Bay Road Lane entrance, entranced. The corridor through the trees leads to open fields and an old farmhouse. I took the right hand turn and kept going until I could split the difference between Leach Pond and Upper Leach Pond, spending half my time in each community.

I came across a bench with an inscription on it: "In wood lies the greatest gift of all, peace." It was a memorial to a lost friend of the community - the community being that of Borderland State Park - and overlooked a serene setting on Upper Leach Pond. Nearby, I found a length of monofilament fishing line dangling from a tree limb, and a red and white bobber securely fashioned to it. If that didn't speak of peacefulness, I don't know what does. The "stress" of losing a bit of fishing line on a quiet spring morning is far down on my list of life's worries. In fact, I wish it happened to me more often.

Good call, Taylor.

139. Norton: Leo G. Yelle Conservation Area

If I had my way, I would have called the plants along the trail for encroachment. Of the many conservation lands I walked on this day two displayed this type of overgrowth. It was almost as if nature didn't want us there...

But who was I to complain? I've always felt that nature should be absorbed through all the senses, with a bit of deferral for each method, of course. We shouldn't eat and touch certain things, while smells can't really do us much harm, despite what we think of skunks. Walking through this wood was like shaking a wet, slippery hand with thousands of plants, over and over and over again.

Making so many contacts, I finally was interested enough to look down and see what it was I was brushing up against. The predominant species was the highbush blueberry, an identification I made very easily once I noticed that they had started to sprout their blueberries. And by the way, am I the only one who remembers the episode from *Taxi* in which Alex Riga and Jim Ignatowski argue over whether or not the blue berries they find in the woods are blueberries, or just blue berries? Ah, childhood re-run memories.

My final turnaround point in Norton consisted of a walk over a small muddy brook that was much more mud than brook. I found, too, thanks to this particular walk, that one of the keys to avoiding mosquitoes is to just keep walking at a great pace so they can't catch you. Especially when you're leaning over trying to take a picture of the first Indian pipes you've found for the year.

140. Raynham: Raynham State Forest

Well, another day, another disappointment with the state. Borderland State Park had closed gates beyond the time they were supposed to be open, this state forest had not had any trail maintenance for at least a year, maybe more, and there would be more problems during the day, too.

Sadly, despite the inviting nature of the place, on maps, even by way of the sign posted outside the trail, one would have to be a hobbit to walk here on a regular basis. Trees from both sides of the trail had overtaken the available walking space, making it so that I had to crouch down to get through some spaces I could not easily push straight through. I fought on for the full half hour, but figure this is a scratch off the list of future visits until I hear that any type of maintenance has been done.

On the other hand, perhaps that was the grand plan, to let it return to its natural glory. I'm all for that. I just wished I knew what was going on. But then, I say that all the time in all phases of my life, from wondering about Red Sox trade deadline moves to my son putting plastic eggs in my boots.

141. Berkley: Dighton Rock State Park

After having wandered in the woods all morning, this park was a revelation. I had no clue what to expect when I saw it on the map. I figured I'd be parking at the beginning and walking to find the rock, but no, one drives to the end of the park.

And I'll tell you one thing, had I walked all that way to find what I did at the end, I'd be beyond pissed off.

Dighton Rock is apparently inside a small museum. I can't tell you for sure because the museum is locked up tightly. I came all this way to Dighton Rock State Park, and couldn't see Dighton Rock. What a downer, man. I tried to appease myself by reading the brochure mounted outside so I could at least learn more about it, but the first sentence said that the rock is a "bolder." I walked away.

The park sits sublimely on the Taunton River, complete with soaring ospreys, diving cormorants and surface-skittering swallows. Across the way a marina sat strangely quietly. Somewhere in the woods, a state employee was munching up some brush with a mower of some kind, while a woman walked her ancient dog by the water. "What happened to Mr. Swan?" she asked me, to which I almost replied that I wasn't a local, and didn't know Mr. Swan. "He's dead, down by the water's edge." Ah, that kind of swan.

A grandfather and grandson pulled up just as I was walking out of the area marked with a sign that indicated it was the approximate site of a former cemetery. They popped their trunk and began assembling fishing rods. The little guy said, "Hey, it rained here." By Jove...the kid was right. I guess in my wanderings I just dodged the raindrops.

There would be more to come.

142 and 143. Freetown and Fall River: Freetown and Fall River State Forest

As the skies began to threaten to release their pent up precipitation, I wandered into another area for the first time in my life. I had heard about, read about and generally wondered about this particular state forest, but again, it had never called me in.

I headed for Profile Rock. I wanted to know why it was that I had never heard of it, especially given the famousness of the Old Man of the Mountain up in Franconia Notch in New Hampshire. I left the parking lot for the trail marked "Overlook" and nearly walked directly into a wood thrush. What a beautiful sight.

I found the rocks, complete with their early twentieth century-style steps to them. I tried to find a way to the top, circling the entire base, reading as little profane graffiti as possible along the way. I could hear voices at the top and began to wonder if my youthful climbing days were at an end. Then it hit me: follow the Dunkin Donuts trash. Sad, but true.

Within a few moments, I was on top of this particular piece of the world, looking for miles across the treetops. It was even better than Abrams Rock. One cell tower here, one steeple-less church tower there, and the rest a sea of green, like the Beatles sang in "Yellow Submarine." Three young men joined me on the stone, but my guess was that when they thought of the word "stone" another meaning came to mind first. I smelled them long before they arrived. But then again, had I said "stone" to an ancient Babylonion, he, too, might conjure up a different image. For a reference, watch the Monty Python movie *Life of Brian*. ("Nobody is to stone anyone, until I blow this whistle!")

To catch the Fall River side, I moved across the street to the general wildlife management section of the park, and there I finally came face to face with Pine Cone Johnny himself. The state owes a lot to the Depression era Civilian Conservation Corps workers who spent so much time in our forests, and here the state had done the right thing, erecting a statue in their memory. As Johnny and I stood together in the rain, I realized that for all my frustrations with the State of Massachusetts during the day, consisting of parking problems, fees, neglect, abuse and more, this one act did a lot to balance the ledger.

And with that, I said goodbye to Bristol County for 2011.

144, 145 and 146. Washington, Lee and Becket: October Mountain State Forest

Y'all ready for this? Fasten your seatbelts.

Berkshire County comprises about one-tenth of Massachusetts, community count-wise. It also represents, by far, the longest distance I had to travel in Massachusetts and still say I was in Massachusetts. As fate would have it, I had work to do out here this summer, for the Breeding Bird Atlas 2 project, and so I blocked out three days to do just that. That gave me 72 hours to get to 33 towns before returning to the lowlands of eastern Massachusetts.

Berkshires: Take One. I arrived at my first destination, atop October Mountain in Washington and stepped immediately into a different world. The background noises were just completely un-Massachusetts-like to me: chestnut-sided warblers, least flycatchers, squawking yellow-bellied sapsuckers, and was that a raven? Was that a beaver lodge?

I hit a dirt road that my GPS said was in the heart of the state forest, despite the fact that there was not a single sign saying anything to that effect. I found a crossroads and began to wander. After a few minutes, another car pulled up and out stepped an older gentleman with binoculars. I had run into the only other birder, possibly the only other human being, in the 16,500 acres of the unmarked park. We exchanged pleasantries and sightings, and went our separate ways.

I had work to do.

147, 148 and 149. Great Barrington, Monterey and Tyringham: Beartown State Forest

There are just those places that you have to stop and take in through every sense. Beartown State Forest slapped me across the face from the moment I set foot in it. And it wasn't just me doing that to keep the deer flies from biting. A thick dousing of DEET took care of that little problem.

As much as I wanted to walk, I wanted to stand. There were moments on the trails at Beartown - and I got to spend an hour and a half here thanks to the fact that it touches upon three towns - that I wanted even the sound of my own feet to cease, so I could soak in the natural gorgeousness of the sounds of the forest floating on the air. I was still getting used to my new friends in the flycatchers and the sapsuckers, but was starting to hear old friends, too, especially the cedar waxwings darting from treetop to treetop.

As I stopped along one trail at a roadway crossing, a guy in a pickup truck stopped and asked what I was seeing. This, by the way, is a phenomenon that increases as one moves away from cities and into the more rural areas of our country. This guy, towing a dirt bike, told me of how he normally caught up with an owl or two on his rides through the park.

"Keep an eye out for bobcats, too," he said as he smiled, waved and drove away.

Oo, I certainly would.

150. Otis: Otis State Forest

In a way, one can look at Massachusetts and compare it geographically to America. First there's the fact that they both start on the East Coast. Then, they both gradually rise to a western mountain range. Think of Greylock as Pike's Peak. There are large bodies of water in the middle: Great Lakes and Quabbin. There are major dividing rivers, the Mississippi and the Connecticut. And one can just imagine that the first settlers who cut through the passes of the mountains in Berkshire County probably put their hands on their knees, panted heavily and said, "Well, at least we got across these darned mountains. I'll bet it's smooth and flat sailing from here all the way to the West Coast, whatever that is."

The state and the country have one other thing in common. The major cities of the east give way to wide open spaces in the west. In the grander scheme, it's the national parks; in Massachusetts, it's the state parks.

In many cases, the state parks bleed from one town to the next. I could have walked the Otis State Forest and checked Otis off my list, or I could have walked a particular section of the Sandisfield State Forest and gotten both Otis and Sandisfield. Or I could have walked Tolland State Forest and gotten both Tolland and Sandisfield. Hmm...

I took the Otis-only route, and was glad I did. I saw my first white admiral butterfly of the year, even if I didn't get a picture of it. I wonder if General Henry "The Ox" Knox saw any when he was passing through here to the siege of Boston in 1776. Did the general see an admiral? Another great question of American history.

151 and 152: Tolland and Sandisfield: Tolland State Forest

I took myself up on that offer of double-dipping in Sandisfield and Tolland, although it didn't matter anyway, as I would double-dip again in Sandisfield and New Marlborough...it's not really as confusing as it sounds, I promise.

The parking area to the state forest was jumping with activity: dirt bikers coming off the trails covered in mud, stripping out of their one-piece togs, fishermen casting from the shore, and more. It was turning out to be a deviously beautiful day, one that fools you into thinking you can do much more than your body really wants you to.

But I had miles to go before I could sleep, to almost quote Robert Frost.

The rush of the Farmington River drowned out much of the passing auto traffic noise as I crossed the old bridge and headed into the woods. When I look back now I realize I only checked off two birds: a red-eyed vireo and a ruffed grouse, the first extremely common, the second a pure chance sighting.

They, though, were simple diversions from a dramatic scene I saw being carried out 50 feet above my head. The scene was straight out of Tolkien. A tree had fallen in the woods and on its way down reached out with what looked like two arms to be caught by its brethren. It looked like a soldier being dragged from a battlefield by comrades. The sight made me see how writers like Tolkien do it. It was enough to get me started on my own fantasy novel.

153. New Marlborough: Sandisfield State Forest

I was on my way elsewhere in New Marlborough when the roadside sign caught my eye. A CCC Memorial, dedicated to the members of the 196th Company of the Civilian Conservation Corps, was just in the woods a few hundred yards.

My ongoing learning about the CCC and its accomplishments in Massachusetts' state forests had been refreshed every few weeks on this project. The thought of it still pulls at my heart: a country so poor that mothers and fathers couldn't feed sons and were forced to send them away to live in camps in the woods to become property of the federal government until suitable work could be found. What a horrible time the Depression must have been.

The marker here was dedicated in December 1934 after five boys were killed when the dump truck in which they were driving to church slammed into a barrier in Great Barrington. The stone notes that they were killed "in the line of duty," a distinction certainly *a propos* despite its military connotation. The marker was surrounded by smaller stones and paired with a flagpole proudly flying the stars and stripes, a scene as American as any military graveyard, and possibly ten times as sad.

154. Egremont: Appalachian Trail

Just like in New Marlborough, I was looking for something else when the Appalachian Trail came along. But I could not fight the urge. I just had to do it to say I did.

The notion that one can walk from Georgia to Maine on mostly open spaces is just incredible, but it can be done and has been done for decades. It's a dream journey for me, one I fear I will never get to take, for numerous reasons. With so many responsibilities on my plate for so many years going forward, it just feels like it can't happen...but who knows. Maybe someday.

I think I expected some sort of magic when I stepped on the trail for those few thousand feet, but nothing was different from the rest of the habitat in which I'd been walking all day. There were waxwings and veeries and common yellowthroats. But there were two new sensations for the day. Part of the trail was being mowed as I was there, so the smell of fresh cut wet grass dominated my nostrils. That, and I looked up to realize that the heat I was suddenly feeling on the upper parts of my body was being generated by a giant yellow orb in the sky. The sun was out! Hallelujah.

So I walked my half hour, and I can't say that I walked the Appalachian Trail, but I can say I walked *on* the Appalachian Trail. I feel so Bill Brysonish. And that is magic enough.

Added bonus: I noticed a granite marker near the parking area, and had to investigate, of course. There's nothing more exciting to me than words chiseled into stone. Somebody really wants to say something important when they go to those lengths. This one called attention to the fact that the last battle of Shay's Rebellion was fought on this spot in 1787. It meant I was standing on an historic battleground. It also meant I was in Sheffield. With a yelp I leapt back across the street to the Egremont side. Phew! That was close.

155. Sheffield: Lime Kiln Farm Wildlife Sanctuary

It had already been a long day by the time I reached Lime Kiln Farm, but I felt rejuvenated, not only by my chocolate almond fudge Clif Bar, but by the notion that I was walking on one of the few Mass Audubon wildlife sanctuaries I had never previously visited.

I immediately met a woman on the trail, walking her dog, unfortunately, which is against the rules. We exchanged hellos and she paused, I think expecting more conversation, but I was already striding past and would have had to make a dainty kind of pirouette to smoothly accommodate her wishes. But I couldn't pull it off. I must have seemed so Eastern Mass to her. Sorry!

The butterflies met me next, beginning with a great spangled fritillary, which made perfect sense. They have one flight per year, starting with the last week in June. Welcome, Frit! It was soon followed by a tiger swallowtail.

Past the fields and a really interesting sedge habitat and into the woods, my old friends came out to play, the pewees, towhees and ovenbirds. The trail wound past memorial markers for the sanctuary's visionaries, to mountain overlooks and an old lime kiln. For just a few short years limestone extraction and conversion to lime took place here. A century later, its physical reminder, the kiln, still stood.

I caught myself lingering a little too long at the scenic overlook, and "punished" myself with an extra half an hour of walking on the trails. Bad boy. Bad, bad boy. Enjoying nature like that.

156. Mt. Washington: Bash Bish Falls State Park

I was nearing the end, and I could feel it. My legs were starting to give out, breathing was becoming more difficult and I was bathed in sweat.

I'd always wanted to visit Mt. Washington, having already driven up the mountain of the same name in New Hampshire, but for probably the most obscure reason imaginable. Back in the 1980s, before I was officially practicing history, a historian in my hometown of Hull did a study comparing the two communities. They were, at one time, the two smallest towns in Massachusetts by population totals.

But things would change for Hull. The Victorian era brought an explosion in vacationing, and eventually a lot of those day-, week- and month-trippers stuck. The population rose from 250 in 1880 to 1,000 by 1900, to 11,000 today. But Mt. Washington never grew. Today 130 people call Mt. Washington home, but, believe it or not, there are two towns even smaller than that in Massachusetts according to the 2000 census.

Mt. Washington is mostly state parks. My visit here coincided with a crossing of the New York border, by accident, and finding a bordering New York state park. *Half an Hour a Day Across New York: 994 Towns in 365 Days.* Bet that would take some walking.

I descended the trail toward the falls, and found some of the headwaters. A brook trickled down across the trail, wet, mossy rocks seemingly forever caught in the constant motion of the waters. Even if I never saw the falls - which were as spectacular as advertised - this scene would have done my heart just fine, creating a perfect memory of this particular state park.

On the way back up I passed a couple in their sixties. The woman said, "How was it? It was beautiful when I was a kid and we came here fifty years ago! This is my first time back."

See? You can go home again, when open land is preserved.

June 27

157. Lenox: Pleasant Valley Wildlife Sanctuary

Berkshire County, Day Two. Captain's Log, Star Date 06.27.11...

I had positioned myself to wake up in Lenox, practically across the highway from the entrance to the Pleasant Valley sanctuary, another jewel in the open space crown of Mass Audubon. I know way too much about this sanctuary to fit it all in here, so I'll stick to the highlights.

When the ladies who formed the sanctuary in the 1920s by buying the old Power family farm started their journey, they hired a young man named Maurice Broun to supervise things, fresh from his stay at a banding station in Wellfleet (that later became the Wellfleet Bay Wildlife Sanctuary, also a Mass Audubon property). Broun left quickly to found Hawk Mountain in Pennsylvania, and his replacement, S. Morris Pell, took charge.

Pell felt the place could use a shot in the arm wildlife-wise, so he introduced beavers to the sanctuary, and they did what they do best - plugged up the brooks to create ponds, which then attracted wood ducks. Mission accomplished.

Several years ago I took a dusk beaver walk with a guide named Butch, a volunteer who brought our gang to see the beavers emerging from their lodge as the sun went down. I was there at the wrong time of day this time around, but I did get to see my favorite parts of the sanctuary, the red barn, the old Power farmhouse, the beaver ponds...

...I could go on.

158. Stockbridge: Laurel Hill

Well, what an adventure I had on Laurel Hill.

It started simply enough, across the bridge, past the railroad tracks to a fork in the trail: observation tower or ice glen? When in doubt, go long. I decided to take in the sights from the heights.

Up I went, and soon I found that I would not have nearly enough time to see it all and stick to my 30-minute plan. So I broke my own rules and kept walking. And sweating. And panting.

If you ever saw that episode of the Simpsons where Homer gets in shape and becomes the poster boy for a protein bar company, and is lined up to climb a mountain to show off his newfound prowess, and the marketing guy keeps telling him that no, it's not that mountain, it's the bigger one to the left, no the bigger one, no the bigger one...well, that's what this trail was like. Every time I took a turn up a switchback on the trail, I felt like the top had to be nearby, but it just stayed out of my reach. I had the sensation once before, on a chairlift. Up and over one crest we rode, only to find we had barely traveled a fifth of the distance to the top of the mountain.

So I climbed, past the olive-sided flycatcher (found another one!), into the mountain laurel, past the boulder fields, until finally I could see green grass along the trail. There had been none the entire way up, with the dense canopy completely shielding the sun's rays from hitting the forest floor. Finally, I reached the top, climbed the observation tower, to find that the entire view was one hundred percent fogged in.

CRAP!

So I walked all the way back down the hill and almost stepped on a red eft. I didn't though. But I did get a picture.

159. Alford: Just Alford

My goodness...was this place beautiful.

I didn't have a park or sanctuary or anything picked out in Alford, and in the end just got out of the car and walked some of the "main roads" of town. This place was as quiet a community as I'd ever seen, and easily one of the most pleasant. The town website says there are no hotels, motels, not even a gas station, but that they're available in neighboring towns. It's almost as if the town stopped growing before the Industrial Revolution and decided that life was just fine as it was. And you know what? They're right.

The rolling hills and mountain overlooks were simply stunning. Valleys dip between peaks of green. I'm sure the light breeze and soft sunshine helped me think that way, but I can't imagine that fall could be unsightly, either. I encountered a group of seventy-somethings on bikes riding up one of the longer hill runs, happy as four-year-olds with ice cream cones.

I stopped at the small cemetery which, of course, overlooked a lush, green vale. There I met Stephen Johns, Civil War veteran and member of Company F of the 12th New York Cavalry. New York. That's right. I forgot I was on the border. In some instances it was easier for Civil War soldiers to sign up with not only units forming in other towns, but in other states. And in those days it mattered. Today, you join the Army and it's just the Army, a national entity. In those days, state pride meant everything.

You know, I haven't thought much about retirement, but this place certainly made me start to formulate the list of places I might like to be in 30 years.

160. West Stockbridge: Main Street

I could have walked a bit of Lenox Mountain and called it a hit, but I decided to do a little downtown action in West Stockbridge. First, it's just so damned cute. Second, I've got a childhood tie to the area, spiritually.

It was all brought back to me by a Shaker furniture storefront, in an old, Gilded Age corner building. When I was young, my mother brought us - my sister Julie, brother Nick, and me - on many a summer vacation journey. Such was the freedom of a schoolteacher working in a public school system. We visited the Baseball Hall of Fame in Cooperstown, did a long run through the sights of Kentucky, from My Old Kentucky Home to Colonel Sanders' gravesite to the Perryville Civil War battlefield (where I first realized, at 11, that I wanted to study history). And we explored a lot of New Hampshire.

I couldn't even tell you today without cheating in which town in New Hampshire we made this particular stop, but we visited a Shaker village. I remember vividly an interpreter explaining how the Shakers were so efficient. They had a broom with an extra long handle for sweeping the ceiling, and hooks on the wall for hanging their chairs when they were done with them for the day.

But that wasn't even the most amazing memory. There was an old woman in the room, in her high 80s, wearing a black dress and white bonnet. She wasn't a Shaker, but she had been raised by Shakers, and that was as close as I was going to get to one. And that's what happens to your way of life when you decide as a group to not have children; it dies out.

So there I was, standing in the middle of the sidewalk in West Stockbridge, peering back into my childhood.

161. Richmond: Swamp Road and Beyond

Again, without any designated open spaces to tackle, I decided to let Richmond take me to places it wanted to show me. Besides, this was one of those locales I had been asked to focus on in particular for the Breeding Bird Atlas, a ten-square-mile block of land ignorant of town borders or other political niceties the natural world doesn't understand.

At various times I found myself overlooking a small pond on a relatively busy corner, on the side of a mountain where a road I had intended to drive had been closed halfway up, and back at the bottom of that road staring across a gorgeous field of green toward white puffy clouds and bright blue sky.

It was then that I realized what Massachusetts' biggest problem is: redistribution. I think that if we could just get a humongous vacuum cleaner and suck, say, 2,000,000 people out of eastern Massachusetts and send them elsewhere, we'd be off to a good start. No more traffic jams, no more noise, no more road rage, no more hatred. I'm not even saying put them in western Massachusetts, as I'd never want to subject the good people there to the Eastern Mass way of life.

The more I drove around Berkshire County, the more I fell in love with it. I still had half of it to go at that point for this particular trip, but I knew from previous experiences that there was a lot of culture in Pittsfield and Lenox and Lee, and this trip was just hammering home the beauty of the natural surroundings for me.

Maybe that was it, then. Maybe it was just me that needed relocation. Anybody got a Hoover?

162. Pittsfield: Canoe Meadows Wildlife Sanctuary

It had already been a fantastic trip by the point I rolled into Pittsfield, but I knew it was about to get even better. I mean, come on, I had to pass Herman Melville's house to get down here to land once owned by Oliver Wendell Holmes. I think I even passed out from the excitement for a few seconds.

It's not easy being a history geek.

I was here once, a long time ago, back when I was researching my history of Mass Audubon. I had arrived too early for my appointment at Pleasant Valley in Lenox, and decided to see what Canoe Meadows was all about. Keep in mind this was before I could be described as a naturalist in any sense of the word. I saw a deer. It was *soooo* cool. Little did I know how many hundreds I'd be seeing in the next seven years.

I walked the main trail out to the observation blind on the pond, and listened to the green frogs twang. I walked past a flooded area obviously designed by beavers, along the carriage road out to a pasture, where a giant tree once stood. I found the spillway that was already etched in my memory from my last visit, and did my best to swat the deer flies that were probably direct descendants of the dozen or so that harassed me the last time I was here.

My favorite short Holmes quote fits my life quite well. A history degree? Really? Well, I've made the best of it, and today can't keep up with the work I'm asked to perform on top of my own chosen pathways. "Every calling is great when greatly pursued," the great man once said, and I'll stick to my decision 'til the day I die.

Reinvigorated by a self-perceived spiritual bond with the long dead gentleman, I walked on.

163. Hancock: Pittsfield State Forest

Oh...my...god. Just when I think I've found the most beautiful place in Massachusetts, another rises to the top of the list.

I took the Berry Pond Loop to the top of Berry Mountain and got out of my car to the deafening sound of silence. I took everything out of my pockets, took off my shoes and stepped onto the Taconic Crest Trail. I, in no way, would break that silence. It was glorious as it was.

I walked among chest-high ferns, out to a scenic overlook - the Berkshires do have a few, I'd started to realize - and just soaked it in. Weymouthites, Reverians, Swampscottsmen, Scituations, you just have no idea what it's like. "Back east" our homes are crammed together in disagreeable little lots, privacy having been thrown out the window decades ago. We're intruded upon by planes, trains and automobiles, avoided by the indigo buntings like the three I heard on Berry Mountain and laughed at by those folks who found early on that life just doesn't have to be like it is in and around the cities of the northeast.

Even the air itself was different, light, thinner, of course, and clean. I could almost taste the difference when I breathed.

And I breathed. In deep, deep breaths, I breathed.

164. Lanesborough: Balance Rock State Park

I can't tell you how disappointed I was when I reached Balance Rock, as it was one of the landmarks I had long planned to visit when I got to western Massachusetts in 2011. But, of course, like almost every other rock formation in Massachusetts I'd seen this year, it was covered with graffiti.

Son of a bitch.

It was, strictly geologically speaking, an incredible sight. The rock, an erratic, weighs in at 165 tons - that's 330,000 pounds, or thirty male African elephants, if that's how you personally measure really big things - and is balanced perfectly on a slab of bedrock in a way that seems to defy gravity.

I was quite perturbed about the sight of the graffiti until I later visited an exhibit at the Mt. Greylock headquarters and saw an old Bill Tague photograph from the 1950s. There was Balance Rock, covered in graffiti, in black and white. Graffiti, as stupid as it is, is now a part of the history of the rock. One just can't help but think that if the rock could think, all it could be saying to itself is "Idiot humans, I'll be here long after you're gone, and your petty work will all be washed away." That's what I would say, if I was a talking rock.

Hmm, it had been a long couple of days.

165, 166, 167, 168, 169. Adams, North Adams, Cheshire, Williamstown and New Ashford: Mt. Greylock State Park

Well, the time had come. Despite creeping fatigue, a tiring back, weakening quads and mental droopage, to coin my own new term, it was time to scale Greylock. I had about three hours and wanted to be true to my plan - a half an hour in each town - so I picked my trails accordingly.

That didn't matter one damn bit. This whole place was outrageously beautiful. I found plenty that made me smile, but only one thing that made me laugh out loud, a sign that said "Entering War Memorial Area - No Firearms."

I found the white-throated sparrows and dark-eyed juncos I'd lost at the end of winter in eastern Mass. Most fly north, some just fly up, right up the sides of mountains in western Mass. For some it's not a latitude thing, but an altitude thing.

I found the story of the CCC boys told once again, this time in the main road running across the spine of the mountain, and I resolved then and there that someday I would do more for them, after all they've done for me. Their legacy of open space creation in Massachusetts is unparalleled. Here I was eighty years later enjoying the fruits of their work, and until I started this project, I didn't even know it.

I found that when I reached the pinnacle and the state's war memorial, I was not alone. It was slightly jolting to see how many cars were at the top, after having passed but a handful of people on the various trails. This had happened to me before. I took a young woman to see the Anne of Green Gables historic site on Prince Edward Island, leaving forlornly desolate roads to find a parking lot overflowing with Japanese tourists. How did they all get there?

Three hours wasn't enough, and I made myself late for my last few rounds of the day, but as you probably know by now, it didn't bother me in the slightest. I always have time for the next adventure.

170. Clarksburg: Clarksburg State Forest

In one of my few human interactions of my Berkshire County trip, I met two young men working on Mauserts Pond. From what the park ranger had told me, there was an issue with invasives in the pond, caused by Canada geese. He said there was "removal" going on, and I wanted to see it.

The pond was obviously a beach-type oasis in summer, but late on a Monday afternoon there wasn't bound to be much activity.

The pond itself averages only six feet in depth, with an eight-foot deep trench running through it at one point, and that can be a problem. If an invasive plant species gloms on to the pond floor, where sunlight easily reaches, it quickly can spread. Such an event can easily occur when a bird species flies from one place and drops the seeds in the new place. If the conditions are right, it spreads like Skippy peanut butter on a nice slice of Wonder Bread.

Sorry, all this walking has me hungry.

I asked the guys working on the pond what they were removing, and they said they didn't know. They just were removing, and that was just fine. The pond obviously needed a fresh start, and they were giving it the chance to be natural again. They boarded their sidewheel barges, dropped their rakes and hit the next section.

Which was exactly what I needed to do, make one more stop before declaring it a successful day.

171 and 172. Florida and Savoy: Savoy Mountain State Park

The sunblock had worked, that was for sure, and the bug spray I had added on top of it had certainly done its job as well. Luckily I didn't need to talk to any more people for the next day or so, as I don't think I'd have been very good-smelling company.

But, as Emilia said in *Othello*, that 'tis neither here nor there.

I was surprised to find bathers in North Pond when I arrived in the northwest corner of Savoy Mountain State Forest, but they, like me, were wrapping up their day. It wasn't quite time to start listening for owls, but it was late by swimming standards and the sun was giving up its struggle against the horizon, as it does every single day. Quitter.

As they moved on, so did I, to other parts of the forest, down dirt roads into deep woods and finding an odd grassland near the top of the mountain. A Cooper's hawk flew out from the field, one of the few, rare raptors I had seen in the Berkshires, a complete surprise to me. A raven, though, did add its spookiness to the surroundings. They always seem to be just distant enough to be background noise, like in a suspense film from the 1950s.

I wound down the mountain, then wound down in general. It was a remarkable day, and I had just a few towns to go before I'd finish Berkshire County for the year. A good night's rest would be unavoidable, and I was thankful for that.

June 28

173. Dalton: Wahconah Falls State Park

Berkshire County, Day Three. Twenty-eight towns down, four to go. I'd be done before lunchtime. And that meant I could do some more damage to the map as well, as I could split the long ride home into shorter treks with interspersed walks along the way east.

I'm glad to say that I'm not the type that gets tired of waterfalls. Each year I lead a trip to the Finger Lakes that features two visits to falls. Whenever I visit the Poconos, I take in my favorites on my way through the Delaware Water Gap. And now, heading west across Massachusetts, I'd developed a punch list of favorites just within the Bay State.

There's not much more for me to say about them, though, that I haven't said before. I'm silenced by them, which is just a Pisces thing. Put us near running water of any kind and we get all dreamy and wussy. Maybe it's the inner fish pining for release and return to the wild. Whatever it is, it's internally reactionary, nothing I can control.

In all, Dalton wasn't a bad way to start the day.

174. Hinsdale: Ashmere State Park

Are you kidding me, I say again? Of all the things I expected to see in Hinsdale - to be honest, a small list as I barely knew anything about the place before I arrived - an osprey was on the absolute bottom rung of the ladder.

This is not me just being a coast-dwelling chauvinist pig. I know for a fact that ospreys are everywhere, on all continents save for Antarctica (and who could blame them), but the Massachusetts story is well documented. Practically extirpated during the *Silent Spring* era, when our free and rampant use of chemicals that escaped into the landscape was driving them to extinction, ospreys clung to Massachusetts in the Westport area. A champion, Gil Fernandez, rose and began building nesting platforms for the birds, and soon they were on their way back. In fact, on June 30 and July 1 I would be visiting about a dozen nests on the South Shore in order to help band the year's youngsters. Ospreys are here and thriving, a true success story in the face of overwhelming odds, given an assist by human hands.

But Hinsdale? In my mind, it was far too west. Yes, I had seen them in central New York State, but it didn't click that I might find them in between there and the coast. But I did, and gleefully so.

175. Windsor: Windsor State Forest

For all intents and purposes, not to mention intensive porpoises, I was at the halfway point of the year when I emerged from Windsor State Forest.

351/2=175.5

I would officially be there fifteen minutes into my next walk, but that number 175 was a blessing to see on my list. It would all be downhill from there.

Now, the question is, do I really have enough stories in me to keep you interested for another 175 journal entries? The challenge is on. So here's one for you.

As I stood staring at the particular wildflower, I realized that I was probably staring at a math lesson. There is a peculiar growth pattern in nature that affects not only flowers but seashells, broken down by the concept of Fibonacci numbers.

Take a line and divide it at the point where the ratio of the whole to the greater portion is equal to the ratio of the greater portion to the smaller, and you have the Golden Ratio, or Phi, or about 1.6. Now imagine you've got a rectangle using the same theory. Draw a line across the width of the rectangle at that point, and you have another perfectly Phi-primed rectangle. Draw a line where the Golden Ratio manifests itself in that smaller rectangle, and you start to get a spiraling effect.

That effect is exactly what you see in the face of a sunflower. The Golden Ratio, a number that has baffled mathematicians, historians and scientists alike for millennia, arises naturally in the woods and on the beaches.

Did that do it? Onto the next lesson, class.

176. Peru: Dorothy Frances Rice Sanctuary

If ever I saw moose country, this was it. Yet I did not see a moose. I did, though, have a perfect viewing of a white admiral butterfly, and unlike my earlier encounter on the trip, this time my camera was at the ready.

Technically, I had already seen and photographed this butterfly earlier this year under its other guise, the red-spotted purple. Oddly, the *Limenitis arthemis* has two widely variant forms, one without the white band, one with. Now I could claim both for 2011.

I took the main trail into the sanctuary and swatted at the mass of deer flies that slurped and salivated at my arrival. There was no doubt I was still in Berkshire County, as the bird sounds were all the same, but something in the air was different. Perhaps I had lost a base altitude, or perhaps it was simply delusionality on my part. Either way, one fact was definitely true. As I walked back off the trail past the same butterfly still clinging to the same plant on which I had left it thirty minutes earlier next to the pond, about ten feet from the dead meadow vole (*Microtus pennsylvanicus*) in the center of the trail, I had finished another county's worth of walking for 2011.

Berkshire County - Galluzzo out.

177. Middlefield: Glendale Falls

The smell of the stream hit me square in the face. It probably was more the smell of the stagnant pools that formed off to the sides of the Glendale Falls, but it certainly reminded me of every pond and stream I'd ever had the privilege of getting to know in Massachusetts. It evoked primal memories, physical more than mental.

But it was hard to focus on anything not moving in the din of the falling water. And it made me backtrack a bit, to the top of the trail, where the water was still in stream mode and not falls mode. It was a little mind-bending to consider that the same water that was trickling along here just a few feet down the trail would roar, simply by the addition of a touch more gravitational pull.

It made sense. I'd make a lot more noise if I suddenly started to fall off the side of a hill.

There was a single couple here to enjoy this moment with me, New Yorkers. The guy had a mustache, but didn't seem like a mustache guy. I had to look for a few seconds to try and figure out what he would look like without it. I shook my head to clear it like an Etch-A-Sketch and went back to the falls.

178. Huntington: Huntington State Forest

Another dirt road, another metal state forest gate, another immersion into the wonderful woods of western Mass. I figured if I was not tired of it by that moment, I never would be.

The most interesting facet of this particular state forest, though, had to do with what was just outside of it. A stoic old farm building, in deep-shaded shingles, stood guard over the entrance. Standing alone, it was in an era all its own, a sight unlike anything I had ever seen.

I could see the old farmer with a horse drawn wagon, driving it over the craggy road. I could see him in the woods with a saw and perhaps a son or a farmhand, taking down a tree to be cut up for firewood, to heat the old building in winter.

I could see his wife in her apron, and his granddaughters running in the yard among the dandelions, very *Little House on the Prairie*-ish, I guess. But it was all there in my mind.

My last thought here was about the state and its overreaching conservation plans. Was this it for this forest? No signage, no real trail maintenance? I know, from working with the state in the past as the head of a nonprofit "friends" group that Massachusetts has more land than it can currently deal with. I hoped it would not always the case. I hoped the land is forever protected in Huntington.

179. Westhampton: Lynes Wildlife Sanctuary

With about an hour of walking left in me for the day, I visited Westhampton and Easthampton. You know, the Hamptons.

After I walked at Lynes, I met a friend of the donor who gave the land to Mass Audubon who said that the former owners believed there were places on the sanctuary where no human being had *ever* walked. I could see that, with dense swamps that held no attraction for any man. But, I thought, one must be careful with such thoughts. For a millennium, at least, man has walked this land. And man has many reasons to run and hide, from animals and other human beings. A deterrent swamp might be just the perfect hiding place.

My walk on this day was a tough one, as the trails here had not yet been plowed down or cut back. The first field, in particular, was almost impassable because I simply couldn't see the trail. Luckily, someone recently through - and that last someone may have been on a horse, judging by the droppings - had placed a marker at the first main intersection, giving me guidance.

Not far beyond that, I was looking at a wildflower when I noticed a purely white spider crawling on it. It ducked underneath a petal when it sensed me, but I partially caught it with my camera before I moved on. I don't know enough about arachnids to be either scared or not, but I was smart enough to know not to mess with it.

I entered the woods and was about to emerge onto another old field when I heard...wait, could it be?...no, that couldn't be right. It's an endangered species, extremely rare. There's just no way, although the habitat is perfect...

180. Easthampton: Arcadia Wildlife Sanctuary

I'll admit it, I stumbled to this finish line. More than once during the trip, I found that extra reserve of energy, the one that propelled me over yet another finish line. But this was nearly my fortieth sanctuary visit in three days. I was cooked.

I let the mosquitoes have at me as I walked the trail to my favorite overlook on the oxbow, the tower that shows the heights of the historical floods of the region. This is another place I know too well for the purposes of this book. I know the story of the land owner who experimented with bird boxes on his property, inviting outside guests to visit his land and experience the wonder of nature. I know how he sold it to Mr. Chafee, who wanted to turn it over to Mass Audubon in honor of his son, dead at a tragically young age. I know about the old tobacco barns, the corduroy road, the raccoon that raised her young in that very observation tower overlooking the marsh.

When I emerged from the trails, drenched in mid-day humidity sweat, Mt. Holyoke stared me down. "Come on, you know you wanna!" it teased, "I'm in another town, one you haven't walked this year." It wasn't easy, but I blew it off with a quick turn of my head.

I'll get you, Mt. Holyoke. I'll get you if it's the last thing I do.

June 29

181. Burlington: Mill Pond

I was starting to get a little worried that I'd have to write about frogs again. I didn't want Halfanhouraday.blogspot.com to turn into a Frog Blog. Or did I...?

I found another good one while on the main trail into Mill Pond, took another pic, and kept moving. Soon, though, the stories started to unfold: the powerline, the pond, the four guys, two girls, a radio and a rope swing.

I heard the voices first - after hearing the yellow-billed cuckoo calling from the trees, of course - and was unsure of what I would be stumbling upon. After the chatter came the splash, and it was a good one. I found a break in the treeline and watched as one after another the kids climbed onto a sawhorse well up the little island, held on for dear life, timed their releases and crashed into the cool water. Good for them. And it wasn't the least bit obnoxious, which was amazing. Imagine that - music kept low, just enjoying the outdoors, with a touch of daredevilry.

My next encounter was with a garter snake. Typically when I run across them, they slither away and keep going. This guy, maybe a foot and a half long, turned and tried to take me on, staring me down and flicking its tongue angrily. I had no beef. I moved on to July.

July

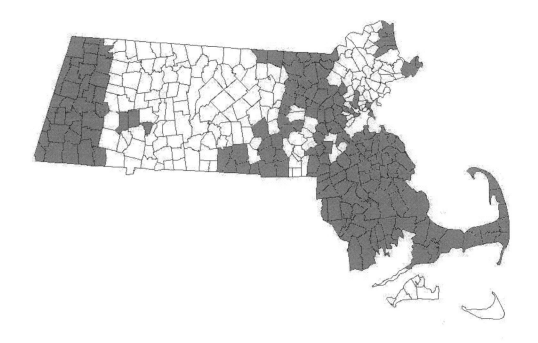

Benchmarks

Aww, yeah. Now that's what I'm talking about. After six months, I had visited 181 towns, more than half of the state in half the year. And I felt like I was just hitting my stride. I thought about calling my 58-town month a Herculean effort, but it just didn't fit. "Hercules, you must slay the hydra. Hercules, you must clean the Augean stables in a single day. Hercules, you must capture Cerberus. Hercules, you must take 58 half an hour walks in 30 days." Not quite Herculean. We'll call it a Galluzzoan effort.

At this obvious reference point, halfway home, I decided to do a bit more research on the state, looking beyond the first letter of each town,. There had to be other ways to look at Massachusetts.

How about by founding date? There were 72 towns in Massachusetts in 2011 that were founded in the seventeenth century. It's really rather amazing, when you think about it. The tradition carried from Europe was one of religious schisms, of breaking away from the larger community when you felt your village got big enough to support a parish of its own. And in the beginning, it was all about the churches. I know one house in Hanson that, without moving an inch, was in four different towns. Plymouth (1620) starts the 17th century list, of course, and Attleboro (1694) ends it.

It was the eighteenth century when Massachusetts boomed. There are today 187 towns that trace their roots to the 1700s, from Framingham (1700, though technically that year should be the last of the previous century; there was no year 0) to Burlington (1799). And as if anyone needed to ask why, the greatest single year for incorporation in Massachusetts history was 1775, when 37 towns came onto the rolls, more than one-tenth of the state. It's almost as if there was something in the air that year.

Things slowed in the 1800s, with only 89 new towns still around today, by that time being driven by economic factors rather than whether or not the walk through the woods to the nearest church was too far or too dangerous (why Pembroke left Duxbury). Communities split when economic centers shaped by the Industrial Revolution shifted, and backwater villages long underrepresented in town politics found themselves in better financial positions than ancient town centers. Only one town sought secession during the Civil War, when Gosnold broke away from Chilmark in 1864. But it had been trying to do so since 1788, so it was old news by then.

Only three towns incorporated in the 1900s: Plainville in 1905, Millville in 1916, and East Brookfield in 1920, our youngest community, not even a century old yet.

How about by population? Of the 54 cities and 297 towns in Massachusetts, five had populations of 100,000 or more in the 2000 census: Boston, Worcester, Springfield, Cambridge and Lowell. Twenty-seven towns had fewer than 1000 residents, all but three west of Worcester, and those three were in Dukes County. Two towns had fewer than 100 residents, the aforementioned Gosnold, and Monroe.

And it was Monroe that would haunt me in the coming months. After my triumphant June, Monroe represented the northwesternmost white space left on my map, a tiny town of 96 souls that represented the work I had left to accomplish, I kicked myself for not using the last day of my Berkshires trip to knock out more of that section. With a sigh significant of that lost opportunity, I marched into July.

July 6

182. Walpole: Walpole Town Forest

Eww, dead raccoon.

I stepped past it and rolled into the forest. Actually, I rolled through a short section of woods and into a big open area with a path leading directly to a reservoir. The main path was manmade, but it was pretty obvious that deer had made the rest. And where there are deer, there are deer ticks. I found out just how uncomfortable it is to walk through tall grass while constantly looking at your shins.

The woods were nearby, but I decided to stick to the open grasslands and the view of the water. A mother and father mute swan were herding their only cygnet - probably a sign of snapping turtles, perhaps some local coyotes, as swans produce much larger broods - while a gray catbird resonated in the woods with an eerie echo. Typically, the catbirds I meet are in my face, a few feet away in the thickets, and don't get the chance to play with things like reverberation, at least in my ears.

Other, closer, sounds, though, had my attention, as buzzing insects dominated the grasses around me. Oddly, I couldn't see any of them. That pleasure was left solely to the dragonflies, which were out in force in the bright sunshine.

As was I...

Oops! Dover: Noanet Woods

Well, it was bound to happen. When you have to coordinate 351 towns, 351 spots on a map, 351 open spaces, there's at least a slight chance that even the brightest mind will mistakenly double-up on a community. So imagine how easy it was for me to do it.

But in my defense, it was my friend Joy's fault. She works at the Broadmoor Wildlife Sanctuary, which is in Dover, Sherborn and Natick. When I walked there...whenever the hell that was...I walked two of the three towns, Dover and Sherborn. Although I recorded all of that in a blog entry soon thereafter, in my head - that dark, dank, scary place, full of roller coasters, 1970s television commercial jingles, M*A*S*H quotes, century-old baseball statistics, *Mike Tyson's Punchout* codes...I could go on - I had walked Natick and Sherborn. So I walked Dover again. I have no idea why it's Joy's fault, but you have to blame somebody. It's the American way.

Well, it was fun anyway. There were grand old wooden farm gates, a beautiful walk to the crest of mighty Noanet Peak (387 feet - about a tenth of Greylock!) and strange black feathers with white circles on them on the trail. There was an odd screaming at one point, and I finally realized I had stumbled upon helmeted guinea fowl, which completely explained the feathers.

Back to work.

183. Norwood: Shattuck Woods and Highland Cemetery

I'd really have to have a low opinion of you to think I could honestly tell you I walked for a full half hour in Shattuck Woods. But I think more of you than that.

I walked it, for certain, but it lasted a few mere minutes. I knew I had to extend my stay in Norwood, and so took to the neighboring cemetery.

And what a place it is! There's a burial chapel with stained glass, gargoyles and a plaque that mentions that it was dedicated in MDCCCCIIII, which was...a wicked long time ago. There's a beautiful memorial - if you, like I, can find beauty in ancient artillery - to the men of Company I, 35th Massachusetts Volunteer Infantry. As with many towns in Massachusetts, the post-Civil War years were supremely important to the history of Norwood, or as it was known until 1872, South Dedham.

Work crews were spread throughout the cemetery, cutting grass in the bright, blazing sunshine. I kept them at a distance, in my ongoing quest for noise mitigation, and enjoyed the shadier trees whenever I could. All in all, the cemetery was impressive, from its war memorials to its civil servants' memorials to its intriguing names, like Olmsted. It may not have been *the* Olmsted, but fame by association can be a cool thing.

July 13

184. Blackstone: Blackstone Gorge

Living on the South Shore for most of my life, I was shielded from the harsher realities of life. Let's face it, when you grow up in Hull you think hard work is defined by how many times you have to run the carousel during the day or how many cotton candy cones you have to spin. That's not to discount the work the lobstermen do, or the firefighters or the Coast Guard, but Hull was just never a great center of manufacturing. It never went through the Industrial Revolution mill phase that many other towns did.

Blackstone was all mills, even before its incorporation in 1845. The grandest evidence of its heyday stands today in the form of the Blackstone, Roaring or Rolling Dam, constructed in 1886 to harness the power of nature for the betterment of society, or at least the financial benefit of the Blackstone Manufacturing Company.

The path from the dam leads to a gorge. Following the trail, suddenly the walker finds himself 100 feet above the water, a neat trick. As I walked, it was strangely silent. On a beautiful day like this one, in a gorgeous natural setting like this, there should have been birdsong...

Finally, I found the gang, cardinals, titmice, chickadees, blue jays, red-eyed vireos, even a wood thrush. I also found the spot from which the recent Fourth of July fireworks had been launched, and probably the Fifth of July and the Sixth of July as well. Independence rocks on in the American soul, as does the desire to hear things go "boom."

185. Millville: Millville Lock

And when your town is named Millville, well, I guess there's no escaping Massachusetts' industrial past either.

My planned green-blob-on-the-map visit fell through as I could find no access to the parcel I had chosen. Instead, I followed signs to historic sites, figuring that if all else failed, I'd walk downtown Millville. That was when I tripped over the Millville Lock.

At least I found the entrance to the main trail that leads to the spur trail to the lock. But do you think that I could find the lock itself? *Grr...*

And it was a damn shame that I couldn't. It had statistics. I dig historical stats. Of the 49 locks that once defined the Blackstone River, this one was the best preserved, or so they tell me. Looking at the map now, I see that I apparently walked right past the spur trail off the old railroad bed on which I trod for nearly an hour.

Perspective time. There are a lot of bad things happening in the world right now, and me not being able to embrace a bit of history is not one of them.

Serenity now! I'd go back someday.

186. Mendon: Veterans Park

I find it hard to believe I visited Mendon, New York, before Mendon, Massachusetts, yet here we are. I did the same with Millville, New Jersey, and Millville, Massachusetts. Go figure.

Veterans Park is one of those multi-use green blobs, playground, sports fields and short walk through the woods all rolled into one. Thankfully no baseball was being played today, due to the excessive heat. I remember those days as a kid in my Corkin Lumber uniform for the Hull Little League. Sure, the Alice blue uniforms reflected most of the sunlight, but there was nothing like baking on a hard dirt surface for two hours while your pitcher struggled to throw strikes, and there were perfectly good episodes of *Hulk Hogan's Rock'n' Wrestling* and *Dungeons & Dragons* on TV, not to mention a perfectly cool *ocean* two blocks away.

The local killdeers had taken to the field in Mendon, despite the heat. It looked like mom was playing second base while the kids overloaded the left side of the infield. They could never defend against a bunt that way, but who was counting.

In the woods, I found (well, a baseball, which I high-tossed back to the field) the answer to a question that had always bothered me. Beetles! I found several sassafras trees with pockmarked holes on their leaves, and found two Japanese beetles munching away. I remembered how my dad had a coffee can with a little bit of kerosene in it in the garage, into which he dropped them to kill them after picking them off plants in the garden. Talk about invasive species. They came in around 1912 in Riverton, New Jersey, and have since spread from Minnesota to Florida to Maine.

Persistent little buggers.

187. Hopedale: Hopedale Parklands

A kayak class was forming as I set foot on the trail, in the shadow of the giant factory for which the river had been dammed to form the pond that now shines as the centerpiece of the Hopedale Parklands.

Other than that, it was pretty quiet, just how I like it. I shared the start of the trail with a woman with a very small dog, knowing I'd most likely see her again on my way out. I walked along the water as closely as I could, which meant that at one point I diverted from the old macadam road that probably came with the dedication of the park more than a century earlier. I also found the stone dedicating the nature trails to Willard W. Taft, "For his many years of dedication in preserving this special landscape for the enjoyment of all." An appropriate quote from Henry David Thoreau followed: "If the fairest features of the landscape are to be named after men, let them be the noblest and worthiest men alone." Sadly, he probably meant men, specifically. When asked about his friend and fellow writer Margaret Fuller, he once replied that she was an amazing woman, she almost had the intellect of a man.

I stopped on the macadam on the way back when the tiniest of critters, even smaller than my co-walker's dog, caught my eye. A miniscule wood frog hopped once, then posed for my camera, whether it knew it or not.

Gotcha, froggy!

188. Milford: Upper Charles Trail

Sometimes it's nice to just stare straight ahead at a wide open trail and hoof it.

And I did just that until I came across an opening to a small section of woods...sigh. I just couldn't help myself. The Centennial Park diversion from the trail was certainly interesting, with lots of wildlife and infrastructure to draw water from the river for town purposes. A dozen chimney swifts loomed overhead, most of them youngsters, chittering away behind mom and dad in search of food.

Back on the main trail, I passed more roller bladers than I had seen in years. I, once, was a member of that fraternity. But my hometown, Hull, was so sandy, that it was a cost-intensive proposition. Sand and ball bearings aren't supposed to mix, but they do.

As I neared my turn back into the parking lot, I noticed a bald man with a saggy, shirtless body pumping the pedals on an old bike that looked like all it was missing was a handlebar basket, and I thought to myself, "Oops, should get out of the way so the old-timer can come through." But when he turned the corner, he stood up on those pedals and blasted past me with a brisk "Good morning!" I recognized the tats on his forearms and knew: ex-military. That discipline never goes away.

189. Upton: Upton State Forest

I've been boxed.

I love boxer puppies. Young dogs, in general, are full of so much spunk that it's hard for me to dislike any of them, but I'm definitely not into the little nervous yippy types. An old friend had two boxers, and I had a fantastic time walking and taking care of them from time to time.

But they come with a punch. Boxer pups have a tendency to stand on their hind legs and jab a paw directly into your midsection (if you're lucky), and if you're not braced for it, man, do you feel it. One such creature happily and slobberingly charged me on the CCC road at Upton State Forest, and although I knew it was coming I stood there and took the jabbing. OOF! Ah, that brings back memories...

Apart from the obvious and ubiquitous Civilian Conservation Corps history, I found stonewalls and cellar holes. The more that I do, all across Massachusetts, the more I want to travel back in time to see the homes that once stood in these woods. Maybe it's the constant chomp of the research bug, but I always yearn to know more every time I see stones piled up in unnatural ways.

Come on science, get with the program and get the time machine done! After all, it's been more than a century since H.G. Wells came up with it. On second thought, I think I could become obsessed with it, and might never spend much time in the present. My wife would constantly be telling people, "Sorry, he's not here - he's in 9th century England watching Alfred the Great fight off the Danish invasions. But I'm sure he'll be back before he leaves for the Renaissance tomorrow afternoon."

190. Hopkinton: Waseeka Wildlife Sanctuary

The drive into the parking lot, between two about-one-car-width-apart trees reminded me of walking the Polar Caves in New Hampshire as a kid, squeezing through sets of rocks that never intended for human intervention.

From there, I hit the buggy trail, and by that I don't mean horse-and, but swat-and-run-as-fast-as-you-can. I took the Pitch Pine Trail for starters, which was probably a mistake, but eventually popped out onto a body of freshwater to a familiar sound: ospreys.

I've become quite used to the sounds of ospreys defending their territories over the past few years, and though I was several hundred feet from their nest, they wanted me to know I was too close for their comfort.

But look at that! The nest was not on a manmade platform. For the first time ever, I was looking directly at an osprey nest built on a dead tree, as nature intended. To me, this symbolized a triumphant moment in the life of the osprey in Massachusetts. Nearly extirpated during the 1960s and '70s, here was a pair that had foregone human help, had not even chosen a cell tower, but instead selected what their great-great-great-grandparents had chosen ages ago, a prime real estate spot in a completely natural setting.

For one brief moment, I was universally proud of the Bay State.

191. Ashland: Ashland State Park

The sign up front said it all. The state couldn't afford to staff the park. Pride? gone.

A group - two moms and a bevy of kids - walked ahead of me in bathing suits, so I knew the pond I saw on the map wouldn't have much wildlife on it, which was just fine. I was certainly learning the distinction between "state park" and "state forest" in Massachusetts as I walk it from end to end.

The main road into the park, which was cut off from the start, leads to two completely unused parking lots, a damn shame considering the temperature and the relief the pond could have provided. Perhaps the state should consider how much less electricity is consumed when options like this one are utilized rather than air conditioning, and figure that into the budget. But I'm not going to bang my head against that wall any more than I just have.

At the lake there was light activity, a man walking two yellow labs, a father teaching his son to cast his fishing line, and a handful of swimmers, soon joined by my fellow walkers. I found a shady area overlooking the pond, and took advantage of it. Four hours of walking had scorched me, physically, but invigorated me spiritually. Time for a break. I was off to downeast Maine for the next four days. Hmm, *Half an Hour a Day Across the*

Pine Tree State: 433 Towns in 365 Days...better start at the northern border. Don't want to be up there when the snow flies. No suh, don't want that. That would be a numb move.

July 20

192. Natick: Hunnewell Town Forest

So anyway, back to the story. When I walked Dover-Sherborn and then double-dipped on Dover, I mistakenly skipped Natick, which I thought I had walked. So here we are at the Hunnewell Forest. Got it?

At first, I thought, it was more wetland than forest, but then the magnificence of the tall pines struck me. I was also presented with a choice: tower, memorial or woodland loop? OK, I'd had more than my fair share of water towers during this project, so that was out. Nature or history?

So I set out for the memorial. I stepped past even more wetlands, marveling at the nest boxes on the water, which ran from brand new to heavily-used. At one point I paused to pay homage to an unborn robin, finding a striking blue egg on the ground, in the heart of the trail. A wood duck blasted out of the reeds with its wistful cry. Who said nature and history don't mix?

I found the memorial and snapped a pic, to join the hundreds I've taken of other similar stones in the past. Thank heavens for digital storage. I do have to admit, though, that Hunnewell certainly sounded like my kind of guy, a man who strove to enrich his hometown with "the beauty of trees and the spaciousness of parks."

See? Moe Howard of the Three Stooges was right. The big solution to life? "Spread out!"

193, 194. Framingham and Marlborough: Raymond J. Callahan State Park

I smelled the wild raspberries before I saw them, and they brought me back to my grandfather's garden in Hingham thirty-five years ago. It's amazing what the olfactory senses can do.

The trail surprised me as it opened onto a wide open field, sloped down the side of a hill. I found a bench at the top, but bypassed it, as I was intrigued by what was in store. I took a trail to the right, and climbed a hill in Framingham. I descended and swooped down to a pond in Marlborough, all the while listening to two women ahead of me chattering incessantly. We never actually saw each other, and I doubt they even knew I was there. I hope the one who was walking on the left gets that toe looked at.

I never found the powerline referenced in a note on the fence when I came in. The sign was apologizing for the unsightly condition of the cut, apparently bushwhacked back in August 2010, and promised that the plants there would regenerate. No need to apologize, if you ask me. Cutting the powerlines back provides habitat diversity and therefore wildlife diversity.

Circling the pond I found the human history I just knew had to be there, from barbed wire to stonewalls to a free standing chimney. Painted turtles slid off logs at my approach.

Of course, none of that mattered in the face of milkweed beetle sex. Just can't get enough of that. Might have been the sighting of the year.

195. Hudson: Danforth Falls

Well, if you want proof of my visit to Danforth Falls, check the police log.

I walked the trails in quietude, not even the Danforth Creek providing enough of a rush to make a noise, until I smelled smoke. It was pretty overpowering, making me wonder if there had been a recent forest fire. I reached the falls, which were not moving, and the source of the smoke, a grill.

Oh, big no-no.

I decided that when I got back to the car I would call the local fire department and tell them that it looked under control, but that there was a fire in the woods, even if it was in a backyard barbecue set-up. But then, the oddest sight I've ever seen in the woods happened upon me: a policeman in full uniform walking the trail. Seconds later, a fireman followed, also in uniform. So incongruous.

I reached the parking lot and was glad to see that despite the presence of one fire truck and two cop cars, I was not blocked in. No idea how bad the busting was, but somebody did get busted that morning.

196. Clinton: Rauscher Farm

Big maps, easy-to-reach and read handouts, accessible parking - now this was my kind of open space.

The walk was dominated by a wide-spreading pond and thankfully by two species of flycatchers, although I wish they'd developed more of a taste for mosquitoes. At this point in the year they almost had all of my blood. I was trying to save the last few drops so I could play with my son from time to time, but mosquitoes apparently have no such paternal instincts. "MUST DRAIN HUMANS..."

I found a beaver-chewed tree and thought that judging by the age of the damage, there had to have been beavers here within the past decade. Then I turned the corner and was met with a massive beaver lodge, the biggest one I'd ever seen in person. I mean, that thing could be rented out by a family of five unworried about getting a little wet on their summer vaca. I'm sure this one was about average, but it struck me as larger than normal.

Stepping back, I realized that there were in fact dozens of recently chewed trees, and that the beavers had been active not that long ago. Who knows what goes through their minds? I've heard stories of how someone can destroy their dams in one day, then come back the next day and see them already rebuilt. The Massachusetts Institute of Technology chose beavers as their mascot a century ago, for their industriousness in engineering; they couldn't have made a better selection.

197. Boylston: Wachusett Reservoir

I respect "No Trespassing" signs, and as such was ready to go elsewhere, until I found a publicly accessible section of the Wachusett Reservoir. It's a biggee, more than 4,000 acres of fresh water, all dammed up over a twelve-year period at the beginning of the twentieth century (remember that?). Some of the water seen at the reservoir will someday soon be in the stomachs of people in Boston. Weird thought.

A few small islands escaped the damming of the Nashua River, and the trees still stand thereon, although it seemed to me that the water level was quite low comparative to recent weeks. Still, it was a spectacular 'scape across which to gaze.

Wildlife here was nearly nonexistent, a chickadee here, a towhee there. It should have been the kind of place where wildlife thrives, as the sign at the entrance to the trail showed that there were a couple dozen things you can't do when you enter the park. Of course, when read properly, the sign says that the following things are prohibited: not swimming, not walking your dog, not horseback riding...

I'm not sure, but I think I was in violation of a whole mess of rules.

198. Shrewsbury: Dean Park

Decisions, decisions. Which park to choose? The first one looked nice, but the second one had the General Artemus Ward House directly across the street from it.

So call me a history slut.

The temperature had climbed well into the 90s by the time I reached Shrewsbury, and I was beginning to really feel it after three hours of walking. But the show had to go on. First things first, I photographed the house. Ward was one of those Revolutionary War heroes who survives more on a local level, partially on a regional, than national. Think of him like Henry "The Ox" Knox, though one wonders if even he would have retained that nickname with the surname Patterson or Tannenbaum. History might never remember a Henry "The Ox" McGuillicuddy.

I swept past the pond and took note of a sign that said that the fountains installed therein had been the gift of residents in honor of a family member. I couldn't see any fountains and moved on. Then they erupted, shooting water into the air, a feature unique to my travels during this project. I rushed back to the water's edge to photograph them, not knowing when they might quit. Well done, Shrewsbury. Bravo.

I commiserated with a camp counselor shutting down her position for the day, telling her to stay cool. It was becoming a day unfit for man or beast, or, like me, both.

199. Holliston: Brentwood Conservation Lands

It took a while to find it, but once I stepped into the Brentwood property, I was entranced.

Sand. Why was there sand underfoot this far inland? I think I need a geology lesson, as being from the water's edge, I tend to associate sand solely with the beaches, yet here it was. I guess a refresher couldn't hurt.

The sandy section quickly gave way to a swamp that looked like it belonged in Louisiana. I felt that at any moment an ivory-billed woodpecker would soar through the trees, but that, as we know, is now impossible. Or is it? Yes, it is.

Or is it?

I spent a good solid two minutes attempting to photograph a blue dragonfly, but never got it in focus. Maybe that was the problem, as comedian Mitch Hedberg quipped about Bigfoot. Maybe it was just blurry. "There is a large, out-of-focus monster roaming the countryside," he said, "and that is extra scary to me."

Ehh, I rolled onto my final stop of the day, dragonfly-less.

200. Bellingham: Center Cemetery

BAM! 200. Or should I say "Ding"? *World of Warcraft* popularized the ding as the audio symbol of level advancement in their massive multiplayer online world. But "bam" feels much more forceful when reaching a milestone in the real world.

I hadn't, of course. Two hundred was just a nice round number and not significant in any way to 351. It falls just short of meaning that I'd walked in four out of every seven towns in Massachusetts, and that I still had three out of those seven to go. And they keep getting farther and farther away.

With no other open space to speak of, this tiny cemetery was it for Bellingham. I had to walk slowly to make it a full half hour.

There are a lot of Bates buried in Bellingham, a name I associate strongly with the South Shore, like the famous War of 1812 keeper of Scituate Light, but they obviously moved west at some point, as there are just Bates everywhere.

Two Greek families had recently gone with the new fad, color photographs inserted into their stones. Cemeteries are getting a whole lot spookier now that the dead can gaze back at us in color, instead of in the bas-relief way they used to on occasional memorials. What picture would you choose? College graduation? Driver's license? Mug shot? Which one will I choose?

Ugh, I don't want to think about it. Besides, BAM! My day was done. BAM!

July 23

201. Topsfield: Ipswich River Wildlife Sanctuary

Rain? Are you kidding me? The forecast had called for hot and dry, yet there I was, standing near the Rockery in heavy rain. Eh, why fight it?

I ran into a photographer who had arrived a few minutes before me and set up shop on the one dry spot on the boardwalk. Two great blue herons flew by as we spoke, while a third stood silently in the marsh. I promised to do my best not to spook it as I walked past, and my promise held.

A green frog croaked at 8:17. I add it here only for dramatic effect.

I walked through the Rockery itself, thinking back on my research for my *Images of America: Mass Audubon* book from years ago. Thomas Proctor, who owned the land, had paid a lot of Italians a lot of money over a lot of years to create this marvel, and today it's entirely enshrouded by nature, probably not his original vision for it, but who can tell with eccentric early twentieth century millionaires?

Another green frog, 8:27. The drama grew.

Thunder boomed, somewhat softly, as I retreated up the Innermost Trail, with the deer flies rhythmically tapping my head like a bongo. By the time I reached the parking lot the sky had turned steel gray and was shaking its first menacingly at me.

I shook mine back. Rain wasn't going to ruin my day.

202. Hamilton: Bradley Palmer State Park

With rain still coming down, and more thunder rocking the sky, I stuck to the main road of the state park, passing two women with the only dog I had met in 2011 that did not treat me like a milk bone.

The air had grown terribly thick, and I wondered how far the fumes would travel from the fuel truck rollover that had closed Route 1 for the weekend.

A big boom sent my heart fluttering a bit, and I considered retreating to the car, but I stuck it out. The rain, which was falling steadily but not heavily any more, had not penetrated certain places. The multiple-canopied trees along the roadway had dry spots under them, which seemed impossible. I found a couple of side trails, but refrained from taking them, unsure of how unstable the weather truly was.

On my return trip, two men stopped me and asked me if I had the key to the gate to the road on which I was walking. I must have looked official. I said no and accepted their frowns in the manner in which they were intended.

203. Essex: Athletic Fields

I could have walked the extensive marshes in the northern part of town, but I had two reasons for avoiding them. First, I prefer them with snowy owls in them. Second, in a particularly buggy week, when deer flies and mosquitoes had already done their damage, I, in no way, wanted to add greenheads into the mix.

Instead, it was the enchantment of the old town hall and library that brought me to a halt on Main Street. What a fantastic old building! Behind it were youth athletic fields which even had tarps over the pitcher's mound and home plate, keeping them somewhat dry for upcoming games. Behind the fields were a part of the marsh system that dominates the rest of Essex. I'll bet the kids who played ball here learned how to time the onset of greenhead season.

I stopped to photograph the Civil War memorial. The base was unique, but the statue part came out of a catalogue. And why not? While practically every town needed a monument - Essex sent "186 Loyal Sons" to fight in the war, for instance - not every town could afford to commission a statue. Some entrepreneur somewhere figured out how to mass market his Union soldier sculpture and made a fortune, though I'll be there's a warehouse still full of them somewhere out in Indiana.

But it's all in the sentiment, and Essex did the right thing by their Union men.

204. Manchester-By-the-Sea: Agassiz Rock

I guess I learned a lot about myself on this one. When presented with the choice of Big Agassiz versus Little Agassiz, I didn't even hesitate. I went big.

That meant descending from the hill on which I was walking and finding what looked like a huge slab of bedrock, although I wonder now if it was an erratic. I would hope so. I'd hate to think that one of the greatest naturalists in Massachusetts history would have lent his name to such a basic feature of the landscape. Does that make me a geo-snob? So be it.

I was much more impressed - after scaling the rest of the loop trail in the by then oppressive humidity - with Little Agassiz. One problem: I couldn't tell which one it was. There were two, side-by-each, as Rhode Islanders say, ginormous erratic boulders standing atop a hill.

I swear I have no idea where this uncomfortable and unnatural love of erratic boulders comes from, but I think I need to start keeping a checklist. That, or regular appointments with a therapist.

205. Wenham: Wenham Lake and Cemetery

You just can't go to Wenham and not take a look at the lake. It's sacrilege.

Unfortunately, it's cut off from access, so it has to be seen from afar. I started in the cemetery and moved my way across.

But the cemetery was a study unto itself, a collection of Perkinses, Conants, Peabodys, Dodges, all the names that make the North Shore famous. Wenham has done well in memorializing its fallen soldiers, firemen and policemen, and even has a stone dedicated to the town founders and "Sons of the Revolution Now Buried in Unmarked Graves."

Future historians will have no way of capturing this following tale in its entirety, but it's as much a moment as any political election or natural disaster. There, at the back of the cemetery, was the grave of a U.S. Marine at rest. He was obviously a dad, and I say that without really knowing, but the grave decorations told me all I needed to know.

In 2004, Boston Red Sox fans who watched their team win the World Series for the first time in 86 years moved en masse to local cemeteries, bringing word of the championship to their lost fathers, uncles and grandfathers, and even mothers, aunts and grandmothers. Baseball is in the New England blood. Here, though, in 2011, a whole different fan base had reason to celebrate. The Boston Bruins won the Stanley Cup! Bruins fans, perhaps due to the nature of the sport, are even more diehard than Red Sox fans. There, in a banner and even a puck, was a son telling a dad (again, assumptions) that their common dream had come true.

The emotion was palpable. What else would you travel to a grave to tell a lost family member? A birth, a death? The Bruins winning the Cup ranks right up there with life's most important moments.

Lake? What lake?

July 27

206. Shirley: Mulpus Brook Wildlife Management Area

I got to Shirley early, and not just for the rhyming, although I will admit that was a very big part of it. I had a wonderful day planned.

Of course, nature had its own plans, complete with heat and humidity. Yet other factors would quickly make Mulpus Brook a forgotten adventure for me. It was overgrown, which to me was just fine. As a wildlife management area and not a state park, it was designed for heavy usage by wildlife and little impact by humans. Go to it, friends!

But with the good side of nature comes the bad. I was guarding against ticks, so wasn't worried about that, but there, in the early dawn, as the sun slipped sideways through the trees, the mosquitoes began their work. I *Offed* up.

But it did not matter. My hands and lower legs were exposed, but the former were slimed in bug spray and the latter were so toughened by a summer of thorns, barbs and bites that I barely felt anything down there at all anymore. No, they weren't the problem. The mosquitoes were bypassing open skin and biting me directly through my shirt.

29 minutes, 58 second...29 minutes, 59 seconds...30 minutes. Bye, Shirley! I know it's not your fault.

207. Lunenberg: Cowdrey Nature Center

So I strolled out of the woods of Shirley into the woods of Lunenberg. I still stand behind my early 2011 decision. Had I done things in reverse, and walked the woods in the winter, I would have been spending my summer trying to walk the seashore towns, among the thousands of sun worshippers at the beaches...I shudder at the thought. Give me a quiet forest path any day, even in the height of summer.

With every stop in Lunenberg, I was vindicated. A gravelly brook meandered under a wooden bridge here at Cowdrey, where I was, according to the parking lot, anyway, alone. My only friends were the hermit and wood thrushes, the scarlet tanagers and a belted kingfisher working the brook.

I stopped on the Mayflower Trail while heading for Tall Timber, names which, of course, meant nothing and everything to me. I noted big chunks of overturned mushrooms in the trail, but something more. Newts! Red-spotted newts, to be specific, two of them, were munching on the mushrooms, standing over them as if protecting them like a 3-year-old with his favorite Thomas the Tank Engine toy screaming "Mine!" after he'd banged it into a table leg too many times and was told to stop or he'd lose his toy privileges. Not that I'd gone through that recently.

Well, I, for one, was not going to be the one to take the mushrooms from the newts. *Mangia, mi goombahs.*

208. Fitchburg: Flat Rock Wildlife Sanctuary

Flat Rock Wildlife Sanctuary, a Mass Audubon property, had long been on my list. It's now off the list, and on another one: places I want to visit again.

Up the trail I went. Apparently I never read the brochure. Up, up, up...it was fantastic. I've got low-level mountain climber fever. I see a hill, I want to climb it. Having visited the Colorado Rockies in 2011 and planning on visiting Glacier National Park in August, I realized I have a limit. I hit 12,000 feet in Colorado, but watched people get out of their cars with snowboards and start hiking up to 13,000. The urge to tag along was there, but faint. Maybe it was altitude sickness.

I needn't have worried about that at Flat Rock. I soon reached the final stretch to the top, the Flat Rock Road. So cool! It's not an actual road, but a long stretch of exposed bedrock in a generally straight line that looks like a road. It leads to a spot atop the hill called "the Bald." And you can thank the sheep for all of this, I believe. Mid-19th century herders kept their sheep in places like this one until they ate the plants down to the soil that blew and washed away, leaving these hills bald; they then moved to greener pastures in Ohio and environs.

But at the Bald I found what I figured had to be a pestle, a carved round depression in the rock that I imagined was used for grinding corn or other grains long, long ago. Now I'm no fancy-pants archaeologist or even some high-fallutin' big-city anthropologist, but I do have one hell of an imagination.

Heck, I thought I even smelled bread baking...

133

209. Ashburnham: Mid-State Trail

This was a toughee, or a tuffy, depending on your particular spelling. I found the Mid-State Trail, but was unable to crack much of it. The pathway wound into the woods next to a mobile trailer office for a failed development project. The problem was that the trail had been neglected for far, far too long to be very passable. There was a dumpster and a big sign that said, in good old-fashioned stenciling (a lost art, if you ask me), **"HIKERS WELCOME PLEASE STAY ON TRAIL**." What trail?

I puttered around for a half an hour with the goldfinches, chipping sparrows and black-capped chickadees.

But something felt terribly familiar about Ashburnham. I started to remember a birding trip with a friend on which we stopped into a sub shop, grabbed sandwiches and then drove down the street to eat in an old cemetery. I drove back to the center of town; if I remembered correctly, there was a statue of...yes, there it was! Johnny Appleseed!

This time, I actually got out of the car long enough to read the sign about...*The Schoolboy of 1850*? Argh, foiled again!

210. Gardner: Lake Wampanoag Wildlife Sanctuary

Well, if the world was all painted turtles and colorful butterflies, Lake Wampanoag Wildlife Sanctuary would be the poster child for the earth. That, of course, makes no sense, but, warped by thousands of advertisements in your life like I have been, I'm sure you understand my meaning.

The fields were in their splendor, dragonflies abuzz. I walked a short loop past a small pond - Lake Wampanoag is not on the property, but nearby - and a ruby meadowhawk landed on my arm. I watched as a blue dragonfly, possibly known as the blue dasher, hopped from plant to plant. I'd been trying to photograph one for days! I froze and waited, and the moment came. Got it!

Dozens of butterflies rose from the trail just ahead of me as I walked. I strolled in a flutter of wings under the smooth blue sky. It was almost too idyllic, too good to be true, but Mother Nature doesn't deal in falseness. Except when it comes to camouflage. Or a caterpillar that has spots on its tail that look like eyes to trick a predator. Or a mockingbird that can make you think you're hearing another species when it sings.

OK, Mother Nature is full of it. But how fun would life be if everything was exactly what you thought it was?

211. Winchendon: Fern Glen Conservation Area

I took the turn into the drive like the website told me to. Despite the fact that it didn't look like a road, I kept going, like the website told me to. And when I got to the end, I found the open area in which to park, like the website told me I would. From there, it was into the woods, where, among other things, I found loppers and gloves, signs of recent trail work.

I drove away. Near the end of the drive I ran into two people on foot, one of whom looked slightly annoyed by my vehicular appearance. "I did what the website told me to," I said. He admitted that he had not been on the site, and trusted me, though he was surprised to see me coming out this way by car. He said he worked for the town and was helping with the preservation of this precious open space.

His friend, in the meantime, had retreated to move her car so I could get out. "Wendy!" he called when she reappeared, "This is John, he's working on the bird survey, too."

"Wait...John Galluzzo?" she asked as she saw me.

"Yes," I said. She obviously knew my name from the state Breeding Bird Atlas 2 project.

"This is John Galluzzo!" she said with a flourish, turning to her friend. "He's famous!"

Oh, oh my God, I'm going to faint, I thought, as all the blood in my body rushed straight to my ego. If I wasn't already sitting down, I would have needed to sit down.

212. Templeton: Templeton State Forest

In the end, I never got in. I circled the forest by car, got out and walked along its edges for more than my slotted half hour trying to find an opening, but I never did.

I retreated to statuary.

Near a town center I found the World War I memorial, and what a sight it was. A doughboy - and let's stop right there. Where did that term come from? We know that World War I soldiers bore that mantle, but why? In fact, rumors say it goes back to the Mexican War of 1848 during which many soldiers found themselves covered in the dust of Northern Mexico, like they were covered in dough. Yet we don't refer to Civil War soldiers as doughboys...hmm, a mystery.

Anyway, this doughboy was being as symbolic as possible. He was in the act of laying down his gun, while leaning over the makeshift grave of what I interpreted as a fallen brother in arms. In his free hand, a sheath of wheat. Take that as you may - peace, the harvest, the fall, time to rest.

Well done, Templeton.

213. Hubbardston: Hubbardston State Forest

I paid for my dalliances at Flat Rock with this visit to Hubbardston. While I climbed the trail to the Bald, I always knew that in the end, I must come down, like the "Spinning Wheel" that Blood, Sweat and Tears sung about. In Hubbardston, things were exactly the opposite. It was the Flat Rock Bizarro World.

Down, down, down I went...

The breeze certainly helped as the mid-day heat threatened to roast me. It's not easy working both the sun and mosquito protections at the same time. With coatings of both on concomitantly I felt like my skin couldn't breathe, that I was sealed in a light film of my own devising. But it was better than the alternative, sunburned mosquito bites.

Great spangled fritillary! A new butterfly species for 2011 drifted on past, and made me take notice of something below, a partially consumed russula mushroom. I usually start looking for mushrooms in September, after the heat is gone and the rains have given them a chance to sprout, but it seems those days are gone, that they start early every year now.

Up, up, up I trudged...

214. Westminster: Leominster State Forest

Do deer flies call ahead?

I'm serious about this. I left Hubbardston with a wave - not *to* a friend or a stranger, but *at* a deer fly that was trying its damnedest to get into my car with me. As I walked in the Lemo State Forest, it took mere seconds before the first deer flies came at me.

And they don't stop at just coming *at* you. They hit you. They ping off your head like someone's throwing large pebbles at your skull. My defense, when bug spray has stopped working? Well, first, I go with the right-hand whatever-I-have-in-my-pocket swing. In most cases, that's a bird list, a small, white piece of card stock. I can hear the stupid things smacking into the card, but they keep coming back for more. Next, two arms, in throwing motions, waving them away from my ears, forward.

Having pitched as a baseball player through high school, my right arm knows the motion well. My left, not so much. Either way, if things kept going at this pace, I'd definitely need double rotator cuff surgery by the beginning of the next spring training.

I got back to the car noticing two things: the laurel blooms had fallen away, and I hadn't noticed a single bird call, the first town in 214 for which I would not be making a visit to the Cornell Lab of Ornithology's ebird website.

Wait, was that a chickadee...?

YES!

215. Princeton: Wachuset Meadow Wildlife Sanctuary

My memories at Wachuset Meadow go back beyond my earliest days. Don't get me wrong, I only started visiting here in 2004. But the connection I feel to this land is remarkable and stretches back through time.

It was one of my earliest targeted Mass Audubon sanctuaries, when I was writing my book on their history. I met the director, shared a UMASS alumni bonding moment, climbed Little Wachuset Mountain, and more. In the years since then I'd walked the sanctuary in search of butterflies, tracked fishers and porcupines, worked on winter tree identification in the dead of winter and sat in the barn just inches from the door as torrential rain poured outside.

But it's the history that gets me, the Goodnows, the carriage line that ran past the front door, the Crocker maple, the award-winning cattle. It's all here, if you care to close your eyes and see it.

It didn't matter what trail I walked on this day, it would mean something special to me. And it always will, even long after I'm gone.

216. Sterling: WMA

Nameless, faceless. That's how this place will always be to me. I was heading for another map-bound green blob when I struck dirt parking lot. Sometimes they turn out simply to be turn-offs, but this one was different. It had a kiosk.

Still, that kiosk gave up no secrets, like a name. I walked down a slight hill and hit a macadamized road. Ah, human history, in the woods again. All I knew was I was walking in a state wildlife management area.

It went straight, and for a very long, long time. It was obviously an old passageway for vehicles, but to what? And from what? I would never find out, as no matter how far I walked, it continued. Without even a clue as to what was nearby, without a foundation to be found, without a name to which I could attach a legend, I retreated.

On the way out, I found lilies. For whom were they planted, I wondered? Someone long gone, no doubt.

217. Leominster: Lincoln Woods Wildlife Sanctuary

My fourth Mass Audubon wildlife sanctuary of the day brought me into a nearly urban setting, in Leominster. I parked the car, learned a little bit about the woman who donated the land for nature study for the kids of the community, and moved into the woods to work on some of my own questions.

Then, I threw them all out of the window, despite the fact I was standing outside.

There had been a fire. A couple of trees rested in their death poses on the ground, blackened by the experience. Arson? Maybe. Lightning? Much more likely. Me, detective? Ha!

The burned area proved to be more extensive than I first thought, as I wound slowly down the trail. Patches of earth were scorched, but as far as I could deduce, they were in connection with the fallen trees, as if the trees were hit, fell to the ground burning, and set the ground around them ablaze. Yet it was remarkably controlled. Perhaps the fire department responded quickly? Perhaps the rain was enough to put it out?

I got in close enough to take a photo of the burned bark of one of the trees and nothing else. It was superficial. Between the cracks I could see the brown of life. The tree was prematurely dead, like a man in a coffin before he was completely lifeless. It stared out at me as if asking for help. I felt useless.

218. Lancaster: Blood Town Forest

And then there was one...for this day, anyway.

As I entered the Blood Town Forest I expected a lot of things. The trash in the parking lot told me it was a party spot. OK, blind eye to that; see through it to the natural beauty of the forest, I said in my usual mantra.

I expected the eastern wood-pewees. They'd been singing all over the state for the past three months. And so it was in Lancaster. I expected American goldfinches. Ditto.

But there were things I wasn't expecting, pleasant surprises. There was the great blue heron that I spooked from its hiding spot into a tree. It led me away, flying a few more feet ahead, stopping, turning back to see me, repeating the process numerous times. It led me back to the parking area. Perhaps it knew something.

I met a small, older woman there, with her hair pulled back in a bun. She was loading her big van with trash. The garbage, she had explained with a wide smile on her face, had come from the woods. People had left it there, but she felt that her fellow townsfolk shouldn't have to see it, so she collected it and disposed of it. She did this every few days as necessary.

Humanity got a big boost in my eyes on this day. And I think I was in love.

August

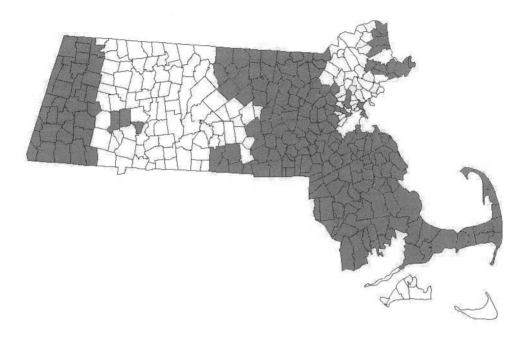

351

I guess, in a way, I was still trying to justify the project when I took off for Glacier National Park in Montana in early August. I started to think about the number and its significance, if it even had any.

And, of course, being an American male, I thought in terms of sports. Two men, Jeff Kent and Dick Allen, hit exactly 351 home runs in their careers, good for about 85th place all-time. Nobody ever hit 351 triples (Sam Crawford's 309 being the record), but Sam Rice did steal 351 bases, which placed him at 109th all-time in 2011. Charlie Buffinton - that complete rarity, a professional baseball player of whom I'd never heard - pitched 351 complete games. It quickly became obvious that baseball and the number 351 had little in common. The same could be said for professional football. Eric Metcalf returned 351 punts during his career, second all-time. Roy Gerela, a kicker with the Houston Oilers, Pittsburgh Steelers and San Diego Charger in the 1970s, kicked 351 extra points. Boring!

So why was I walking in 351 towns? Was it to match the 351 feet in height of the Jefferson Davis Monument in Kentucky (about 70 times taller than the man himself) or the 351 foot tall Pecos River Bridge or the 351 foot tall Albuquerque Skyscraper? Mmm, probably not. Plenty of things are or were 351 feet long - *USS Oregon*, several dams, piers and bridges, the cars on Stockholm's SL-X60 commuter train. There are 351 people named Lewis Wilson in the White Pages in the United States, and 351 Wallace Browns.

The year 351 started on a Tuesday.

What about math? 351 is a triangular number, meaning that if you started with one ball at the top, two in the second row, and kept adding one on down to the last level, you could form a perfect equilateral triangle. 351 is also the sum of five consecutive prime numbers, 61, 67, 71, 73, and 79.

Oddly enough, the 351 area code since 2001 has been assigned to Massachusetts. How random is that? Still, that wasn't why I was walking 351 towns.

I was walking 351 towns because that's how many there were in my home state in 2011. I would have walked 400 if that was the number, but I doubt I would have gone much higher than that.

To me, 351 was the perfect number, holding uniqueness, a number that meant more to Massachusetts residents than most others around the world.

But what did I know about 351 at that point? I was only at 218.

August 10

219. Salem: Salem Willows

Wow, it'd been so long since I really thought about weeping willow trees. I see them every year in their splendor on the Finger Lakes in New York, but seem to overlook them here at home in Massachusetts. Well, not on this day.

There was my youth, standing right in front of me. We had a weeping willow, right in my backyard in Hull. It was everything: shade, a place to build forts, hang *piñatas*, and most importantly, it was second base. The roots were, anyway. And any ball hit into the tree was in play. We - Charlie, Danny, Jimmy and I, the longstanding executive committee members of the Backyard Baseball League (with occasional appearances by J.P., Mark and others) - became experts at tracking tennis balls smacked into the upper branches, and catching them before they hit the ground. Freddie Lynn (you're still my hero!), eat your heart out.

But Hurricane Gloria took that all away in 1985, when I was just fourteen, and at the height of what should have been my wiffle-ball-bat-and-tennis-ball stardom. I slowly forgot about weeping willows.

But this place today, it brought it all back. I remember a rumor from my youth, that a ship carrying the seeds of the weeping willow trees wrecked off Boston, and cast the seeds ashore, where they planted themselves and gave us places like Salem Willows. Of course, I later heard the same legend about *rosa rugosa*. Whether it was true or not, it was a beautiful story. *Of the spread of invasive species!*

220. Beverly: Sally Milligan Park

Hmm, I thought to myself, it seemed all just a little too easy. And perhaps it was.

The water spots at Sally Milligan just seemed to me to be too...formalized, like perhaps someone had dug them purposely as wayside attractions. Not that there's anything wrong with that - some of my best friends are way too formalized.

This place was a home to rocks and dells, to trees and mud, apparently to some kids that liked to make false houses in the woods. Bring it on! Let's not lose touch with our inner cavemen. Embrace the earth, sometimes literally if you have to, to get the point.

Sally never walked the trails in the park named for her, but that's not unusual. There are plenty of places in Massachusetts named for people who never saw them. It's the spirit that counts. Sally walked the woods of the Berkshires as a kid, and went west to the Ohio Valley from there. She knew what it was all about, and hopefully her spirit is sharing that knowledge today with the kids of Beverly.

221. Danvers: Proctor Farm

I started to worry a bit on my way to the main field of Proctor Farm. The pathway to it is a nightmare of phragmites, but saved by the presence of boardwalks, bridges and a neat little picnic area unexpectedly tucked into the woods.

It was the lack of color. After spending a week in Montana, I was used to the bright yellows of the glacier lilies, but then, the brief Montana spring was just beginning in late July. The colors of the woodland plants were just gone in Massachusetts. I had made a trade-off, a little Massachusetts for a little Montana.

But once in the field, it all came back to me; to find the color in Massachusetts in August, you have to go to the fields. There was the jewelweed, the Joe pye-weed, the milkweed. I felt better as I entered the woods on the far side of the field, squeezed through the trees to meet the witch hazel, the sassafras and the stonewalls once again. And the slug. We cannot forget the small yellow slug that stopped me at the bridge like a troll waiting for a bribe. I left a $50 bill and moved on.

And if you believe that...

222. Middleton: Aunt Betts Pond

Lush, lush, lush (the boys are mar-ching!). Wow, was the world green on this day.

Aunt Betts Pond was a tough nut to crack. From what I could see it used to be an open pond, but has closed in. At least to the naked eye looking at it sideways, which is the least optimal way to see a pond - it was like looking at a flat piece of paper at table level - it was hard to discern.

But that just meant that there was a lot going on there nature-wise, and you know my vote on that. Leave the dead trees be; the woodpeckers will love them. Let them fall when their time comes for the insects and mushrooms to eat. May the thickets grow fat with catbirds! May you always be surrounded by house wrens, and may the forest be with you.

I walked the access road along Aunt Betts Pond, my head turned to the right. I was passed by a man on a scooter with a teddy bear, or vice versa, I'm not sure. I found the remains of old walls - wouldn't an archaeological map of post-1620 structures in Massachusetts be just so cool? - and let my mind play in the playground of history.

223, 224. Andover and North Andover: Harold Parker State Forest

I still don't think I truly know what all the sounds are that comes from the trees in Massachusetts in summer. There's a single daytime sound that you can't miss that I guess I've just taken for granted. It's a long, metallic buzz that has a slightly musical quality to it. It rings out loud and proud.

I was always told that it was a beetle. More specifically, I was told that it was a beetle burning in the heat. Like so much else about the natural world in my youth, I socked that info away into the deep, dark recesses of my mind and just let it fester, right next to the cobwebs and the pictures of girls in bikinis that take up most of my brain matter.

Yet here it was again in Andover and North Andover, a full hour of it playing over the sound of a single eastern wood-pewee. My mind dropped the bikinis for a second (haha) and came out of its fog long enough to take note, and get frustrated. What? Me, not know something? Unpossible!

I would get to the bottom of this.

225. Boxford: Boxford State Forest

For many birders on the South Shore, the Boxford State Forest is known as the first stop on the "Century Run." That's a cute name for a "Big Day," which is a cute name for trying to score 100 bird species in a single day. I always found it funny that South Shore birders felt they had to go to the North Shore to see that much variety, but hey, what the heck did I know.

So they stop, listening for owls in the Boxford State Forest. My first experience here was to hear not an owl, but my first ever winter wren, which, if you haven't heard one, is a breathtaking experience. And not like the doctor at the beach house thought Elaine was breathtaking on *Seinfeld*, but in the literal sense. They sing for 5 to 10 seconds, and here in the east they sing approximately *16 notes per second*! You have to wonder how this tiny bird, weighing no more than 2/5 of an ounce, can hold on for so long. But that's in spring, when mates are on the loose. My walk on this day in Boxford featured the American goldfinches, black-capped chickadees and cedar waxwings that seemed to be everywhere in Massachusetts on these days. It also involved sunshine, a small pond, broken glass, "no swimming" signs and wondering where I could sign up for the next "Century Run."

August 16

226. Saugus: Breakheart Reservation

So it was August 16th. I was back from Montana, it had been raining for two days, and I was on antibiotics for a virus I somehow picked up over the past weekend. Must mean it wa time to go to Saugus, I thought.

I still haven't figured out how to predict my state parks experiences in Massachusetts. It seems that there have to be political pushes and pulls at work. Some parks are neglected, shut down, forgotten, perfectly delightful places where Massachusetts residents should have the right to walk, to hike, to swim, closed because of apparent budgetary issues. Then, I find places like Breakheart, uniformed staff up front and visible, open trails, frequently refreshed bulletin boards and clean facilities. Is it proximity to Boston, or is it simply proximity to large blocks of influential voters?

The constant hum of a television news truck faded into the distance as I walked away from the parking area and into the woods, and away from all thoughts of politics - thank god. I heard my favorite frying beetles again (cicadas singing, and not what my mother always told me they were; it took me until I was 40 to question her definition. Lesson: never trust anything your mother ever told you). The main trail, paved, wound between hills covered with loose, large rocks and under young trees that bent over the road in a reach for sunlight. Croaking green frogs called from what were obviously wet places beyond the walls of the trees.

I usually don't care for paved roads through the woods, but I have to admit, under the circumstances - the rain, the allergies, the virus - it was nice to get an easy start to what would be an eleven-town day.

227. Lynn: Great Woods Reservation

Another Great Woods? I thought the one down in Mansfield was the only one we had. And another Walden Pond? Ok, who came first, the chicken or Henry David Thoreau? I'm so confused.

Best way to beat that? Go for a walk! I headed up the trail at the Great Woods Reservation in Lynn, avoiding the ditches created in the gravel by the recent rains. It meant a lot of wandering the trails from side to side, but I eventually got where I wanted to go.

And that was never really a primary stated goal, having a destination. I had no idea where I was going. I was just walking until I saw a sign that said "tower." Hmm, I thought, I dig towers, as I watched a chipmunk scurry up a tree and disappear inside it.

I was not disappointed. From the top of the tower I could see the Boston skyline, Revere Beach, and a half dozen water towers above the trees to the west. I also picked out an old fire tower that was obviously no longer in use, as its ladders didn't reach anywhere near the ground. That's when my phone rang. I booked a date to give a lecture, then began the walk down the hill, which was not nearly as strenuous as the one up to the tower. An idea then struck me, my next book idea: *Half an Hour a Day on Foot: Just the High Points*. Oh, the possibilities...

228. Lynnfield: Kallenburg Quarry

As much as I enjoy a good statue or a revered piece of stone architecture, quarries make me sad. Believe it or not, I don't get heartbroken over a tree being cut down, at least not on the small scale. Yes, denude several acres, and you've lost a friend in me, but lose a tree to a storm, cut one down and replant two more, and it's all good. Trees have finite lives anyway, and can be replaced. But when we blast a ledge to create additional parking spaces at a restaurant, we're permanently altering nature. That rock isn't growing back.

The old quarry land in Lynnfield features a stand-alone fireplace, with no house around it, and then trails to a powerline that puts one almost on top of the world, at least as far as coastal Massachusetts goes. I found a rock upon which to sit atop the hill, and took in my surroundings. At my feet was a coast and geodetic survey marker. The powerlines, which looked like parallel ski lifts, reached down to a major, slow-moving highway, and for a brief moment, I felt sorry for every person in every one of those cars - and that is a remarkable achievement for a Massachusetts driver who has to share the roads with them all on a regular basis.

In the distance, I could see a bright blue pond, the green areas around it, and spreading as far as the eye could see, were patches of goldenrod. I could have sat and watched for hours.

Back in the woods, I spooked a snake, apparently out to get some sun after all the rain of the previous few days. I then noticed some odd graffiti on a flat wall of rock. Someone had drawn a perfect representation of an AT-AT, one of those huge four-legged walking robots from *The Empire Strikes Back*. Hmm, *Star Wars* graffiti, three decades after the movies came out.

There's a lot I'll never understand about Lynnfield. But I sure was glad to visit.

229. Ipswich: Willowdale State Forest

With Saugus, Lynn and Lynnfield out of the way, I shot to the northeast a bit to continue my quest. Ultimately, I had plans to reach Methuen. I had to. The library was expecting me. More on that later.

A few feet down the trail, I did it again, spooked another snake. A few feet beyond that, I found a dead field mouse, and wondered if they were somehow connected. I took my hat off my head and realized it weighed about a pound from sweat. The library wouldn't like that. I kept walking anyway.

There was no denying it was summer, sweat aside (I can generate that much sweat in mid-December. Just put a snow shovel in my hands and watch my smoke). No, there were other clues. Chipmunks were scooting around everywhere, and had quickly become the most dominant species of the day for me. Green frogs burped from the woods, and I spied a pond down to my left that was so thick with green scum that I had peripherally mistaken it for forest floor. A deer bounded away upon seeing me (not that that is a particularly summer phenomenon). The sweet pepperbush was in bloom everywhere, giving the forest a fragrance that would last for a few short days.

At one point I wandered around a large puddle, listening to the frogs squeak and splash upon my appearance into their glade, and found myself at the edge of an enormous swamp. To my right, a Canada warbler sang. A great blue heron flew off a branch and disappeared deeper into the swamp.

When I turned to leave, I spooked another garter snake! Geez! Sometimes, they're so big, their noise makes *you* jump. I was getting to that point.

147

230. Georgetown: Georgetown-Rowley State Forest

My frog-scaring ritual continued. As I walked into the Georgetown-Rowley forest I came across more puddles - in the middle of the trail, mind you, where *I'm* supposed to be, and not the frogs - and sent more and more of the little green monsters splashing into the muddy abysses.

Catching a patch of sunlight, I came across a spectacular little dragonfly, the ruby meadowhawk, or as my friend David calls it, the *Sympetrum rubicundulum*. No, he's not from ancient Rome. He just had the misfortune of getting to know dragonflies before anybody decided to give them easily memorable names in English. When we're out on the trails together, doing some odes work, I'll point one out. "David - common white-tail?" And he'll shout back, "How do I know? It's *Plathemis lydia*, if that helps."

So I did my act-like-a-tree-and-stand-wicked-still routine and began to stalk the dragonfly. I looked around before each step to be sure I wouldn't spook any more snakes and finally grabbed my shot. Yes! My first ruby meadowhawk photograph. I figured I could file it under "R" for both ruby and *rubicundulum*, and keep everybody happy.

231. Groveland: Veasey Memorial Park

I was only in a play once, and it wasn't even a live performance. Several members of my senior class wanted to do a taped performance based on a work by Mark Twain and they needed one more body, someone to play...Mark Twain. They dressed me up in a white suit, powdered up a white wig and slapped a droopy white mustache on my face and nudged me out on stage. I only had one line to deliver.

Those memories came back to me at Veasey Park in Groveland. I walked through the woods, down a hill and into a gorgeous little pine grove, called...the Grove. There had been a recent small campfire, and out on the water of the adjoining pond I could see four men in a small boat, fishing. The sun was shining, there was no traffic noise, and the few birds that were still active - a downy woodpecker, two tufted titmice and a white-breasted nuthatch accompanying the ubiquitous chickadees - were chattering softly in the background.

It was at that moment that my line came back to me. And I did exactly what it called for.

"I set still and listened."

I love summer in Massachusetts.

232. West Newbury: Mill Pond Recreation Area

Well, now I had seen everything.

I had to see a few more things before I could officially make that statement. I set off down the trail, past an old building that reminded me of pictures I'd seen of old boat clubs from the 1920s and 1930s. I walked past a sign that I had to stop and read twice: "Horse & Dog Wading Area 500 ft. south." Huh? Were they serious?

So I walked, 500 feet south to the foot. And there it was, another sign telling me that I'd made it. But without horses and dogs around, I couldn't really make any call as to the sign's validity. So I walked on, knowing I'd be coming back the same way.

Out on the water, a woman in a kayak had two yelping, swimming dogs sharing her day with her. She passed from my sight, briefly, as I entered the woods, though the dogs were certainly audible at all times. They were offset by eastern wood-pewees that seemed to be forming a communication chain through the woods, like one car alarm setting off another. I wandered through the beautiful little patch of forest for what seemed like hours, stopping once every few moments to admire another view.

As I headed back toward the wallowing area, I took note of a particularly well-endowed young woman with a chocolate lab (author's note: I've prided myself on my powers of observation and accuracy in reporting, and do not see any reason to change my style now. It was definitely not a black lab). A few bounding steps, and the dog was in the water, turned to face its owner, who had a tennis ball at the ready.

Yep, that was some good wading that dog was doing. I'll be damned.

233. Amesbury: Amesbury Town Forest

Oh, the woods, the woods! Eight towns in, I didn't want this day to end.

I wandered down to a powerline that runs through the Amesbury State Forest, and immediately turned back. Been there and done that on this day, and numerous times in the past. Not that there's anything wrong with powerlines, as I've stated. I just knew there was more to find in the woods.

First of all, there was plenty of red squirrel scaring to do. I didn't set out to do it, I wasn't planning on making any squirrel uncomfortable, but apparently I'm just what the red squirrels think of when they tell their youngsters about monsters. But I often wonder about their senses. Gray squirrels hide on the other side of the tree at a human's approach. Red squirrels stand their ground and start squawking, and they're half the size of the grays.

As that little game played out around me, a squeak, a jump and a squawk, I moved to Char's Hillock and to the intersection of Lion's Brook, Skunk Cabbage and Ashley Brook. And I could see that Bear Wall wasn't far away. I meandered, taking them all in.

As I walked, a bug flew inches from my face, causing me to lurch, but not swat. I looked towards its destination and saw where it was going. A bald-faced hornet's nest. I stood back and looked through my binoculars, but decided not to linger. Stings are not my thing. Luckily, for me, it had rained recently. When things are dry late in the summer and bees - bald-faces are technically yellow jackets - can't find food, they get very aggressive and can sting multiple times. Believe me, I know. The lushness of the forest allowed them to concentrate on their needs, and not turning their wrath on me. I took the opportunity to escape while they were distracted.

234. Merrimac: Lake Attitash

Hmm, there was something strange about the town logo for Merrimac, especially when placed next to the one from Amesbury. A covered carriage, facing to the left, without a horse, rimmed by the name of the town and its incorporation date. They're nearly exactly the same.

There is, of course, an easy explanation. Amesbury and Merrimac were both once part of Salisbury, but broke away together in 1666. Then in 1876, on the one hundredth anniversary of our fight for independence from the tyranny of England, West Amesbury broke away from the tyranny of Amesbury (really just an economic thing as the village had reached self-sustainability) and became Merrimac.

None of that helped me in my search for open space on this day. I tried to get into the Indian Head Park and Wells Site, but found a big "closed" sign on the way in. So, I did what I've often done in Massachusetts this year, I headed for the water. I found Lake Attitash, and walked around the neighborhood adjoining the boat launch area, which included a protected wetland. In all, it was a nice break from the humidity of the woods.

235. Haverhill: Winnikenni Park

I had never seen so many cars parked in one area related to an open space parcel. Not everybody was walking the woods, but many, many were. It was obvious that Winnikenni is a community gem.

Wildlife usually stays at bay during these times, opting to hide or skulk or retreat when humans overwhelm the landscape (others acclimatize and accept handouts). Chimney swifts flew overhead and a few Canada geese honked over the water of Kenoza Lake, but they were pretty well otherwise alone.

And who could blame them? At one point I was walking on the wide trail, staying well to one side to accommodate two young women approaching from the other direction. We exchanged hellos and I was instantly hit smack in the face with a blast of fruity perfume. PHEW! My immediate thought, as I tried to regain full consciousness, was of the 8-foot, 2-second rule publishers use when designing their covers for their books. It has to catch you as you glance at the shelf walking by in a book store, from eight feet away for two seconds.

If it had that affect on me, what would it do to a chickadee? Luckily, I'll never have to know. Heck, I rarely even wear deodorant. Just ask my wife.

236. Methuen: Nevins Bird Sanctuary

I finally reached my destination for the day, the little bat-shaped town of Methuen. The library would be so happy.

I found the Nevins Bird Sanctuary pretty quickly and readily, thanks to pictures I had seen of it on the internet. To enter, I had to walk down a set of railroad tracks, over a bridge through which I could see the water below.

Unfortunately, I spent most of my time on the phone. I was double-booked for the evening, a meeting on the South Shore and a lecture on the North Shore, so I took in the former via conference call.

And so it was that I was on the phone when my fourth snake of the day decided to make a slither for it. My heart jumped when I heard the movement at my feet and knew it was definitely not a garter snake. Nope, much bigger. I high-stepped, practically dropped the phone, and watched as a water snake, easily two feet long, sprinted for the edge of the small bridge and dove into the water. It looked like someone had pushed a stick out over the edge of a cliff and let it drop when gravity deemed it was time. The snake tilted like a seesaw and dropped into the water with a loud splash. Through it all, I could not say a word. I watched as it swam away, unable to work my camera with my phone in one hand.

From what I could see of it, and sight was the main sense I could dedicate to it, the sanctuary was full of bird life, from white-breasted nuthatches to belted kingfishers. Soon, I left the meeting, left the sanctuary, remembered everything I had ever known about lighthouses, changed my clothes and went to the Nevins Memorial Library to talk before a crowd. No one there ever knew what my day had entailed. To them I looked as fresh and crisp as if I'd just stepped out of the shower and put on my fancy lecturin' clothes.

It was my reverse superhero moment. I had changed from The Wanderer back to Clark Kent, mild-mannered maritime historian, able to leap water snakes in a single bound.

August 21

237. Gosnold: Penikese and Cuttyhunk

Aha, my ace in the hole.

I'm privileged in my fulltime work to have the opportunity to share a specific bank of my own personal knowledge. I lead trips - sometimes two, sometimes just one per year - to Cuttyhunk and Penikese Islands at the end of the Elizabeth Islands chain off Woods Hole and Falmouth. Since the rest of the Elizabeth Islands are privately held, it's the only way to visit the tiny town of Gosnold.

The islands are a study in contrasts. Cuttyhunk has a sizable population, relatively, numerous homes, some even year-round, and a harbor filled with boats of all sizes in summer. Penikese is a former leper colony and until very recently hosted a school for boys that was off-limits to the general public.

We visited both on this day, my co-leader Ian and I, interpreting the histories of both islands, sharing everything we knew about these two special places. We walked on Penikese to the spot where the leprosarium began, where Louis Agassiz held his naturalist training courses, where the lepers were buried; we walked on Cuttyhunk to Barges Beach, to the town center, up to the top of Lookout Hill.

For this project, it was an all-day adventure to mark off one town out of 351, but I'd do it all again. And on September 11, 2011, I did.

August 24

238. Boston: Boston Nature Center

If there's one thing I enjoy about walking Mass Audubon's trails, it's spying on my colleagues. Let me explain.

Public programming for naturalists can be a challenge. Think about it! How many people do you think will come back week after week to a wildlife sanctuary or nature center to learn about the world around them if there was no pizzazz in the presentation, no hook to bring them back in? Anybody can throw together a catalog of programs and hope for the best, but it's those folks who watch trends, understand the competition and market accordingly who attract the best crowds. Even then, it's a matter of message delivery. But that's another story.

So, at Mass Audubon's Boston Nature Center, I put on my spy goggles. I reached for program catalogs and watched the way staff interacted with the kids gathered for the day's programs. I examined bilingual signs in the woods on the trail, and thought about how I would interpret this place if I was an educator there and not in Marshfield. I'll admit it. I stole some ideas from them. But that's a good thing. We're lucky, being a statewide system, to have so many fantastic, dedicated educators working together, so far apart, willing to share our best practices. I only hope they all know they can steal from me any time they want.

On the trail, on the grounds of the old state mental hospital, a muddy brook ran past me on my left as the leaves on the trees suddenly turned upwards with a gust of wind. Was rain on the way? Eh, even if it washed me out, it had already been a great day.

239. Brookline: Larz Anderson Park

Finally, a return to the scene of the crime.

No one was ever charged for the crime, and no one ever actually committed it. But I was definitely the victim. A few decades earlier - and let me state here and now that I never thought I would be old enough to say *those* words in relation to my own life - my mother brought our little family to Larz Anderson Park. I had no idea where it was. I just knew it as a place of slides and baseball fields and kites and Weaver batter-dipped chicken drumsticks. *Mmmm...Weaver batter-dipped chicken drumsticks...*

The last time we were there was the last time I was there, and it ended traumatically for a seven-year-old. I was wearing my new straw cowboy hat, purchased at Six Gun City in New Hampshire. I was standing near the backstop of the baseball field, simply playing, being a kid, when the bees attacked. Two of them stung me simultaneously on the side my head, very close to my left eye. I dropped the hat and ran for my mom, crying uncontrollably as I went. She magically produced ice and started the hugging and healing process.

Meanwhile, my brother, all of 5, ran toward the scene of the disaster. He returned with my hat and a story of beating up two kids who tried to walk away with it, although we were clearly the only people in the entirety of the park. No wonder he became a cop.

So there I was, back to see the park for the first time in more than 30 years. The Boston skyline loomed over the ridge in the distance, willow trees dangled over ponds with fountains a-tumbling and the auto museum standing atop the hill.

I didn't remember any of it.

240. Watertown: Dr. Paul Dudley White Bike Path

Now that I think of it, I suppose I should have expected more from a town named Watertown, and should not have been surprised by the passage of boats on the waterway to my left as I walked.

I definitely have a blank spot in my knowledge of certain parts of the state, although I was taking on a little project in 2011 to try to correct that problem. Perhaps you've heard of it.

The bike path I followed followed the Charles River. I was dinged off the path by a woman on a bike with a nasty little bell she seemed to constantly be ringing annoyingly. I hadn't been thinking about boats when I saw the first one approaching me from behind out of the corner of my eye. Whoa! A boat? Out here? Say it ain't so!

It so.

The path eventually opened up to a wide vista of the river, and I could see that the lone boat was not a lone boat. There were other small cabin cruisers heading in the same direction, upriver, under Route 20. Coming out from under the bridge, kayakers and scullers slowed to deal with the wakes of the larger boats before continuing on. Soon, full rowing teams stroked into view. The Charles was alive and rocking.

Hmm, *Water*town. Now I get it.

241. Arlington: Menotomy Rocks Park

I looked at the map and decided that due to the postage-stamp size of the place, I might have to walk the trails at Menotomy Rocks Park twice to get in a half hour, which would be good. It would give me extra time to figure out what a Menotomy was.

I am an idiot.

I started out by Hills Pond, and wound around its edges. Up into the woods I went, and started to realize that my eyes were deceived by the map. Menotomy Rocks Park - named for the early name of Arlington and the rocks that dominate the park - was much bigger in practice than theory. For that, I was glad.

And what a band of merry-goers was here on this day! Two girls played on a huge rope swing dangling from a supporting tree. Moms and dads watched over bands of kids climbing the rocks mostly for acknowledgment from their parents. A young boy fished in the pond while his mom sat nearby reading a book, supportive of her son's pursuits, but also thankful for the few moments of escape she could get from diving into frivolous fiction. Benches throughout the park offered views, of woods, of water, of rocks.

Vandals had struck here in the past, but I decided that I was just glad they weren't followed by the Goths and Visigoths (that was my second Ancient Rome joke of the year, and, I promise, my last). I left with a wonderful amount of appreciation for all that the Friends of Menotomy Rocks Park had done to create and maintain that special place.

August 31

242. Oxford: Huguenot Fort

You know, where the Huguenots built their fort.

Isn't this state *amazing*?

Everywhere I turned, I found something new, a bird, a butterfly, a memorial, a bit of history I never knew happened. And the connections were incredible. John Eliot and the praying Indians of the Natick area visited this area in 1656. Isaac Bertrand DeTuffeau brought a settlement here in 1686, which was then abandoned, resettled in 1699, abandoned in 1704, and finally settled by the English in 1713.

At one point, there was a 30x18 blockhouse here, designed not for comfort, but for safety from Native American attacks, the legacy of King Philip's War being fear that the natives could strike at any time. We know that because of archaeological digs conducted in the area, with one survey being completed by Oliver Wendell Holmes' father in 1819.

There's nothing like starting a dewy morning with a smile upon your face, placed there by the discovery of something you never knew existed, right under your own nose. Now, if only I could figure out how to pick the right shoes in the morning, so my feet weren't completely soaked within the first half hour of what was supposed to be a double-digit-town day.

I squished happily on.

243. Auburn: Worcester Hebrew Cemetery

Let me just say this about the Jews...

Oo, dangerous way to start a paragraph. But let me say this: they like their tombstones tall, if the cemetery in Auburn is at all reflective of the rest of the culture.

And they like to laugh. My favorite marker was for a woman who had died at 98 years old with the epitaph "An Untimely Demise." How's that for going out with a bang?! And I say this all with true respect and admiration for my Jewish friends. I grew up in a town with a strong Jewish community, and have always been amazed by their commitment to their faith, and to the strength of their own community.

That said, the cemetery tells more than jokes. Among the Katz, Cohen, Silverman, Levy and Feldman stones are many more that I will probably never be able to read. They were in Hebrew, and only Hebrew, names, dates and I don't know what else. I've seen a few around the state in French, but not much more than that in foreign languages. They probably dated back to the earliest immigrants fleeing the pogroms at the beginning of the twentieth century, but I can't tell you for sure.

What I can tell you is that the cemetery is surrounded by some excellent wildlife habitat, thickets full of catbirds, a nearby pond, a powerline crossing a railroad track.

When I die I want my family to look at it like the family of Rose Pelletz Cohen. Get one last laugh out of the story of my life! Perhaps, if I outlive the average American male's life expectancy, we can go with "A Timely Demise."

244. Leicester: Pine Grove Cemetery

I found Russell Park, and it wasn't what I thought it would be, so I skedaddled. I found a cemetery that looked like it had a good, thick forest behind it, and took my chances.

And there I found the sad tale of Julia Julia.

No, not Julia Gulia. That would have been the name of the Drew Barrymore character in *The Wedding Singer* had she married the Matthew Glave character instead of falling in love with the one played by Adam Sandler. This was, in fact, two Julias born to a Clapp family. One died in infancy, so they named the next one after her, who also died very young. That ended this particular Clapp family's usage of the name Julia.

I decided, after divining that saga, to poke and prod at the back wall of the cemetery. There had to be a way into the woods beyond! It was a perfectly wet day, and I just knew that if I broke the wall down I would find treasures within that piney realm. Bingo! I shouted aloud, thankful that no living soul was around to hear it, lest they think I was playing the game with the dead.

I found a trail and started walking, dodging a few downed trees here and there, recent casualties of tropical storm Irene. But I hit the final, impenetrable barrier: "no trespassing" signs. Aw, shucks.

But all was not lost. A barred owl called, "Who cooks for you?" See, I knew there had to be more to this place!

245. Spencer: Spencer State Forest

The way I see it, I'm up for honorary membership in the Spencer Snowbirds. But we'll see how things turn out.

In my continued study of Worcester County on this day I found the state forest and began my muddy walk, only to find that much of the trail was under assault. Branches, limbs, small trees, thrown haphazardly about by a lady named Irene, crossed the trail at numerous points. Although I spent thirty minutes there, I didn't get very far. I spent most of my time cleaning the trail - taking the burden off the Spencer Snowbirds, who have claimed the task as volunteers.

That's OK, no need to thank me. But you can send the patch to my name at Mass Audubon...

Seriously, though, it was wonderful to see such community engagement in open space. And that is a huge key to its success as a concept, user buy-in and, well, parent-like commitment. Love and care for the land like it's your child, and it will live forever. In this case, the users are snowmobilers. In a perfect world, power-driven machines are kept entirely out of natural environments, but at some point down the line, the land owners decided to allow it here. Thankfully, the group that has grown up around snowmobiling in this part of the state has taken stewardship seriously. Without the land, they have nowhere to practice their pastime. The same goes for hunters, birders, fishermen and more.

Have fun, Snowbirds!

246. East Brookfield: Quabog Pond

Well, this little storm we had certainly did its share of damage. News came in from as far away as Vermont and central New York about flooding and other problems, so I guess I shouldn't have been so surprised about high water levels out by Worcester, considering how badly damaged the eastern part of the state was.

Shore Road in East Brookfield was washed out at one end, leaving the other end a nature trail, so I just got out and walked right there. I passed by a broken down house with a small boat named the *Footloose* - how *a propos* for 2011, as the movie had been remade (as if it ever had to be!) - and listened to the unrelenting sound of crickets. Water swirled in dancing eddies as I looked skyward to find the most bizarre looking plane I'd ever seen, and believe me, I've examined quite a few in my time.

I had no way to judge how deep the water was, or, should I say, how different it was on this day from the way it was a week earlier. I could see that fishing was pretty popular, going by the number of bobbers wrapped around the powerlines.

A fisherman approached and started casting from the road. Why not? There wouldn't be any cars through here for days. I asked him how high it was and he responded, wearing his tie dye concert t-shirt unironically, by pointing to a spot six feet below the surface and saying, "That's where I usually stand."

Yeesh.

247. Brookfield: Quacumquasit Wildlife Management Area

That corn was as high as an elephant's eye and it was well past the Fourth of July! Harvest it!

Birders often get excited when they see crops growing - crops produce seeds, seeds attract birds - but in this case, on this day, there was no real avian excitement. There were exactly four bird species nearby, song sparrows and American goldfinches, both of which were hanging out near the cornfield's edge, and distant blue jays and American crows, unnecessarily squawking, at least in my opinion.

Sometimes, though, the crop thing can work in the wrong direction. A small kitchen garden, for instance, might attract a bluebird, an evening grosbeak, or something like that. But a thousand acres of grain could bring in swarms of blackbirds, which, for the birders, are nice, but for the farmers are pests. Too much of a good thing can be too much of a bad thing. Part of the problem for farmers during the Depression was the swarms of insects that found and grew fat - and abundant - on monotonous crops that fed them well.

Such was not the problem there in Brookfield. This particular section of the town was dominated by open spaces connected to the Quabog River, Quabog Pond and Quacumquasit Pond. Unfortunately, though, there was a problem, an invasion of Eurasian watermilfoil. If you had an aquarium as a kid, you probably had some of the feathery-looking stuff. In ponds and lakes it forms mats that shield other plants from sunlight, changing the ecosystem. Ugh. Yet another invasive.

But then there's corn. Good old corn, the stuff of Pilgrim legend. There's a plant you can sink your teeth into.

248. West Brookfield: Rock House Reservation

Yeah, baby, now we're talking.

My love affair with big rocks continues to flourish and grow with each passing day. Every once in a while I find a place like this one, where I can let my love fly, like a bird on the wing, and let my love bind me to all living things. Thank you Bellamy Brothers.

I was, though, duped. I followed the map to the spot where the Rock House was supposed to be - you know, past Carter Pond, past the tent caterpillars, past the gray tree frogs trilling from the...trees - but thought I had found it, when I hadn't. I reacted like Homer Simpson when he got a huge beer placed in front of him in Australia. "Well...it's pretty big...I guess." Then I turned the corner and my heart jumped. It was the Rock House!

Without placing myself in the middle of it - what I considered the living room - I couldn't take a picture to justify its grandeur. I felt puny as I looked up at the mass above me. One of the rocks looked like it could easily just slide right over on its side and crush me in an instant, but it had been there for so long, I doubted it would pick today to make its move.

I was in rocky heaven (not *Rocky* Heaven, where Sylvester Stallone will be some day). By visiting this site, it meant that I had been to both Rock House and House Rock, in Weymouth. Long live erratics! At least until the next Ice Age.

249. North Brookfield: Town Forest

By mid-day, most of the bird activity has quieted down. Some birds go to sleep mid-day, and they, like the Mexicans and the Italians, have it right - why exhaust yourself in the noontime sun? *Siesta* time!

And so it was quiet when I rolled into the last of the Brookfields. I found a trail on which to walk, and took note of the scarcity of noise, and the powerful smell of the pines around me.

I also found white wood-asters. Their presence told me two things. First, that it was perpetually shady where I was standing. Wildflowers in the woods are odd creatures. Some, like the spring ephemerals, take quick advantage of the early sun before the trees leaf up and get the nutrients they need for the year in that short period. Others, like white wood-aster, wait until August to even throw their flowers out, more of a field or meadow plant's gig.

Second, it told me that where I was standing was usually pretty dry, as that's the habitat this particular plant likes. But that was not nearly the case today. They would be in force for the next month or two, a dominant plant in dry forests around Massachusetts. I'd probably meet many more.

250. New Braintree: Evergreen Cemetery

That mid-day sun was still cooking as I moved onto New Braintree. Without any luck locating open space parcels, I found my third cemetery of the day.

That last sentence should come with a disclaimer. New Braintree is sparsely settled, especially in comparison to the old Braintree, well to the east. There's a lot of space there that is open, beautiful rolling hills and farmlands, but none of it is *open space*.

The cemetery was small, triangular and finite. A wall surrounded it, and I found it odd that there was a plaque that memorialized forever the names of the men who built that wall. Wait a minute, I thought, let me go back and take a look at this thing. I stood at one end and looked straight ahead. That thing was as unwaveringly true as an arrow shot from a taut bow! That was real craftsmanship, and I could see why its makers would be recorded for posterity.

It reminded me of marveling at two old-timers in Hingham who were trimming a hedge at a church. I could not believe how straight, how perfect, they could make it, in not a substantial amount of time. I guess if you've got a steady hand, you've got a steady hand.

251. Oakham: Oakham State Forest

Oops, scared a frog. Damn, I do that a lot these days.

I found the Oakham State Forest on a newly-paved road. It was so new that I was leaving some of the first tracks on it, bringing dirt from the sides on the bottom of my shoes and staining the otherwise perfectly black surface with a light brown.

I had to. I was like a little kid understanding how a bridge works for the first time. I found the outflow area, a dramatically enclosed, dense pine grove with a stream running right through it. Gorgeous! I then ran back across the street to Foley Pond to see the stepped spillway and the manmade channel directing the water under the road. I ran back to the outflow. And back to the pond. It was a rusty red stream coming from a deep blue pond into a black pine wood.

The only thing that could snap me from my boyish discovery was an unfamiliar sound overhead, or at least an under-exercised one in my head. I knew what it was; I just had to find the right connection in my brain to put the species of hawk with the sound I was hearing, a double-whistle.

Ah, got it. Before I even saw the bird, I had two memories pop into my head. One from downeast Maine, one from high atop a mountain pass in Colorado, which, ironically, was a place a broad-winged hawk was not supposed to be. But it was there then, and it was here now, probably not the same one.

252. Rutland: Rutland State Forest

I was entering the Promised Land. No, not Rutland. No, I had broken the plane of the final 100 towns to walk in Massachusetts. It meant nothing, of course. It wouldn't until I crossed the finish line - wherever the hell that would be. What, do you think I actually planned anything like that?

I walked up a hill, and realized there was nothing new here, and that in itself was exciting. After 251 walks, I had seen it all, or so it seemed. An old railroad bed. People on bikes, some towing dogs. I found an old maple sugaring bucket, but I could count on my hands and my best friends' hands the number of towns in which I'd seen them already. I found a "Moose Crossing sign." Been there.

I heard a blue-headed vireo. *For like the fiftieth time!* I thought to myself, in a Napoleon Dynamite-type voice.

It wasn't repetition to me, it was truth. I was finding the heart of Massachusetts. I expected I would still find some surprises along the way - in fact, perhaps by the end of the day - but for that moment I was content in the knowledge that I was accomplishing what I was setting out to do: getting to know my home state in ways I never had before.

253. Paxton: Moore State Park

Forget everything I just said. Every last word.

I figured that Moore State Park would be just like the rest, and the pathway into the park was proving me right. But then I found the experimental orchard. And I found the rhododendrons.

Rhodies were, at one point, the bane of my existence. As a landscaper I pruned them continually, arguing with people over the efficacy of planting them next to a home. It just makes no sense. They get big fast. They block windows. They give ants and other bugs quick transport into parts of the home they don't think about approaching from the ground. And this whole foundation planting fad only started about 100 years ago, when we had to start hiding gas meters. Get the rhodies away from the house.

So rhodies, not native to our area, are a pretty good sign of human settlement. So, too, are old mills, and my goodness, what a beautiful arrangement they had at Moore. Among the many old foundations of the mill town that once thrived here is one building still intact. A short walk down the hill past the rushing water finds a spot called the "Artist Overlook," from which I'm sure thousands of folks have photographed and painted the scene before them: water splashing past the old wooden mill building, which itself is perched at a three-quarters angle.

Yup, I've got so much to learn about Massachusetts.

254. Holden: Eagle Lake Wildlife Sanctuary

Wow, miraculously, for some reason, I stopped sniffling. Allergies had been pounding my senses all day long, but moments after I stepped into the woods at Eagle Lake, they disappeared.

The sanctuary had its own special layer of sylvanity (how's that for a made-up word?). There was a peaceful brook and at different times I encountered cheery toads and hyped-up chipmunks. I even got to know a few mushrooms, though not in the Groovy '60s kind of way.

There were trees down, and not just the typical blow downs. These were big, massive, recently-felled-by-the-wind warriors of the forest. It seemed so unfair, to have lived for 200 years and have the end come so violently. Sorry to make such a crass analogy, but it was like the way we lost David Halberstam, the author. A car accident took him, when he should have been allowed to drift into eternal sleep when his time came. The trees I saw lying on their sides should have been allowed to stand in place long after their deaths.

I found one waymarking post with dueling arrows. When viewed from either approach, the arrows made sense. pointing either up or down the trail. But standing directly in front of the post, if I pointed my camera lens just right, I could make it look like the "Which way did he go? Which way did he go?" cowboy from the cartoons of my youth.

I so totally did it.

255. West Boylston: Goodale Park

Once again, the end of a long day of walking stared me in my sweaty face. Eight months down, fewer than one hundred towns to go. I was well ahead of pace.

I found Goodale Park as school was letting out, and as such, felt a bit on edge. The park is near school grounds, and there were a lot of young kids around. The park itself - if I read it correctly - consists of athletic fields, a failed fitness trail and some open space. Although I confined myself to the open space, it's never really good to be the guy walking around near the varsity girls' soccer practice with the binoculars and camera.

But the birds gave me plenty to focus on, so I looked legit, or at least hoped I did, as I didn't want to offend anybody. In actuality, there were only a handful of species, but they were active as heck. Chipping sparrows and eastern bluebirds led the charge, seeking seeds with their youngsters, teaching them how to fend for themselves. As I walked on - oops, that was a field sparrow! - I bumped into a granite marker that designated the bounds of Goodale Park.

It turned out that I had just missed the centennial celebration, marked by extensive improvements to the property by the town. As far as I can tell, it was named for one of the many Aaron Goodales who have called West Boylston home, probably the one who lived from 1851 into the early years of the twentieth century and served as overseer of the poor, chairman of the board of selectmen, and more.

I love it when a town honors their past and the people who built their community. It so rocks.

Home, Jeeves.

September

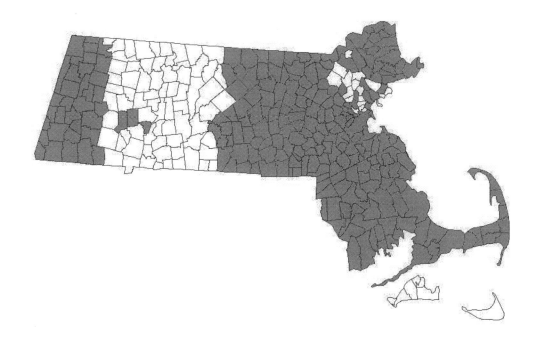

Belted Galloways

When I looked at the map on September 1, I had to laugh out loud. It looked like a Belted Galloway.

Vas ist das? you ask. A belted Galloway is my favorite species of cow. It's black on one end, white in the middle, and black again at the far end. It looks like a giant Oreo cookie, or, if you prefer, a Whoopie Pie turned on end. And if you look really hard, you can find them in farmyards around Massachusetts.

And that's what I do.

Before I started this project, back before I had kids, my friend David and I would spend full days exploring little known corners of the state. We simply called them nature days. If we went north, he drove, I paid for lunch. If we went south, I drove, he paid for lunch. We searched for birds,

165

flipped rocks and logs for amphibians, sought grape-ferns, wildflowers and more. Call it OJT - on-the-job training.

The funny thing was that no matter where we went, we found Belted Galloways. We could be on the Mass Pike, blasting west for High Ledges Wildlife Sanctuary in Shelburne Falls, or climbing Turkey Hill in Hingham.

But there's more to the story. Our previous boss, another David, was the one who introduced us both to Belted Galloways. He had a weird vibe about him that drove domestic animals crazy. By the time I met him he had a long history of being chased by dogs, and even cows. I remember once being in a van with him, driving along the dirt road that led to the parking area for Cohasset's Wheelwright Park. A big dog approached my side of the van wagging its tail with smiling eyes, hopping along beside us. When we turned to leave, and David was on that side of the road, the dog lurched at the van and yelped at him with all fury. We figured it was the mustache.

That David retired, and the other David and I took to the hills and valleys, the seashores and the mountain tops. Whenever we saw a Belted Galloway, we laughed, in honor of our friend and mentor.

But it's not like he's dead or anything. We still bird with him. Sorry if that sounded all sentimental-like.

September 7

256. Holland: Quinebaug Woods

I came up with a theory a long time ago, one that would make Staples proud. It was raining again, this time in Holland. I still didn't care, as it doesn't bother me in the slightest until it becomes obviously unbearable. While a walker in the woods sacrifices some things in the rain, he gains others. As I've said so many times this year, let me explain.

The rain, you see, if it hits during just the right season, is nature's highlighter. I often find that the greens of the understory are never so vibrant as they are during a steady spring or fall downpour. Mist and fog don't make the cut, and tempests, well, I don't walk in many of them. But a good, steady rain, one worth donning a raincoat for, one worth clearing one's pockets of paper goods (books, bird checklists, the list of stuff your wife wants you to pick up at the supermarket after you take ten nature walks in a single day, you know, like that), they bring out the best in the woods. Such a rain fell on this day.

Of all the sights in the woods on this day - hairy woodpecker and hermit thrush among them - the most spectacular was a mushroom known as a varnish shelf. Already imbued naturally with a rich, red color that seems as if it's been hit with a coat of Minwax fast-drying, the varnish shelf picks up the sheen of water and glows in the rain.

A beautiful brook, one that had me wistfully pining for the American dippers I had seen in Colorado and Montana, and the Louisiana waterthrushes I had last seen in Pennsylvania, rushed right at me, but was unable to hold me in perpetuity.

257. Wales: Norcross Wildlife Sanctuary

As I stepped into Wales, I began to feel the butterflies in my stomach. I knew I was edging ever closer to the tornado zone. I had purposely waited well into the year to avoid the worst struck areas, which included nearby Monson, but, sadly, the hits just kept on coming. Tornadoes in June, a heavy windstorm in late July, tropical storm Irene in late August, they all targeted this section of the state. Stories had developed of sections of Route 2, farther north, closed indefinitely. State forests and parks were closed, with the same time schedule. If I was truly going to walk all 351, I would have to see these towns at some point.

Wales, though, and specifically the Norcorss sanctuary, was open for business. And what a weird little place it specifically was. Among the many anomalies I found there were a vernal pool, a kettle pond - I thought that was just a coastal plain thing! - a sandplain, pitcher plants and Labrador tea (found in anoxic bogs) and a widespread invasion of stinking squids.

"Wait a minute!" you may say. "I'll believe you when you speak of insectivorous plants and sand-based habitats miles from the state's beaches, but there's no way a squid is in Wales." I am sorry to report 'tis true.

Stinking squids are mushrooms that travel in wood chip deliveries - the trails here were well-covered in wood chips - and stink. They are technically stinkhorns, and if you're dumb enough to grab one from the ground and put it in your car to show to a friend later in the day, well, I don't want to tell you what the inside of my car smelled like. I mean, what the inside of your car would smell like. If you did something dumb like that.

258. Monson: Keep Homestead Museum

It was as horrible as advertised.

I was at home in Weymouth the night the tornadoes struck. There is no stronger feeling of powerlessness than sitting in front of the TV listening to the news broadcaster say, "ETA for Weymouth, 16 minutes." It's the randomness, like that of a lightning strike, that instills the fear. It might only take one life, but chances are just as good as the next person's that it would be mine. The line used to be "Smoke 'em if you got 'em." Now it's just a silent resignation to fate.

I stopped at the Keep Homestead Museum and could see the path of the tornado that tore through the town. It was unnerving, tear-jerking. The trees had fallen in the path, a perfect cut through the woods. Two black vultures, as if wishing to add a sense of the macabre to the scene, flew up and over the hill as I took it all in.

I headed onto the trails behind the museum and saw, at first, what I thought was the extent of the damage. I could discern the tornado's path, off to my right. But then, the trail turned, and headed into that area. For the next forty minutes or so, I walked *in* the path.

The fact that the trail was open at all was utterly remarkable. But it was passable from end to end. One section, known for its Christmas ferns, won't have ferns in a few years. An entire section of forest had been laid bare, and without shade, the ferns probably don't stand a chance. A ten-year study of the plant life of this particular plot would be fascinating - how often do Massachusetts scientists get to study the aftereffects of a tornado in their own backyard? The same goes for the birds. Without their trees, do they return? Piles of chainsawed debris reached well above my head. Pits created by the uprooting of massive trees had filled with water during the morning, making for hundreds of small pools on the hill.

All was not lost, of course, as goldfinches, pewees and woodpeckers flew through the area, still finding food. Life amidst all the death.

I'd never felt so sad while walking in nature, and never pulled for a community I didn't know as much as I pulled for Monson that day.

259. Hampden: Laughing Brook Wildlife Sanctuary

I had barely noticed that the rain had more or less stopped in Monson, I was so consumed by the tragic story. When I started on Mass Audubon's Laughing Brook Wildlife Sanctuary trails, the atmosphere re-energized, forming a mist that promised to keep me well slicked for the next half hour, at least.

But what a lyrical place! Hemlocks, witch hazel, stonewalls, a rushing brook to cross and run shoulder-to-shoulder with. A split rock formed a perfect Nike running shoe, when viewed from the right angle. And I found the biggest chicken mushroom I'd seen to date. Don't tell the Italian side of my family. They'll make me go back and get it for preparation as a meal. I'm not going through that again.

Even as I heard the thump-thump-thump of a retreating white-tailed deer, I knew that I had to keep one other notion in mind. This spot once belonged to one of the greatest children's book writers of all time, Thornton

168

Burgess. It was here that he walked the trails examining the squirrels and the other critters of the woods, giving them names and personalities, divining stories that would appear in his books.

Imagine that, somebody being inspired by walking among the trees. Whodathunkit.

260. East Longmeadow: Watchaug Meadow

There's a story in East Longmeadow that I'd like to chase down, once I get over the trauma of the mosquito bites. And it all has to do with the long history of the town.

It started in the early eighteenth century for East Longmeadow, settled in 1720. Obviously, being an "east" there's a tale of political separation, and that happened in the late 1800s. Now there's a study for you - this town was the 347th of the current 351 to form, older only than Westwood, Plainvillle, Millville, and East Brookfield. Wouldn't it be fun to randomly pick a year and figure out how many towns there were? This project, for instance, would have been much easier in 1639. *Half an Hour a Day on Foot: 23 Towns in 365 Days*. Of course, back then, I would probably have had to walk *to* all of the towns themselves before walking *in* them. And I'll bet there was a lot more open space back then, too.

But East Longmeadow, with its sandstone quarries, supposedly supplied the raw materials for the construction of the Smithsonian Institution. I ask you, good gentlepeople: how cool is that?

So, someday I'll dive in. Like I did to the trails on this day. And someday I'll truly learn about the proper way to protect oneself from the damaging advances of the insect world. Meadow + humidity + summer = one chewed up wanderer.

261. Longmeadow: Fannie Stebbins Wildlife Refuge

I had this old boss named Rick when I was growing up, who was larger than life in the eyes of a teenager. He only had about six jokes, but he delivered them with such gusto and panache, not to mention a constant ear-ringing laughter, that you felt as if you were in the presence of one of the world's most confident, important people. He had this one saying, just two little words, that often heralded his appearance in a room. They were initially words of discovery, used when he found out something ribald or slightly off-color, and wanted to call attention to it. It later became a simple greeting. All day long he had us all smiling and chuckling whenever we bumped into each other in our mad scramble around the video arcade. "Hey now!"

Such were my initial thoughts as I "discovered" Fannie Stebbins. "Hey now!"

Were it not for the rain, which had grown more intense as I approached the trails, I might have had more fun in Longmeadow. The habitat was there. The puddles on the trail, though, were more than just weak depressions. They were deep, wide, edge-to-edge oceans of rain water. I tiptoed along those edges as much as possible, but in the end found it to be an exercise in futility. I stood on the brink of a pond as a flock of Canada geese blasted in with a series of uncoordinated honks, which term could also be used to describe my coworkers and me during my arcade days. Both hairy and downy woodpeckers laughed at me as I slowly moistened at both ends.

One of the best features of the sanctuary was a water level marker for the famous storms that had inundated the Springfield area. The Hurricane of 1938 was pretty bad, but the winner, at least on this very spot, was the 1936 flood. I've studied it from afar, and know that Coast Guardsmen from my childhood home of Hull responded to the rising waters at the time. Kind of made my ankle wetting today seem a bit of a trifling, sniveling little complaint.

262. Springfield: Forest Park

When I got there, the nature class was already underway. I watched from afar for a while.

I'm no longer in a position to truly care whether or not school is in session. I've been out for twenty years, and my mom, a longtime French and Spanish teacher, retired in the spring. My son is only 2, so we haven't even gone lunchbox shopping yet. And I'll tell you one thing. He's not getting my Dukes of Hazzard lunchbox. That's not to say I won't be jealous of his Lightning McQueen one.

But there it was, a field trip. Our biggee back home on the South Shore was Plimoth Plantation, in the third grade. For these kids, though, there was a bit more hands-on work to be done than we got to entertain ourselves with at the Plantation. They had nets and were standing on the edge of the major pond that dominates Forest Park.

I never saw one swung in anger, though. They milled about, the girls giggling, the boys conniving. There were most likely dragonflies or butterflies about, or perhaps they were heading for some ponding exercises. I'll never know, as their teachers and instructors jabbered at them the entire time I was nearby. I steered very wide of the log cabin-style nature center they were using, although I wanted desperately to know more about it, architecture geek that I can be at times. Instead, I settled for the mallards and the Canada geese, and the fountains spraying water skyward. And hey, look at that - the rain had stopped again.

What a day.

263. Chicopee: Chicopee Memorial State Park

There have been times during my travels that I have broken down to simple solemnity. Emotion drains away and I fall silent. That silence is an inner stillness, for as I walk, I think, heavily.

Mostly these moments come when I'm struck with the stories of fallen veterans.

Why such reverence? Family pride. While my grandfather was of the wrong age to join the fight in World War II, he did work at a local shipyard. He carried his ID card in his pocket for the rest of his life, into the 1990s. My dad, a true hero to me, joined the Marine Corps in 1966, full well knowing he was on his way to Vietnam. It scarred him for life, but he hid it well. That story is yet waiting to be told, and maybe someday will be.

In Chicopee, I stood among his comrades. The park is dedicated to the fallen Vietnam War warriors of the community, fifteen men lost between 1966 and 1970 with the Army, Navy and Marines in that horrid little conflict that changed America in so many ways. A sign bearing all fifteen names was dedicated in a grove of trees planted to represent each of the fifteen. The arrangement of the trees is eerily similar to the statues of the Korean War memorial on the mall in Washington D.C.; it feels as if the trees are a unit spread out and moving toward a destination, each one warily looking into the distance for a hidden foe.

I've given out kudos jokingly along the way during this little project, but were I authorized to do so, I'd salute the people of Chicopee for a job well done.

264. Ludlow: Ludlow Center Cemetery

Argh. After all the emotional ups and downs of the day, from stinking squids to tornadoes to Vietnam War remembrances, I was up for my final push through the last two towns on my list, Ludlow and Wilbraham.

Truth be told, I had already struck out once in Wilbraham, but I'll tell that story in a minute. Ludlow, though, had promise. It had spunk. It coulda been a contenda. But it was not to be.

I picked out a handful of spots in town that showed potential for a foot-weary traveler to enjoy. But everywhere I turned, there were "no trespassing" signs - even at the entrance to the town forest. So I gave up and found my last resorts, cemeteries.

Drained by my frustration, I barely found the energy to be interested, and were it not for the northern flicker in the Ludlow Center Cemetery, and the curious positioning of two, side-by-side utility sheds that had me wondering about the burial process on the grounds, I might have had nothing to say at all.

265. Wilbraham: Red Bridge State Park

I really, really wanted to meet the Pesky Serpent. In the southern reaches of Wilbraham there's - supposedly, I couldn't find it - a meadow in which young Timothy Merrick met his doom after the bite of just such a creature. The tale was told in the "Ballad of Springfield Mountain," possibly America's first folk song. I wanted to connect to that land, but couldn't find my way into it early in this trip.

So I saved Wilbraham, mentally, for another day. Yet, as I was passing out of Ludlow and into Wilbraham, nature invited me to a small boat launch and some surrounding woods. I hit the brakes and felt the final squish of the boots as I stepped out of my car for one last walk.

I walked toward the sound of rushing water and was surprised to find an old mill building straddling the waterway. My first thought, which was weird, I know, was of how I was glad I wasn't in a kayak. The four openings under the building were barely exposed under the height of the water. Decapitation wasn't the fear, but a good, solid conking on the noggin would certainly be within the realm of plausibility with me at the controls.

In the end, I got my Wilbraham, and even thought about celebrating with a bit of locally manufactured Friendly's Ice Cream, but honestly, I couldn't imagine any restaurant would be happy to seat me after my day in the wilderness of the Pioneer Valley and environs. Instead, I slunk home, like a serpent, and made plans for my final 86 towns.

September 12

266. Somerville: Foss Park

Well, I knew that Somerville wouldn't provide me with the deepest natural experience of the year, but it didn't mean I was uninterested in what it had to offer. I found Foss Park.

The park is another urban catch-all, a playground, athletic fields, including a soccer field in serious need of landscaping attention, and a baseball field doing just a little better. There were trees that provided shade and even some wildlife. And I mean this next sentence with all seriousness. The pigeons have to live somewhere.

One marker threw me for a loop. "Route of Middlesex Canal." Here? Through this park? Well, I'll be hornswoggled. It turned out to be true (historical markers are rarely wrong, although they are not 100% foolproof). The canal, which operated for about 50 years from the start of the nineteenth century to 1853, ran 27 miles in length and provided a highway for goods and materials during the height of the Industrial Revolution. This particular section had been filled - Boston's history is of filling wetlands to create buildable land - but much of it remains open today. There's even a historical museum dedicated just to its story, in North Billerica.

So, even in the heart of the city, on a small, well-trodden and urbanized block, surrounded by a steady flow of traffic and its clinging noise, even in a place where the residents looked askance at my approach, Massachusetts surprised me.

267. Everett: Mystic River Reservation

An orange line train crashed by as I walked, trundling over a rickety-sounding bridge spanning the river. In fact, it reminded me of the *clack-clack-clack* of the ancient roller coaster cars at Paragon Park, which reigned in Hull from 1905 to 1985, up 'til my 14th year. Behind me a shopping mall bustled.

But the catbirds, and there were about a dozen of them, could not have cared less. They played among the sumac and the knotweed with the robins. The blue jays were there, too, but I don't think playing is a good verb for them. Mostly they bitch.

Across the water I spied a marina, with far too many boats sitting dockside for such a beautiful day. Is a boat ever worth the purchase? Can you ever really get your money's worth out of it? The double-crested cormorants and herring gulls flew by without monetary concerns.

By the time I wrapped up my walk, I came away with an unexpected smile. This small stretch of Everett, known recently for its horrible fire when a tanker truck crashed in 2007 and as the site where liquefied natural gas comes into the state, will now forever be known to me as the place where I took that nice walk in the waning days of the summer of 2011.

268. Chelsea: Naval Hospital Park

There was the Bunker Hill Monument, and over there was the Prudential Tower. And if I walked far enough around the corner, which I did, I could stand almost directly under the Mystic River Bridge. It was a place of Boston landmarks.

Just across the river sat a tanker, the *Overseas Sifnos*, flagged in the Marshall Islands. One tree in the park looked as if it had sunk directly downward and settled in at the height of its first limbs.

The site, of course, had history. A hospital, built high on the hill abutting the park, was constructed exclusively for the nation's sailors in the 1830s and remained in service for nearly a century and a half. Among its patients were one past President, John Quincy Adams, and one future President, John Fitzgerald Kennedy.

Today, the hospital and its grounds have mostly been turned over to residential concerns, but it is possible to discern some of that old history as one walks even just the park itself without invading the privacy of the people who live alongside it. I divined what I could as I said my hellos to strangers, and hit several of those awkward moments when I ran into people for the second and third times. You know, when you get stuck saying something like, "What?! You again!" Believe me, you're better off just smiling and nodding. There's less embarrassment all the way around.

And, if you're counting, that's another county down. Buh-bye, Suffolk.

269. Malden: Forest Dale Cemetery

When I first started telling people about this silly little idea, I heard all kinds of snickers, harumphs and even a few "goodonya's." One stood out above all else for its randomness, my friend Marie wishing me luck in one town, Malden. At the time, I was Malden-free, completely uninitiated in the history and culture of the community. What the hell did I know? It could be that the entire town had been paved. Like Northern New Jersey.

I picked out a promising looking cemetery, Forest Dale on Sylvan Street. They didn't sound like paved words to me.

So, when I stood in a sea of Civil War veterans on a shady slope listening to an eastern towhee call from the nearby woods on a sunny day, I nearly passed out. There's only so much sensory input a guy can handle.

I wandered among the stones and found the two that stood out the most. George Harrison (go figure), Medal of Honor recipient: "Served on board the USS Kearsarge when she destroyed the Alabama off Cherbourg, France, 19 June 1864. Acting as sponger and loader of the 11-inch pivot gun during the bitter engagement, Harrison exhibited marked coolness and good conduct and was highly recommended for his gallantry under fire by the divisional officer."

Not too far away rested the remains of Sarah Fuller, who fought another war. From 1879 to 1913 she worked for the Women's Relief Corps, the organization dedicated to caring for the needs of the men of the Grand Army, the Civil War veterans who lived into old age. But she didn't just organize suppers for downtrodden soldiers; she served as the national president.

Ha! Take that, Marie!

270. Melrose: Pine Banks Park

After I finished my "In Your Face!" dance for Marie, I turned the corner for Melrose. Pine Banks Park! What a find.

As usual, I headed for the highest point I could find. In this case, at the apex of the hill in the center of the park, I found scraggly pines on a rocky ground. The pines were harboring blue jays as if they were criminals, which, in the eyes of some bird species, they are. Chickadees and goldfinches joined them in making a low level background noise for my walk.

Standing atop the hill and looking outwards across the treetops, I realized I had virtually been there before. It used to be, in the old days - pre-internet - that you could say "virtually" and mean something like "practically" or "almost" ("It was virtually like I'd been there before."). Now "virtually" almost exclusively means otherworldly sensory experience fabricated by means of technology. The old virtual reality had a sense of adventure and imagination. The new one comes with ear buds.

The view from the hill, though, made me think once again to my virtual realms online. If there's one thing computer game designers have perfected, it's landscapes. The scenery, when focused on exclusively, can be breathtaking. I felt like my Lord of the Rings Online hunter standing in the Trollshaws as I took the scenery in.

But Pine Banks Park will always have them beat if just for one thing. Fresh air. But, then, maybe someday Elmer Fudd's newspaper headline in *The Old Grey Hare* will come true, and Smellovision will replace Television. If so, I may be the only man outdoors...

September 20

271. Nahant: Nahant Thicket Wildlife Sanctuary

The fall equinox was virtually upon me as I headed the length of the Nahant peninsula to find the thicket, another Mass Audubon wildlife sanctuary. Despite the grayness of the day, with storm clouds threatening, the birds were singing. Breeding was done, and migration was well under way. Some birds don't give up on their dawn chorus - typically the mark of birds attracting mates in spring - until the sunlight tells them the season is over. Even then, there's the odd fact of the sun crossing back over the equator and at some point in the fall producing exactly the same amount of daylight on a given day as there had been during the rush to procreate. Make that fall day 70 degrees and sunny, and you need earplugs while walking through a thicket.

The thicket was smaller than I expected it to be, but, as thickets tend to be, it was dense. I walked through it twice, then walked around it entirely, and still had ten minutes to spare, so I did it all again.

I'm sure I saw the same Carolina wren twice, and the same gray catbirds over and over. Robins moved through the trees in bunches, and starlings overwhelmed the skies from time to time. I could see how this place had become a "migrant trap" in spring, when birds flying north over densely settled areas dive for patches of green seen from above.

That did it. Just thinking of all those warblers made me put Nahant Thicket on the list for next spring. Sigh...I may never see a May Red Sox game again.

272. Swampscott: Harold King Town Forest

Onto the home of actor Walter Brennan, Swampscott, Mass.

I put in more than my share of time in Swampscott, futilely looking for the entrance to the park. I remembered what Google said. I even had a map with me showing me where the entrance was. But I couldn't find the stupid thing, or, perhaps more accurately, the Stupid Thing couldn't find it.

But then, Eureka! as Archimedes once said in a bathtub. An old dilapidated sign pointed the way. "Oscar Short Land Conservation Area," it said, the alternate name for the Harold King Town Forest, as far as I could tell. I stumbled down a trail and into the woods, so happy to be free of the local neighborhood (no offense to the neighbors, of course).

I bounded over rocks and roots, face-mashing cobwebs as I went, the first one on the trails for a while it seemed. I heard a loud splash to my right, and realized I'd struck marsh, though I couldn't see it through the dense brush. At first I thought it might have been a deer, but then saw, and heard, another crash from another vantage point. Ducks, many, many ducks, floated on the marsh. Occasionally they goosed each other into flight (can a duck goose a duck?) and a quick resettling a few feet away. Sometimes they moved in groups of goosed ducks.

And then the rain started, in little drops.

273. Marblehead: Marblehead Neck Wildlife Sanctuary

And so, the day quieted down. My abbreviated little itinerary, only three towns on this day, was drawing to a close. Fortunately, it ended in beautiful, historic Marblehead. Unfortunately, it came with the sighting of vandalism to the kiosk at the sanctuary.

The rain never really intensified, for which I was thankful. Typically, I wouldn't give a damn, but I had a meeting to attend, and it would be best were I not trudging into it mightily muddy and superbly sweaty. Oh, I was sweaty, but no more than usual. I walked the trails from end to end and all the way around.

I was alone with the usual gang, chickadees, titmice, nuthatches and wrens. A crow cawed distantly, while three mallards floated on the small pond. The grays overhead robbed the greens below of their vibrancy.

I couldn't help think while I was there about an old colleague, Barbie, who grew up in town. She always reminded me to put the emphasis on "head" and not "Marble" - "Marble HEAD." That's how the locals say it. It's like the people of Concord with Henry David "Thorough." I could go on. Oh, the things I'd heard around Massachusetts in 2011.

September 27

274. Agawam: Robinson State Park

(Stretch! Creak! Crack! Yawn!) Another early morning drive across the great state of Massachusetts, and this one dropped me in Agawam at dawn.

Once again, there was wetness to be found. But out of the corners of my eyes as I began my walk down the descending road into the park, I noticed something else: the first vestiges of foliage! Fall is always such a rushed time of year for me - back in Marshfield we run our big Farm Day event at the end of the month, and a lot of prep time goes into it - that I often either miss or just forget that I'm looking at the turn of the seasons. But there, on the ground, was the proof. Yellows, mixed in with the greens, indicated change.

This fact, though, was not the end of the excitement of the morning for me. There was a sign on the entry building that said to look out, that bears had been seen in the area! Whenever my co-leader Carol and I bring a group to Maine to see puffins, we stop on a specific road and talk about its history. When it was laid out, competitors said, "Aw, you don't want to use *that* road. There are wolves on *that* road." People reacted not by avoiding it, but saying, "Oh, cool, wolves!" and hopping into carriages to travel the road to see them.

That was me on this day. Cool, bears!

Didn't see one.

275. West Springfield: Mittineague Park

Norway spruces always tell you you're somewhere unnaturally planted and maintained in Massachusetts. That's not a judgment, just a statement of fact.

The park here in West Springfield was dedicated in 1935, and it's obvious that some decorating went into the early stages of its design. Norway spruces are more typical of cemeteries. They have a tall, robust stature juxtaposed by drooping, seemingly sorrowful branches and needles. You don't find them when you're just walking around the woods in the Bay State.

But this park rambles on! I was amazed to find so many habitats - woods, fields, a brook - as I spent my thirty minutes. I could have spent much more.

Two things caught my eye. First, a squashed eastern box turtle on the side of the road in the park. It's always so sad to see. Second, slightly less depressing, blue jays had begun caching. Yes, like many small mammals sharing their habitats, blue jays store food for the winter. If you see one carrying an acorn or something similar in its bill in fall, that's what's happening. They're preparing for cold weather.

Noooooooooo!!!

276. Westfield: Stanley Park

Well, well, well, if it isn't my old nemesis, Stanley Park! So, my old friend, we finally meet again.

Back when I was a young naturalist, green, wet behind the ears, immature and stupid, I thought I would take a group of folks from eastern Massachusetts out to Stanley Park to see the black squirrels. It seemed like a slam dunk, and something fun to do. The park opened in 1950, and at that time the designers thought it would be cool to have a signature creature. They went out to Michigan and found some black squirrels (really just gray squirrels with excessive pigmentation) and brought them home. The park became famous for them.

So I gathered up the gang, brought them two hours west and...nothing.

Seven years later, I returned, on this day, to exact my revenge on the little bastards. I was all set. I was going to take the first one that I saw, load up my slingshot with Cocoa Puffs and...wait, there was one. And there went another one. And I could see another one over there. And there was one more behind a tree.

I was surrounded. Black squirrels everywhere I looked. And maybe it was just me being paranoid, but I swear they were looking at me. Plotting against me, as if they knew what was going on in my mind.

I turned and headed for the hills.

277. Southwick: Sofinowski Conservation Area

And so up a hill I went, to visit the Sofinowski preserve. The day was getting warmer as I walked, but the wetness that had been there since the start of the morning was not disappearing. The humidity was on the rise.

The dew, though, can do some fun things. I spent a full minute staring at a spider web highlighted in wetness in the woods, wondering if that helped or hindered the spider's process, my guess being the latter. I can't imagine that a fly that can see the web is going to fly into it willingly, although I'll bet there are some suicidal bugs out there.

I could not linger, though, as humidity also brings out other things. Damned mosquitoes! I was back into swat mode at my turnaround point, a forced retreat to the field that had greeted me as I arrived. I knelt for a moment next to a stone marker dedicated to "Jim Miles, Supporter and Champion for the Preservation of Open Space, Town of Southwick." My kind of guy. Thank you, Jim.

Then, an odd thought struck me. Maybe I felt it in my bones. I was beneath the regular line of the Massachusetts southern border. Southwick is one of those odd towns that juts southward, altering the otherwise straight line of latitude ever so slightly. After my walk, I felt an odd urge to move northward.

278. Granville: Granville State Forest

To go north, I had to go west. Whether I wanted to be or not, I was briefly in Connecticut. The Nutmeg State. Home of the perennial NCAA champion UCONN Lady Huskies basketball team. And a state in which I used to live and work, almost two decades in the past.

I found a dense stand of hemlocks in the Granville State Forest, once I returned to Massachusetts. The Bay State. Home of the perennial cranky Red Sox fan. The hemlocks darkened the trail on which I walked to the point of eeriness for mid-day. I found, too, that most of the mushrooms in the area had gone black as well. And I found a perfectly gurgling brook with, yes, another sign celebrating the Civilian Conservation Corps. I'll say this: the DCR got their money's worth out of that sign's design.

When I emerged from the loop trail, I retreated to the Connecticut side for a moment. I had seen a roadside sign that looked like a historical marker. Sure enough, it was. "Milo B., son of Harlow and Mary Coe, died October 18, 1854, age 11 years. He was found dead in front of this monument supposed to have fallen from a cart in which he was riding and instantly killed."

Ugh. R.I.P., Milo. Now I wonder whether he was going into Massachusetts or just leaving it. Not that it mattered to him.

279. Montgomery: Montgomery Center Cemetery

Unable to find any open space in Montgomery, I settled for the cemetery, which is, of course, the wrong verb. I don't think I'll ever tire of walking burial grounds.

A young red-tailed hawk greeted me as I set foot in front of the stones. As far as I could divine, it was testing its voice, calling over and over again in that screech we hear applied to so many birds on television. I got to thinking about the species' history in the state. A hundred years ago, any naturalist would have been overjoyed to see one here in Montgomery. Known as "hen hawks," they were hunted extensively and viciously by farmers protecting their investments. As time moved on, the few that were left in Massachusetts retreated to the extreme corners of the state - the northeast, far west, and Martha's Vineyard - before making a big comeback in the last two decades of the last century. Now they're the default hawk in the state.

I examined stones, as I always do. I found a Civil War veteran, George Kelso, who caught my eye, but it was a Revolutionary War vet who made me stop in my tracks. "A soldier of the Revolution," his stone read. Name, dates, epitaph. Two hundred years later, that's all I got to know about this guy from his tombstone. In the end, is that all we are? Fifteen words and a couple of numbers? I started to wonder about my own inevitable demise. What would I take with me? What would be my brief final statement to the world about who I was and why I mattered enough to have a stone standing in place of my human form?

280. Russell: Carrington Road

Good gawd. The more I saw of western Mass, the more I was glad I was doing this little walking project.

I walked in the woods along Carrington Road. I found turkeys. They always make me laugh. You know, with their snoods and dewlaps and such. They just can't help themselves. I smiled at the Hull Forest Products building, always amused when I see the name of my hometown used in a different context than I'm used to. Stupid, I know, when your town's name is a common noun. Whatevs. I am who I am.

Before I left Russell, I paused on the bridge on Main Street, just to look upriver. Again, I know I'm showing my eastern Mass stripes when I say it, but I will never get tired of peeking at the mountains in western Mass. There's just something that happens internally, a stirring, a shaking of my core. Looking up the Westfield River, I watched a soaring red-tailed hawk - see? default - in the sky, which gave perspective to the grandeur of the landscape. In a way, I was glad I left so much of western Mass for last. I guaranteed myself some special sights as the year wound down.

But the day wasn't over yet, never mind the year.

281, 282. Chester, Blandford; Chester-Blandford State Forest

I believe it was B.J. Thomas who sang it, and it was the only song I could think of as I walked. "Acorns are fallin' on my head..." Probably a different lyric, but you know how that happens.

But it was true. While I never got dinged - can't afford to, with the number of concussions I've suffered - I did unwittingly dodge several thwacks, as they fell around me, urged on by the suddenly developing rain and wind. It was the same in both portions of the forest I walked in order to get both towns in.

The first stop was much more interesting than the second, which was much more vertical than the first. At the first stop, I learned about, well, the CCC, of course, for they were apparently like Klondike Kat's mousy nemesis ("Savoir-Faire is *everywhere*!"), but other topics as well. I read that some of the old stonework architecture on the grounds was not just of local design, but instead the direct result of National Park Service nationwide architectural planning in the 1920s, the "Park Rustic" style.

But the acorns were scaring the hell out of me. I remembered that story from when I was a kid, about dropping a penny off a skyscraper, and what it would do if it hit a person on the top of the head at full speed from 20 stories. Did I have to start walking in a helmet?

283. Southampton: Manhan Meadows Wildlife Sanctuary

It became rather obvious to me as I approached that things would not be working out the way I planned in Southampton. I had hoped to walk the Hazel Young trail, but somebody had gone a little trigger happy.

Years ago, some jamoke came up with hydroseeding, a quick and easy, yet barely effective way of seeding a lawn. It defies the basic laws of planting anything. To make a lawn, you need a few things: seed, water, sunlight, and compaction. The seed needs to be pressed into the soil. Having installed several, I know of which I speak. Yes, the process takes time, but it's a matter of you-get-what-you-put-into-it. Hydroseeding - shooting a green seed mixture out of a tube and landing it on top of the soil without creating that perfect environment - leaves a lumpy, uneven, patchy lawn. Give me a rake, a spreader and a roller any day, and I'll be happy to put in the work.

But I digress. Somebody had recently - very, very recently - hydroseeded the trailhead on the Hazel Young side, and had overshot. I couldn't walk the trail without destroying the potential for grass, so I went across the street instead and walked on the old railroad bed, with the goldfinches and the blue jays.

Fine by me. I got my 30-minute nature fix in beautiful Southampton.

284. Northampton: Connecticut River Greenway State Park

And this one falls under the category of "what the hell was I really doing at UMASS for four years if I missed this place altogether?"

I wasn't there yet, in my life's arc. Although I was studying history, and therefore certainly in the same exploration and research mode in which I operate today, I hadn't fully developed my love of nature yet. That would come later. In my junior year I sprained my ankle so badly that I needed reconstructive surgery; two weeks later I was in a car accident that sprained my other ankle. I had to learn to walk again about six weeks later, and did so in state parks and other conservation parcels. Long story short, despite numerous trips to Main Street Records in Northampton with friends, I never once glanced at the Connecticut River Greenway State Park with the notion of taking a walk.

I walked the old bridge near the end of my day, contented to not be climbing yet another hill. I marveled at the perspective, looking below at entire trees caught by the supports of the bridge in the flow of the Connecticut. A military jet blasted by overhead, as I sidestepped a bike rider. Being so close to Amherst, the old pain came back, the deep desire to be in the Pioneer Valley in the fall, to be simply *learning*, not worrying about the rest of the crap life throws at you after college graduation.

How I wish I could be back there.

285, 286. Hadley, South Hadley: Skinner State Park

I ended the day with a flourish, an hour spent in the Hadleys, with the most spectacular of views.

They were both near and far. As I stood atop Mount Holyoke, it all came together for me. There was the old hotel, the Summit House, just oozing nineteenth century tourism, a specialty subject of mine. Sadly, it was closed at that moment, and not even the deck was accessible. Below it was the view of the oxbow of the Connecticut River, and Arcadia Wildlife Sanctuary in Easthampton. Man, this state is stunning.

A ways away, I heard birdlife. I walked into a small grove just in time to catch unsatisfying glimpses of several warblers, four, from what I could count. Migration was certainly underway, and even if I had gotten clean looks, there was no guarantee I would have intuitively known which species they were. Young warblers heading south for the first time haven't figured out their plumage yet. There's a reason the term "confusing fall warblers" gets thrown into nature program catalogs every year.

And then, there was the plaque dedicated to the loss of a B-24 Liberator from Westover, crashed there on the mountain. As I stated earlier, of all the things that tug at my heartstrings, perhaps because of my love of history, maybe because my dad wore the uniform of the United States, are the tales of unnecessary loss of military life. Throw in an old World War II vintage plane, and you've got me hooked. I held my own moment of silence before the memorial.

And with that, I called it a day, a day I would never forget.

October

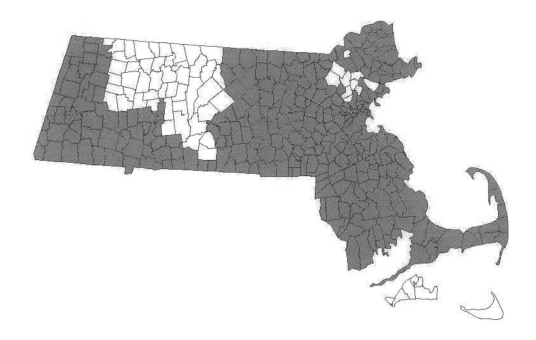

Papa G

I lost a damn good friend over the summer, someone who really put life in perspective for me.

I met him by accident. I was working on an article for my hometown newspaper when he rolled up in his motorized wheelchair and told me I should write an article about him. It wasn't his voice, though. It came from the little machine he had to type into so it would speak for him.

I listened to what he had to say. His name was George. He had ALS.

He had been a plumber, and over the course of several years began losing some basic functions, hurting his back, his legs going out from under him. After numerous misdiagnoses, he was hit with the term ALS, or Lou Gehrig's disease. Slowly, they all started to go, his motor functions. Simple processes became lengthy, deliberate, painful, eventually impossible. But George hung on and fought.

Most amazingly, he laughed. He spent his remaining years raising money for ALS research, even if that meant throwing a yard sale on scarcely-traveled side street. He raised awareness by taking part in 5Ks, by riding his wheelchair the length of the ALS walk along the Cape Cod Canal trail each year. He headed for Florida each winter, and emailed me about the manatees he was seeing offshore, the bikini-wearing women he was boldly riding up to and saying hello to (after all, what did he have to lose at that point?), about the Yankees fans he was tormenting.

When he returned to Hull, I joined him on his porch. The gaps in our conversations became less awkward with time. He would type, I would wait. Sometimes, we didn't need the typing,. We would sit next to each other and stare seaward, each with a beer in hand. It was as if we had been friends for decades. I loved Papa G like an uncle.

That's why it hit so hard when he passed on. He had been strangely silent - and by that I mean via email - for a few months, and it soon became obvious that he had been in decline. He had told me early on that he met ALS patients who had lost the ability to even open their eyelids. He never wanted to be like them. In the end, he bucked the trends, living almost twice as long as a diagnosed ALS patient should.

He was my hero.

And he made me realize I should never take for granted the simple act of walking. My God, he couldn't *walk*. He couldn't move himself from place to place using the basic method of human locomotion. That both saddened me and pissed me off. But it made me realize just how lucky I was. I had already made my peace with my wanderlust ages in the past, but I vowed when I met George to never sit idly again. When he died, I took a second oath, in his memory. I will walk as long as I can.

October 19

287. Peabody: Brooksby Farm

It took quite a while for me to take my next steps in Massachusetts. After finishing up September in Hampden and Hampshire Counties on my last run, I had out-of-state work to do. I spent three days on Block Island in Rhode Island, came home from that, and spent three more at Acadia National Park on Mount Desert Island in Maine. By the time I was able to break free once more, it was October 19.

My course was clear, I needed just one more day north of Boston, so I grabbed at it. Of course, there was rain on the way. I was by this time an official meteorological indicator for Massachusetts. If you see me coming, bust out the raincoats.

I started with a Cooper's hawk at Brooksby Farm, poetically perched on a chicken coop (they were once known as chicken hawks). A farm worker with a thick accent which seemed Caribbean to me pointed and smiled beamingly as he laughed at the bird and the ruckus it was causing among the smaller birds in the area. It was heartwarming to see such a big smile so early in the morning. Separately, a stalking cat was driving the American crows bonkers. Eventually I worked out with the worker where I could walk and he pointed up amongst the apple trees.

I struck sparrow. A bushy edge of the trail chirped with excitement, mostly white-throated sparrows and dark-eyed juncos, but I found at least one oddity among them, a clay-colored sparrow. On the wooded trails, cross-country skiing trail markers were up. Were they posted all year, or was this yet another sign I had to wind this little project up?

I could see that no matter what the long-term forecast was, the short-term one was growing grimmer. The clouds were ready to burst.

288. Lawrence: Den Rock Park

Den Rock Park wasn't the plan, but the sign jumped out at me as I drove down Route 114 and practically caused me to crash.

My first thought was of the Polar Caves in New Hampshire. My dad took us there as kids, and ever since I've been fascinated with big rocks. I think I'm finally starting to understand at least this one of my many, many psychological idiosyncrasies.

But as much as the rocks interested me at Den Rock Park, it was the pond off the back that pulled me in. It was a weird phenomenon as I walked through the year that I rarely had any good bird sightings, anything out of the ordinary. I was doing the *whole* state. You would think that I might stumble onto *something* that nobody else had seen yet. When I walked just the South Shore in 2009, I found a Mandarin duck. I mean, come on.

Finally, it happened. The pond was alive with avian activity. Both mallards and gadwalls swam by a beaver lodge. Yellow-rumped warblers called at my back with the chickadees and titmice. Three species of woodpeckers moved among the dead trees in the swamp like sections of the pond. And blackbirds, oh, were there blackbirds.

But there was something amiss. I had to focus on nine particular blackbirds that didn't seem right. Rusties! A rapidly declining bird in the United States, rusty blackbirds have a fascination with turning over leaf matter in wetlands to look for food. The flock flew my way, picking and flipping. Ha! I finally had a massbird listserv moment to report.

289. Tewksbury: St. Mary's Cemetery

Well, you can't win them all. I had tried on two other occasions to find the open spaces of Tewksbury, even one day while on my way to give a lecture at the public library (very nice place, by the way, and a nice crowd!). But I struck out. I finally resorted to cemetery walking.

But it was sterile. It was a modern place, no real landscape character. In a way, I could see how orderliness can be a good thing, but there was little to see as an outsider. In fact, sight was the problem. I could see everything from anywhere. There were no hills, no dales, and barely any trees. It was all too obvious.

The colors of the season, though, were still in evidence, highlighted by the rain. Here and there, a stone stood out, a well-executed design signifying loss or faith or hope. The foliage was offset by American crows, draped in black and squawking loudly, probably shouting emergency preparedness slogans back and forth in the face of the coming rain.

290. Billerica: Great Meadows National Wildlife Refuge

As I walked, wild animals were on the loose in Zanesville, Ohio. What a bizarre story. Someone broke into a privately-owned animal farm and released all the creatures - lions, tigers and bears - into the local landscape. The police were hunting them down. So, so sad.

In Billerica, I needn't have worried so much. Signs indicated I should be, for it was Canada goose, snow goose and blue goose season, but I found no signs of hunters anywhere that might mistake me for a honker. Besides, I was confused. I thought it was wabbit season. As I walked, I was *vewy, vewy quiet.*

The rain was still building in the clouds overhead, lending an urgency to the calls of the white-breasted nuthatches who were busily gathering food. It must be strange as a bird, or any other non-weather-predicting animal, to not have any idea when the rain starts how long it will last. We can plan. We can run to the store for milk, bread and batteries. They just have to wait it out and hope their food stores will get them through. Some species, like swallows and martins, are ill-designed for three-day rain storms and often starve.

Ah, an old house site, with a set of stairs leading to nowhere. How many of these had I found in Massachusetts this year?

39b. Westford: Nashoba Brook Wildlife Sanctuary

Yup, you're reading that right. It was bound to happen.

Back in January, I visited Westford and walked the East Boston Camps. When I got home and checked the list, I realized that I had missed a Mass Audubon sanctuary. Man, am I dumb. Later in the year, while heading for a lecture I was to give at the Westford Public Library, I tried to find the sanctuary, but was unable to do so. So I made a third trip to Westford, and finally found NBWS.

It was unremarkable, save for the itchiness of a pet peeve. Two women walked right into the sanctuary with unleashed dogs. With signs posted everywhere asking, nay, stating unequivocally that the practice is disallowed, they had no problem doing so, and probably did so many times per year.

I have nothing against dogs. But I do have problems with disrespecting a land owner's wishes.

I seethed in the thick air and walked on, checking off yet another Mass Audubon sanctuary on my list.

291. Wilmington: Wilmington Town Forest

Wow, it's amazing what brings back childhood memories. The Wilmington Town Forest was by no means a big place, and not nearly worth half an hour, but there was a cemetery across the street that supplemented it.

That said, as I strode back and forth through the forest, the swampy terrain in the now light rain sent me back to my earliest days of reading and a guy named Francis Marion, the "Swamp Fox."

He was a Revolutionary War soldier, a leader of "irregular" troops when warfare was fought in straight lines in open fields from a few yards away. I now remember being fascinated by his approach, his guile, his cunning, his ability to negotiate the deepest swamps with his men, his adeptness at angering Banastre Tarleton.

I swear, I must have read a kids' book about him when I was young. There was a series of stories I read as a sixth grader published by a company that ran with a traffic light on the spine. It had to have been one of them. Now that I'm a big boy, I wonder if there are any biographies out there I could pick up.

Thanks, Wilmington, for just being you, naturally.

292. North Reading: Ipswich River Park

It began.

The rain started to fall in earnest as I approached Ipswich River Park. It never let up. It was obvious from the start that mud would be the theme of my second visit to North Reading. My first, in 2009, was to give a lecture for the College Club in an old firehouse downtown. I took a walk that day, too. I saw a red fox in the town cemetery as I was staring at a grave marker for a man named "Deadman."

At Ipswich River Park, though, the story was more about off-road vehicles and the unbelievable amount of damage they had done to the trail system, not to mention the unnerving amount of garbage spread around the woods.

I walked until I could walk no more without completely soaking my feet, as if that mattered at that point. It was a strange thing to ponder. For some reason, although my feet were already marinated, my boots saturated from heel to toe to aglets, I was unwilling to step in water up to my uppers. Instead, I let the large puddle that consumed the trail deter me, and send me backtracking, through the mud, past the downed tree, over the ORV hills and jumps.

For me, it signified the end of a very wet road. But me and the rain, we was just gettin' to know each other.

293. Reading: Bare Meadow

I think I invented a new Olympic sport. I'll be petitioning the IOC for it to replace baseball, since the major leagues have screwed that up for the rest of the world, and there's now an obvious gap in the program. I don't have high hopes, but you can't win if you don't play.

Everything starts with an inspiration. I was walking through the field at Bare Meadow, turning to look back up a hill at a few birdboxes that were being mercilessly pounded with rain, when I started to feel a bite on my shin. Instinctively, I swung my leg forward. Stupid, I know. I had jeans on that were by then plastered to my legs like a cast. I'd have to do a lot more jiggling than just one show girl-style high kick to get it out, whatever it was, if, indeed, it was anything.

But wait, there was more. As I swung, I noticed out of the bottom of my eye that it was more than a kick, it was a punt. I punted a beetle. Up it flew, end over end, completely unsuspecting of its impending free ride, perhaps stunned too much to react just yet.

Amazingly, I tracked it down where it landed - a lone spot of reddish brown in a field of muted greens and yellows - and found that it had landed on its claws. What were the chances! It was perfectly fine, probably shaking the cobwebs out of its head and waiting for the world to stop spinning.

I was hooked. "And now, representing the United States in Beetle Punting...John (John John) Galluzzo (Iluzzo Iluzzo)..." Gold medal, here I come. Never figured out what was biting me.

294. Wakefield: Lake Quanapowitt

It was really just the edge of Lake Quanapowitt. With the rain falling from the skies in sheets, I resigned myself to the task at hand. Three more towns, no looking back. With this run, I would have only two pockets left, Franklin and Hampshire Counties (mostly) and the Islands. I would have to muddle through somehow, as the British said in the early days of World War II.

I walked in the cemeteries alongside the lake. There's an interesting juxtaposition of burial grounds on the spot. One in particular - which happens to be a Hebrew cemetery - is meticulously sculptured and landscaped. Every corner is crisp, every edge trimmed perfectly. The dark-eyed juncos certainly liked things that way.

Just beyond it rests a more generic, homogeneous burial ground. It may have been Catholic - I didn't check - but it felt nondenominational. It also felt shabby. Bushes planted as ornamental reminders of lost loved ones engulfed the stones they at one time flanked like good little leafy soldiers. Grasses were overgrown, trees improperly trimmed, or not at all.

If one didn't think hard enough about it, one might think that there was some sort of religious divide. But it was history. How far back did the old cemetery go? Two hundred years? Three? The Jewish deceased could only have been there for about a hundred years, perhaps a little more. Their mass immigration into the United States came around that time. There were many stones in the older cemetery for people who had been dead for much longer. Families move and change. Some people have simply been forgotten.

But this should not take away from the work our Jewish friends have done in honoring their dead. It was a beautiful place to walk, despite the rain, with character - and I'm sure a lot of *characters* - I hadn't found anywhere else during the year.

295. Woburn: Horn Pond

I finally reached a point when I simply didn't want to get out of the car. This was getting ridiculous. Two to go, I told myself. And at least it wasn't snow. I shivered at memories of January, February and March.

But the walk was pointless. And it was frustrating, if only for the fact that I had finally reached yet another place on my bucket list of natural attractions in Massachusetts. I had been looking forward to Horn Pond for months, hearing about it regularly from naturalist friends from the area. The sky was so darkened by the rain alone that I could barely even see the pond at times, and felt I shouldn't even lift my binoculars because of the chance of ruining them.

I did see a few things. Mute swans floated in the distance. I caught them as the rain lightened for a minute. I could also pick out a double-crested cormorant feeding in the shallower areas, swimming along with its body low in the water before ducking its head under and chasing, I'm assuming, small fish. I thought about how at times at Duxbury Beach I can see them darting about under the water, swimming with the ease of seals as they hunt down their prey.

A great blue heron alighted and flew. Why, I knew not. Typically I find them in marshes in storms like this one with their necks tucked into their shoulders, as hunched over and miserable looking as any animal can look. But something called this bird into action.

I got my thirty minutes in, but knew that I had not scratched it off my bucket list. Someday I'll get back to Horn Pond.

296. Winchester: Wildwood Cemetery

And so I reached the what-the-hell moment. With nothing buy dryness about thirty minutes away, I ducked my head out once more, into the Wildwood Cemetery.

It was an adventure in hills and concentric circles. I took note of my usuals, Civil War vets, comical appellations, people too young to die, the rich, the infamous, the good, the bad and the people that I just guessed were ugly based on their names.

I finally came to one memorial atop a hill that caught me by surprise. I didn't know how many cannons and other guns I had come across during the year, but the number had to be pretty high. The Ancient and Honorable Artillery Company and so many other fraternal organizations of ex-military men had left ordnance behind as reminders of fallen brethren, knowing that someday they'd be buried right alongside them.

But this was cannon art. Three, stacked together in a triangle, formed a tripod. A fourth rose above the rest, and from its mouth there shot forth not shot, but an American flag, resting limply but proudly in the raindrops, tempered as they were by the beautiful canopy of leaves overhead.

I figured that was as good a place as any other to call it a wrap. All rainy days must come to an end, and when this one did, I had filled in a big gap on my map. But, wow, did I wish I had a fireplace.

October 26

297. Barre: Cook's Canyon Wildlife Sanctuary

Boy, I sure can pick 'em. As I set foot on the trail in Barre for the day, it was already raining. And the rain was getting colder as the days went by. I spent so much time walking in the snow in the early part of the year, I made it my goal to get as much of this project done before the snow flew again during the coming winter. So far, so good. Fingers crossed. Toes, too. And eyes.

I could see my breath, for the first time in a long time. I also saw a gorgeous sunrise, granite posts with ringbolts in them, and trees without leaves on them. Fall was hitting in full force. The posts probably didn't care, as they'd lost their *raison d'etre* eons ago.

There was no doubt, though, despite the plain beauty of Galloway Brook, the singing golden-crowned kinglets and tapping downy woodpeckers, what the main attraction of this place was. The canyon! The falls that roared into the canyon were worth the price of admission. Bad analogy. Mass Audubon members get in for free. That would be like saying the sight was worth nothing.

No, it was worth spending a few extra minutes to start my day. I still had that whole Pisces/moving water thing to work through. I became entranced. I tried to watch how the water jumped from spot to spot. But the more that hit my head from above, the more I realized I had to move on.

298. Petersham: Rutland Brook Wildlife Sanctuary

But I couldn't take my own advice. I was so taken with the Rutland Brook Wildlife Sanctuary, that I spent about an hour and a half there. So much for pace. So much for efficiency. So much for lunch.

Somebody had been rock-balancing! I've seen my share of cairns over the past decade. Block Island had an epidemic a few years ago on its beaches. Mount Desert Island is famous for them, too, as hiking guide posts, and I'm sure you can come up with other spots that have them as well. This was a nice surprise.

I looked at the attractions on the map. Big rocks. Swamps. Ponds. I drooled on myself. Along the way I found a flock of 35 dark-eyed juncos, a half dozen kinglets, downy and hairy woodpeckers and the regular cast of post-migration forest birds.

I found a beaver lodge. I found the biggest glacial erratic boulder I'd seen in days. I found Porcupine Ledge. Out in the marsh, I heard the recurring sounds of a sora, a member of the rail family. I checked my migration calendar: 10C, October, third week. Late by 5 days. I'll take it.

By the time I was done, I had stepped on every inch of trail, was very wet, was very late for my next appointment, but didn't care. I'd "done" Rutland Brook. I couldn't wait to go back.

299. Phillipston: Elliot Laurel

It turned out that we had a serial rock-balancer on the loose. I thought I had left him or her behind at Rutland Brook. NOT! (Does anybody even remember what the old lady was saying that about in those commercials? I know she was supposed to be the next Clara Peller, or "Where's the Beef?" lady, but it didn't stick).

And I'll say this for the folks at Elliot Laurel (and, I'm assuming this means the Trustees of Reservations). They weren't kidding about the laurel part. I didn't see any Elliots - didn't see anybody, in fact - but the plants were everywhere once I crossed the field into the edge of the woods.

The rock-stacker wasn't the only one building cairns in the woods. Red squirrels had been at it as well, leaving their piles of pine cone debris by the sides of the trails, mostly at the bases of trees.

The squirrels didn't have to care about elevation changes like I did. My thighs began to burn as I climbed. At one point I slipped on a section of exposed and wet bare rock. To show you just how warped my mind has become after years of television and radio, all I could think, as I looked below me and saw the fall I almost took, was "Down goes Frazier! Down goes Frazier!" But not only was Smokin' Joe not there, Non-smoking Galluzzo didn't go for a ride.

Phew.

300. Athol: Bearsden Conservation Area

Happy Birthday Athol! It's not every town that gets to turn 250 years old.

I didn't have to go far into Bearsden before finding my story for this place. I was accosted by juncos, but there was a singular sound coming from high atop the trees, the exasperated-sounding cry of a raven.

We have three birds in Massachusetts that can cause consternation when taken singularly, the American crow, the fish crow and the common raven (well, I could also throw in some gulls sets, some shorebirds sets, warblers, sparrows, but you get what I mean). But put them side-by-side, and you've got an easy comparison. The raven is the biggest, the fish crow the smallest. No bones about it.

But there's another test, also bone-free. In eastern Massachusetts, we're pretty familiar with the crowing of the American crow. The fish crow is higher-pitched and nasal. While the American crow's call might be characterized as "Auk!" the fish crow might be simply put as "Aunk!" in a higher voice.

The raven, on the other, third, hand, is much more of a call of consternation, like your grandmother when you spill juice on the couch. "AHHH!" And it goes on, over and over again.

But I can't find anything bad to say about ravens. Any bird that chooses to fly upside-down for fun is okay with me.

Congratulations, Athol! You were also number 300 for me in 2011.

301. Royalston: Royalston Falls

Ah, another hidden burial ground, the Newton Cemetery. This state is overrun with family plots.

The yellows hit me first, as I wandered down the trail toward the falls. The colors of autumn were still in full blaze, highlighted, of course, by the omnipresent rain, the same rain which brought me to a crossroads, poetically *at* a crossroads.

Mud.

There was lots of it, and to date, I hadn't been a fan of it. But I really wanted to see the falls, and had to come to a decision. I had to make peace with the mud. I had to embrace the mud. Stepping forward gingerly, I let it squish around my boot (my boots hate me, by the way) and just at that moment a hermit thrush popped into view. I swear it laughed at me. I then heard chainsaws in the distance, a sound of hibernation preparation.

I slopped through to firmer ground, and found myself on a long slow tumble down a hill. The brook that I assumed was either the source of or the result of the falls ran at my feet. I kept walking downhill with it, but never found the falls. I then thought, maybe these were the falls. Maybe that was it.

As I returned to head back up the hill (burn on, thighs, burn on), I noticed a clear dividing line in the make-up of the woods, beeches above, pines below. It was uncanny, and across the breadth of the hillside. It was almost as if they were armies poised to fight.

I fought the mud, and the mud won.

302. Warwick: Mt. Grace State Forest

Uh-oh, unhappy ranger!

I didn't meet him, but he'd left his mark. Somebody had left a camping set-up in a trail shelter near the parking lot of the state forest, and there was a very pointed letter pinned right next to it, basically an eviction notice, stating that the shelter was for the hikers on the Metacomet-Monadnock Trail and not for permanent occupation.

I walked a bit of the trails, but knew I would never reach the summit of Mt. Grace, which would have been so cool. I just didn't have the time. I got within a mile or so and had to turn back, but was rewarded with yet another story about the Pine Cone Johnnies. Of course. They were everywhere.

I pondered the final outcome of the tenter vs. ranger stand-off, if, indeed, there was one, and thought about how Warwick was just so removed from my own living situation that I couldn't just pop back over a few days later to find out the results (the ultimatum called for removal by the end of the week). I guess I'll never know.

Any Warwickians out there? Anybody putting together a Warwickipedia?

303. Northfield: Satan's Kingdom Wildlife Management Area

Well, it was almost Halloween, after all.

I could not turn down the opportunity to visit such a place, especially one that the state of Massachusetts had so embraced. In our PC world one might think the state would want to think twice about placing the name of the region on a wildlife management area. But this was Satan's Kingdom in name on the map, and so Satan's Kingdom it should be called. I love it!

One might also call the place inhospitable, but that is not the fact. Despite the fact that the land in the area is rugged, hilly, mountainous, and generally ready to toss humans out on their wussy asses (and therefore perfect for wildlife), people do live there. The irony, of course, comes with the realization that Northfield was a Puritan stronghold; perhaps that's the point. The land was so uninhabitable in those days, so unforgiving, it represented Satan's Kingdom to them.

But Northfield has two other oddities. It's the only town in Massachusetts on both sides of the Connecticut River, and the only one, that I know of, in Franklin County that can claim possible visitation from Captain Kidd. He and his pirates supposedly sailed up the Connecticut to bury treasure on Clarke's Island.

Aww yeah, baby, pirates in western Mass. This project just gets better and better. I just wished there was someone there besides the juncos to enjoy Northfield with me.

304. Erving: Erving State Forest

And so it came down to this: the picnic tables were back at attention. Back in January, during one of my first walks in the upper reaches of western Middlesex County, I commented about the picnic tables at a state park standing on end, at attention, falling in formation for the winter. Here it was again.

And at Laurel Lake, three other things were obvious. One, the rain had stopped, but I could still see my breath. The day had never really warmed up. Two, foliage at this particular spot was at peak. It was just stunningly beautiful everywhere I looked, out across the lake at the cottages lining it, wherever. Three, once again, they weren't kidding about the laurel. People in eastern Mass have no idea how beautiful this part of the state can be. And I wasn't even seeing it in bloom. I was just imagining what that would look like at the height of spring.

I spoke too soon. The rain started again, but the sky was starting to lighten up despite the shower. I thought that perhaps I might be dry for the remainder of the day, if I played my cards right.

Eh, as if I cared at this point of the day, and the year?

305. Wendell Wendell State Forest

When the rain stopped for good at the Wendell State Forest, I couldn't believe my ears. There was near complete silence, the absence of sound I'd been searching for all year. But the water still had to fall from the trees, from the branches, from the leaves. There were drips, soft, quiet, barely audible drips tapping all around me.

I walked until I found a powerline cut, and noticed once again the preponderance of laurels. I started to feel like the Michael Palin character in Monty Python's "Dennis Moore" sketch. Moore, a twisted Robin Hood, holds up stagecoaches of the rich to steal lupines to give to the poor. Yes, lupines. He comes back to Palin and his sick wife to give them more lupines, and Palin blows up. "We're wearing the bloody things! The cat's just died from eating them!" I was starting to get laurel happy.

I finally came under an arch, a birch tree bent perfectly over the path in a mimicking of the St. Louis Gateway Arch. I took it as a sign that the St. Louis Cardinals would win game six of the World Series that night, if it wasn't rained out, which, I would soon learn, it was. Figures.

306. Orange: Tully Mountain Wildlife Management Area

I don't know what it is I love about these little mountains, but when I see them, I want to climb all over them. They look like little hedgehogs sticking up out of the ground, bunched up humps of dirt and rock decorated with trees.

Tully Mountain was my last stop of the day, number ten. I passed by a small pond and continued up the trail as it slowly wound up the mountain. With the waterworks turned off, the birdlife had started to move again. Juncos, the bird of the day, were the chirpiest, but blue jays held their own. Sadly, for one and all, the fun was about to come to an end.

The sun was going down, the light waning. That fact was as depressing as any other. Winter was moving in as the days grew shorter. I wasn't worried, though. As October ended, I had hit 306 towns out of 351, 45 to go in two months. I was well ahead of pace, and even had dreams of finishing before Thanksgiving.

I won't even mention the traffic jam I found myself in on the way home when a medflight had to close down the entirety of Route 128 for several miles. Sat in that for a while and went from one of the most peaceful days of my life, to one of the most stressful. Argh!

Serenity now, as Lloyd Braun said on *Seinfeld*.

November

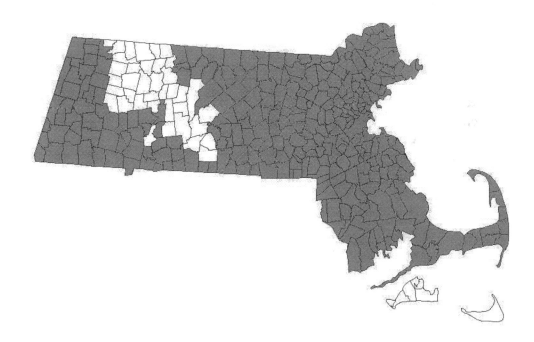

Not Me

I hope by now you've figured out that this book is not about me. It's not about whether or not I'm a person who especially or distinctly differs from the rest of civilized society. It has nothing to do with whether or not I completed this self-assigned task. No, there's something much larger than me that I've set out to do.

And it took me until this late in the year to truly figure out what I was doing.

Mass Audubon, the largest conservation organization in New England, wanted to know what it was up against. Land conservation is not an easy thing, for either the organizations trying to save the land or the owners looking to sell. It's very easy as the seller to get dollar signs in the eyes when a developer talks in numbers of lots and units. It takes a strong belief in the power of open space, of the preservation of a community's identity, to foresee land remaining forever wild.

All that said, Mass Audubon undertook a study of the "changes in land use and their impact on habitat, biodiversity, and ecosystem services in Massachusetts." They released their summary report in November 2003, titling it *Losing Ground*. And that was exactly the case.

According to aerial photography surveys, it became obvious that between 1985 and 1999 Massachusetts lost about 40 acres per day to what Mass Audubon termed visible development, i.e. houses, malls, stores, etc., being constructed. When transportation infrastructure and other less visible side effects of the construction were added, the number nearly doubled, to 78 acres per day. By May 2003, approximately one million acres of open space were protected in Massachusetts, but 71% of the wildlife habitat left remained unprotected. And the trends were disturbing: larger house lots for fewer people who will need, once natural systems are destroyed, more "water treatment, climate regulation and flood control," quoting the report directly.

So why was I walking? Because it was there.

I didn't set out to do so, but I became aware of the fact that I was proving that no matter where you lived in the Commonwealth of Massachusetts, in 2011 it was possible to take a walk in recognized, protected open space in every single community. In places where that was not possible – Plympton, Bellingham, Montgomery, among a handful of others – natural experiences were attainable in cemeteries, on country roads, along the edges of ponds and reservoirs in the cities. Would it be possible in ten years? In twenty? I did not know. Like Mass Audubon would follow up with *Losing Ground II* in due time, so perhaps I would with *Another Half an Hour a Day Across Massachusetts*.

No, it had nothing to do with me.

November 10

307. Nantucket

I played one of my aces, a trick I'd been holding up my sleeve. I called my friend Jeremy.

Jer and I went back about eleven years, to a chance meeting in San Francisco when we were attending the same maritime history conference. It turned out we had both studied under the same history professors at

UMASS Amherst, at the same time, and never knew each other. We had *sooo* much in common. We'd been fast friends ever since.

Did I mention he lives on Nantucket? It's good to have friends on Faraway Islands.

Jer picked me up at the ferry and announced we were going to Stump Pond. Sounded fine to me. I'd been all over Nantucket's open spaces, leading nature trips there for years, but had never been to Stump. Why? "It's a place only the locals seem to know about," said Jer.

We walked the Windswept Bog and found the pond, a few buffleheads and a good spot for Jer to cast a few times. He fished while I observed the nature around me. We walked on until we found a painted turtle oddly walking the scrub forest floor. We talked of celebrities who had tried to buy that particular piece of land, but who had failed for one reason or another.

And then he showed me one of the Underground Man's homes. The Underground Man had lived in these makeshift, surprisingly furnished subterranean caverns in the woods for a long time, until he was picked up for heroin tracking.

With only the possibility of doing one town that day, we did the whole property, walking for almost two hours. We had time to drive around the island a bit, chat, and brainstorm. We parted with numerous new ideas we wanted to tackle in the history museum world over the next decade, and promised to meet again in person soon, wherever that would be.

November 19

308. Holyoke: Mt. Tom State Reservation

It was a warm Saturday afternoon when I returned to Easthampton to deliver a lecture for the crowd at Mass Audubon's Arcadia Wildlife Sanctuary. I had led a bird walk in Scituate in the morning and had to be back in Marshfield for an owl demonstration at night. But I figured I had time to squeeze one town in on my way back.

I had to reach another zany avian history hotspot, although I'll bet that I was the only one in the park thinking about it in that way. I reached a scenic vista, went for my 30-minute walk on a veritable feather bed of downed leaves, and then headed for the tower. Before I could ascend, a photographer had to descend. He was wearing shorts. On November 19. As the kids say, WTF? But it was just that warm.

The shot wasn't there, he said, the light was too flat, so he gave me the tower. I scampered up and took in the view, breathtaking as it was, despite the overall grayness. Then, I thought about the significance of the place. Back in 1851, on a spot not too far from where I was standing, the last native

Massachusetts wild turkey was shot and killed. Wiped out. Gone. None left. It was an awful moment for Massachusetts.

Since that time, though, there have been several reintroduction attempts, including one that stuck in the 1970s. Turkeys are back, baby! As I thought about it, I finally decided to make a declaration. I looked around to make sure I was alone, then yelled, "I claim this mountain and this state for the wild turkey!"

Just then, the shorts-wearing photographer appeared from directly beneath the tower, and looked up at me.

Oops.

November 28

309. Gill: Nature Study Area

Life took a disgusting turn. On Monday, November 21, I received a call that my father had gone into a coma. I flew to Florida that night to be with him. I stayed through Thanksgiving Day, came home at night. He never batted an eye as long as I was there.

At that point, I had 43 towns to go. I could have stopped and called it a hell of a good year, but my dad would have been pissed at me. When I did my first book on walking, he read it and told me it was the book he always thought I'd write, full of personal anecdotes and observations. I had told him about this idea early on, walking every town, and he thought I was crazy, but was genuinely interested to see how it would turn out. I decided I would finish the project, but that I would do it as quickly as possible.

On Monday, November 28, I set out for the first of three very tiring days. I was stressed like I never had been before, but let the natural world work its healing powers on me. I needed mental diversion, spiritual grounding, emotional evening out.

I hit Gill, and found the small Nature Study Area near the public school. The fog and the mud made for an interesting combo as I tried to start my day. I had been preceded by large ungulates, or somebody walking in a pair of deer-toed shoes. I could hear distant mooing,

I walked along Boyle Road for a while, finding ravaged apple trees, and that the birds were in motion, cedar waxwings, downy woodpeckers, a red-shouldered hawk. I took a deep breath. It was a good first step for the now pretty well-defined last leg of my journey.

310. Bernardston: Satan's Kingdom Wildlife Management Area

Onto Bernardston! And back to Satan's Kingdom? Had I examined my map more carefully the first time around, I might have knocked this town off the list already. {Tapping finger on the side of my head} Brains!

My best nature sighting in weeks materialized as I turned the corner to find my trailhead. Five ring-necked pheasants wandered the roads! Probably not a rare occurrence out in Bernardston, but in eastern Massachusetts, good luck finding even a single one. It's a strange, double-sided coin, pheasants in the Bay State. We can thank Mr. Sullivan Forehand of Worcester for bringing them into the state in 1894, introducing a non-native species to be bred in Winchester for hunting. But they've been overhunted, and they're hard to come by now. Should we care?

Either way, I found a snowmobile trail that crossed onto a farmer's land, and some horse droppings. Chickadees flitted alongside me as I walked, keeping pace with my movements as I did my best to obey the local "Respect Land Owner" signs.

For more on that topic, read *A Rambler's Lease* by Bradford Torrey of Weymouth. It takes a lot, especially these days, for a landowner to open land to the public, and we should be grateful and respectful, lest we lose the privilege. Torrey argues that he felt he had a wanderer's spiritual ownership of local farmers' lands, and I couldn't agree with him more in that sentiment. After all, I've been known to wander myself, and know of which he speaks.

311. Leyden: West Leyden Cemetery

I could see the Leyden State Forest in the distance, from atop a high, open-sky road, but couldn't see how to access it. I saw cows, an old dog, and a farmer on a tractor in the fog. I loved it.

Finally, in West Leyden, I found the small local cemetery. Blissful! It was across the street from an apple orchard, and the birdlife was in a whirl. It was an all-American crowd: American robins, American crows and American goldfinches. Then - WHOOSH! - *they* arrived.

Cedar waxwings move in large flocks in winter, operating under the time-tested theory of "if one finds food, they all find food." The back wall of trees was suddenly overwhelmed with them. At that point in the year, and in that portion of the state, it was imperative to stop and look for the oddball, the Bohemian waxwing, but, alas, he was not there this time around. Too bad, it would have been a lifer for me.

Instead, I "settled" for 61 cedar waxwings. In typical fashion, they ate the place clean. If you've ever had a fruiting bush in your yard and had it attacked by waxwings, you know what I'm talking about. And just like that (and just as it should have been), they vanished.

Time for me to do the same.

312. Colrain: First Meetinghouse Site

The weirdest thing happened as I was on my way to the Catamount State Forest. I passed by a historic site marker and a humongous magnet came out from the side of the road, dragged my car into the parking lot and sucked me into the woods.

First, it drew me through the Chandler Hill Cemetery, where I learned the story of the first settlement of Colrain in 1738. Then, I climbed the hill and found the marker for the first meetinghouse, a small granite post surrounded by stonewalls. I noticed that there were trails beyond it and walked on, giving a wide berth to the guys working on the antenna building behind the historic marker.

I got to thinking about catamounts, once I got the history bug out of my system. They don't exist, or that's the prevailing theory. Let me correct that. They exist in human basketball form at the University of Vermont, but claims of sightings of the legendary big cat of the mountains have been dubious. The last famous Vermont "catamount" - a puma, mountain lion or cougar - was shot in 1881. Since that time, numerous sightings have been reported. And while I state definitively, tongue firmly planted in cheek, that there are none now in Vermont, I, of course, have no way of knowing. Vermont was practically treeless when the last catamount was shot, and it's now reforested. The habitat that harbored them has returned.

Wolves had been extirpated from Massachusetts 160 years in the past when one appeared in Shelburne in 2008. Nature can do amazing things, when we let it runs its course. Catamounts? In some way shape or form, I wouldn't be surprised to find big cats in Vermont, New Hampshire, even the deep woods of central and western Massachusetts.

313. Heath: Warren W. Smith Memorial Forest

Time for me to put on my know-it-all hat.

I found this place by accident, a New England Forestry Foundation parcel. The foundation believes in the practice in its name, in periodically thinning the woods to foster growth. It's a different approach than those taken by many other land conservancies, who just want their properties to remain forever wild, lowly-impacted by human traffic. A sign here at Warren Smith noted that the forest had last been harvested in 2004.

An old farm road ran along a stonewall downhill, and I followed that road. I noticed that every few feet, I found a large white, quartz or limestone-like stone tucked into the wall. Decorative? Hardly.

Sit right here on my knee and let me tell you a story. At the beginning of the twentieth century, Scituate had a copper magnate, a guy named Thomas W. Lawson. When Lawson's wife died, young, he buried her in a spot he called "The Rest," directly behind the cottage they used as their escape from the nonstop social responsibilities of the grand Dreamwold estate. They had called that cottage "The Nest."

One of the first things Lawson did in the days after her death was walk down to the beach and find as many white stones as he could. He placed them along the path between the main house and the Nest. When he wanted to visit her late at night, and the moon was shining brightly, the white stones lit up the path.

I have no doubt this farmer did the same thing. Coming in from the field, from a town meeting, whatever it may have been, late at night, if the moon was cooperating, he had his own runway lights.

I'll take off my hat now.

314. Rowe: Pelham Lake Park

The ground underfoot was spongy, and when I looked down, I got retroactive vertigo. I had been here before.

Not here, of course, this was my first visit to Rowe. But the habitat, that was where things were familiar. The ground was mossy, the hemlocks almost palatable. I was back on the Bold Coast, walking to Boot Cove in downeast Maine.

The birds, though, were not the same. Had it been Maine, it would have been all boreal chickadees and spruce grouses. In Rowe, it was black-capped chickadees and golden-crowned kinglets. The one oddity was a single pine siskin, a winter bird that hits us in occasional waves in Massachusetts. One chickadee even posed for me.

I stopped along the way to read every sign about the different tree species in the woods. When I got back to the lake itself I watched several common mergansers gliding along peacefully, a mountain looming over them in a fatherly, doting manner in the background. I didn't want to leave.

315. Monroe: Dunbar Brook

It's a good thing I did the Berkshires when I did. It had been one hell of a year for western Massachusetts. First, the tornadoes. Then, at the end of August, the region got walloped by one of the most bizarre of episodes, the tropical storm that decided to go up the Connecticut River rather than go out to sea. And I haven't even talked about this, because I never encountered its after-effects, the freak Halloween snowstorm that left folks without power for days. I won't even mention the earthquake, which was extremely minor, but which, nonetheless I felt in Marshfield. It was quite a year for the weather, and, I guess seismology.

Monroe, it turned out, was about as far west as I could get on this day, which was fortuitous for me. Route 2 had sustained major washout damage during the tropical storm, and three months later repairs were still underway. In fact, I couldn't even get to my first chosen hiking spot. But Monroe had haunted me since my Berkshire County trip, tucked way up there in the northwest, saying, "You ain't done 'til you got me."

I found Dunbar Brook and a hydroelectric dam site, now being operated by a Canadian company. I watched as two young men in hardhats poked, pulled and cut up branches blocking up the dam. Then I walked, and walked, and walked, high above the river, through the pines.

When I got back to the trailhead, I climbed one final small hill. Looking down again, I could see a tiny burial ground. Like I could let that pass, even though technically it was outside of Monroe? I visited with Lawson Legate and his family.

I concluded that there was nothing like the combination of fresh air and lactic acid. What a great day.

316. Charlemont: Hail to the Sunrise Park

I found the roadblock on Route 2. Luckily, it was just beyond Hail to the Sunrise.

I needn't wax philosophic about our state and country's legacy with the Native Americans. I think I stated my case clearly back in Dennis, many months ago.

This place caught me. I wandered in circles around the monument, taking in the names of all the fraternal orders and tribes that were represented. There was a time when claiming Native American ancestry through the "Red Men" organizations was a point of pride. The term has been eliminated, of course, with the rise of political correctness, and so it should have been.

The fact is that we will never know the full story of "prehistory," itself an obnoxious term. I often lament history being taken to the grave. I think of all the people who die every day who have tales to tell who either, A) were reluctant to talk, or B) were never asked about their lives. We get the filtered version of our planet's history, what we can glean from scraps of paper left behind, from photographs, and now from babbling bloggers.

But who chronicled the lives of the Native Americans? Their oral tradition is wonderful, but do we know the full story of Mohawk life in pre-Charlemont, along pre-Route 2?

More importantly, do we even deserve to?

317. Shelburne: High Ledges Wildlife Sanctuary

The fog that had bothered me early in the day was not present in the extreme western towns of my journey, but returned toward the end of the day as I headed back east.

As for High Ledges, it was a return to Nirvana. Years ago, a friend turned me onto it, and we made several daylong explorations of its sprawling acreage. I still have dreams of chestnut-sided warblers and yellow-bellied sapsuckers, of grape ferns (all seven Massachusetts varieties can be seen here), newts, dragonflies and singing dark-eyed juncos on roasting summer days. I've even read Dutch Barney's book about living there, *In a Wild Place*.

But, with only a half an hour to walk, my scope for the day was limited. I walked up the main trail, but knew I would never reach the overlook where Dutch's house once stood (I got to see the chimney before it came down, but now the spot is bare). Instead, I savored. I walked slowly and took in what I could around me.

The last time David and I left High Ledges, we had spent a rough June night sleeping in Rindge, New Hampshire, after giving a dragonfly identification class for Mass Audubon camp counselors. Unbearably hot, we tossed and turned in our cabin bunks until the thunderstorms started. They shook the building, violently. When the rain stopped around 4:30 in the morning, the robins started singing. We got up and said, "That's it!" and stormed off ourselves. We spent the morning at High Ledges, then got on the highway to go home around 1 p.m. A black bear ran across the road in front of my car.

High Ledges hasn't seen the last of me, and vice versa.

318. Greenfield: Temple Woods

Another hill, another tower. I don't think I'll ever get tired of that combo. Of course, I can't speak for my legs.

As the day began to fold in on itself, I climbed one last time. Atop the hill I found the Poet's Seat. The tower was dedicated in memory of the many poets who had taken the same walk to gain the same perspective in ages past. I'll bet theirs was much nicer, which is not a knock on Greenfield itself. I'm just saying the Greenfield of farms and fields and open spaces, the one that Frederick Goddard Tuckerman saw in the early 1800s, was probably more inspiring than city streets, automobile exhaust fumes...but again, it's not Greenfield's fault. Life moves on.

I climbed the tower, of course. Even in town number ten for the day, I could not pass it up. When I reached the viewing platform, I went from window to window, and finally was inspired to write a poem of my own.

Why, oh, why,
From the corner of my eye,
Do I suddenly see
Undies hanging in that tree?

See? Tuckerman knew what he was talking about.

319. Montague: Montague Plains Wildlife Management Area

I reached the end of the road, town number eleven for the day. It had been a soul-saving journey.

As I wandered the Montague Plains Wildlife Management Area, I stopped focusing on the specifics. Oh, things caught my eye, like smashed pumpkins, sights that would have made me stop and think, earlier in the day. About Halloween, juvenile delinquents and just how the orange innards ended up spewed across the ground.

I stopped to photograph the cleanly broken and recently exposed interior of a tree, to capture its story. It's easier to read from the top down, or the bottom up, even though I'm by no means a trained dendrochronologist. But I could see good years and bad years, lots of water, little water. I could see life.

I widened my personal lens, and saw the forest, and not just the tree. No matter what happened with my dad, I knew that this was a normal process. It made sense he would, *should* go before me. We'd had a wonderful life together, and I loved him like no one else.

As the end of the day came, I knew I had made the right decision to walk. I feared I was becoming a transcendentalist, a Thoreau in waiting. I let nature wash over me, take control of all my senses. I celebrated all life, while quietly, fervently hoping my father could reclaim his.

And I couldn't wait to tell him all the stories of my adventures.

320. Granby: Dufresne Recreational Park

I awoke the next morning feeling both tired and refreshed. My legs hurt, but like the cowboy in the old *Far Side* cartoon said, it was "a *good* kinda hurt."

Under yet another overcast sky I popped into Granby's Dufresne Park to find that it had become, in the wake of all the year's storms, the town brush pile. The wood was separated into think limbs, small logs and wood that could be split. A man driving a tractor was pushing against the tide, doing his best to tighten up the piles.

Beyond that scene played out a woodsy one-act play. Squirrels cached nuts in the overpowering scent of pine, moss-covered rocks and false turkey tail mushrooms stared blandly up at me as blue jays screeched their famous calls. I walked through it all on a nicely laid out trail. I even found some snow.

Yup, a *good* kinda hurt.

321. Hatfield: Cemetery - Old Mill Site

Onto town number two. I had no idea what I would find for open space in Hatfield, as the spot I picked was chosen for its name more than anything: "Old Mill Site." *Well, ya I wanna see an old mill site!*

I parked at the back of the cemetery and walked downhill. Whoa! Let's just say that if you live in Hatfield and have no idea where your 13-year-olds are after school, I found their hiding place. The kids had carved up a section of the woods to become BMX trails, a complete course with jumps and turns and I'm sure the occasional crash or two. Here and there stood artistically inspired rusted metal sculptures, made from parts from bikes gone by.

Richard Louv argues in *Last Child in the Woods* that we need to let kids explore their outdoor world more. This was it in spades. Give kids the space and time and freedom to create, and they'll come up with treehouses, design their own worlds of adventure, and, most importantly, understand what dirt and trees and plants and wildlife are.

For, despite the slight disturbance to the undergrowth in the one sloped corner of the woods, wildlife rumbled on. Juncos, red-bellied and downy woodpeckers, blue jays, Carolina wrens and goldfinches all greeted me as I explored BMX Land. Down the hill and not far away a belted kingfisher rattled its call as it flew.

Let the children play outdoors. Remember what we had when we were young. Take it from the Big Child in the Woods.

322. Goshen: D.A.R. State Forest

Uh-oh. Fog. Can rain be far behind? *Again?*

As soon as I set foot outside my car at D.A.R., I transported back to a 1950s movie about the 1930s. It was spooky. Through the fog, I could hear whistling, and occasional singing. But the air was so thick, I couldn't see the source of the sounds. More than spooky, it was ghostly.

I finally wound my way towards the pond, echolocating, and there, in the distance, silhouetted by the fog, was a man fishing. He was fishing in the rain. Whistling in the rain. Singing in the rain. And not like Gene Kelly. He looked like a 1930s drifter, finding sustenance at the height of the Depression. I snapped my pic and kept my distance.

I thought about the Daughters of the American Revolution and their many good works. In the past, I've covered local scholarship award ceremonies for high school super-achievers for newspapers. The D.A.R.'s past is grounded in an anti-immigration search for Americanness, but they've moved on from that. Let's face it, at the end of the nineteenth century, the United States was changing. Some folks felt they had to prove their American roots, which, of course, when examined juxtaposed to the descendants of the Native Americans - keyword "native" - was a pretty silly concept. Today, rather than a badge of nationalistic purity, I would think being able to trace one's roots to the Revolution would be a cool thing. I'm Italian. I can barely trace mine past the beginning of the twentieth century in America. After that, it's all written in Italian, which is all Greek to me.

I wondered how far back the drifter could go.

323. Plainfield: The Beach

So I hate this about myself. I grew up in Hull, a beach town. Scratch that - a beach. Three and a half miles of sand, bastion against the encroaching ocean, doomed to be gone in a hundred years if the climate continues to warm up. I know beaches.

As I headed for the Dubuque State Forest, knowing that access would be most likely impossible due to storm damage, I saw a sign saying "Beach Ahead." I instinctively laughed.

Argh! I'm a beach snob, I find. It's completely unfair of me to laugh at what others consider a beach just because I grew up on a sizable one, one, in fact, that residents of the Caribbean or Florida would consider puny.

Then I think about how it must be nice to have a place like this to which one could escape in summer, and I get all paternalistic. I go all *noblesse oblige*, if you know what I mean. "It's nice the little people can have their beaches." Then I get mad at myself all over again.

Grr.

While stopping in Plainfield in the mist, I did find that there was a Mass Audubon sanctuary there, but not accessible to the public. Phew! I thought I had missed one.

324. Williamsburg: Graves Farm Wildlife Sanctuary

And, boom went the rain. For the most part, I'd been dealing with fog as the day rolled on, but once I got into the woods at Graves Farm, the rain, and then the snow, took their turns. They'd burst, then ebb.

The trail system at Graves Farm was laid out in two loops, and since it was a Mass Audubon site, I decided to walk it in total. A quaint crossing of Nonnie Day Brook was the first highlight. I'd say the drumming pileated woodpecker was the second.

But a problem developed as I walked in the wet air. I grew a nose whistle. At first I thought I was hearing distant songbird chirps, but then zoned in on my own face. Yup, it was me. I had nothing to wipe my nose with, so, being alone in the woods, I opted for the pick and flick. I then got worried that a squirrel might find the discarded item and think it was food, so I tracked it down and put it in my pocket.

(Sigh.) What I won't do for nature.

Graves Farm has, on the Graves Brothers Loop, a few trees that stand out, and that's saying something, considering how many of them there are in the forest. My favorite was the grand white birch, but there was another one that looked like it was ready to walk away. Its roots had been so exposed over the years that they looked like spider's legs ready to go for a stroll.

Too bad it didn't. I would have enjoyed the companionship on the trail.

325. Cummington: William Cullen Bryant Homestead

Now here's a character for you. William Cullen Bryant and his family moved to Cummington when he was a boy. When he grew up, he went into law, and walked seven miles to his firm in Plainfield every work day. I have no idea if he stopped at the beach.

Along the way one day, he watched a duck flying overhead, and his poetic side shined through, in "To a Waterfowl":

Whither, 'midst falling dew,
While glow the heavens with the last steps of day,
Far, through their rosy depths, dost thou pursue
Thy solitary way?

Eventually, sickened by the court system, he moved onto newspaper editing, becoming the editor-in-chief of the *New York Evening Post* for 50 years. The city named a street corner after him, and then even a school. That's impact.

I wandered his property in the rain, mostly getting soaked in the open field, but wanting to know more, so much more about this interesting man.

326. Worthington: Road's End Wildlife Sanctuary

For some reason, this time the notion of bears unnerved me.

It made no sense. I had spent eight days in Glacier National Park with bear mace on my hip earlier in the year, and there, the problem was grizzlies, the baddest mamajamas on the continent.

I think it was the mention in the literature at the trailhead of scratches on trees at the first intersection. Black bears play hierarchy games. Whichever bear scratches highest on the trees wins. It's as simple as that. All others fall in line. While I knew the old standards rang true - they're more wary of you than you of them, be careful especially around mothers and cubs - and I had certainly walked in many potentially bear-ridden sites during the year, for some reason my head was on a swivel as I trudged through the rain at Road's End.

Nothing happened, of course.

I did manage to note a few things: old car parts that remained from an old farm; another peaceful, gurgling brook; more chainsaws splitting the distant silence; and a nesting box for an American kestrel pair. I wondered if it had been used. That species is vanishing so quickly in Massachusetts, it needs all the help it can get.

Bears or no, I walked the whole property, and loved every step.

327. Chesterfield: Chesterfield Gorge

When all is said and done with this project, I'll have a list of places that I want to see again, and will want to bring others to see as well.

I can't describe Chesterfield Gorge, other than to say it looks like one in a series of nineteenth century romantic sketches intended to capture the grandeur of the New England landscape. Something that Isaac Sprague may have drawn in the White Mountains, or Bill Tague photographed in the Berkshires.

The power of the rushing water drowned out all else that was going on, as it squeezed its way through the corridor of rock. As I strode along the well-trammeled walkway, I thought of the etymological origins of "gorge" and "gorgeous," as it seemed so natural to put the words together. I wondered if there was a relation.

It may be possible. Both words are found in Old French. The former meant bosom, or throat, or perhaps even something adorning the throat. Gorgeous meant showy, as in a necklace worn around the throat. I needed to find an Old Frenchman to confirm my suspicions, but, alas, as usual, I was all alone.

328. Amherst: Holyoke Range State Park

Two roads diverged in a yellow wood, and I couldn't take the Robert Frost trail due to storm damage.

So I took the Laurel Loop. Who's counting?

For the most part, the trail I walked was on an old trolley line, the great regional people mover of the nineteenth century. I often try to put myself on trains of old, and wonder what it must have been like to ride through the New England woods from town to town. The growth of the New England tourism economy rode on them, steam engines, steamboats and electric streetcars, before the mass switch to the automobile.

But what I thought about most as I walked in Amherst was what a fool I had been during my four years at UMASS. The inward pains that haunted me in Northampton stabbed at me again. This place was here all along, idiot. Had you just discovered your love of nature earlier, all this could have been yours. But no, you had to be interested in cheeseburgers and history lectures and college girls and John Wayne westerns and college girls and *The Legend of Zelda* on Nintendo and college girls.

OK, so everything has its place. I just wish that this place had been mine when I was enjoying those magnificent days of my youth.

329. Pelham: Cadwell Memorial Forest

The sun never came out the entire day, and in one way, that was a good thing. A lot of walking in the sun in fall can mean a lot of roasting, totally dependent on the number of layers you wear. There were days when I got home from these excursions basted like a turkey, a nice film of slime covering my body. I don't even want to mention my feet. I was already on pair of boots number three for the year.

With a cellar hole, a swishing brook and an old abandoned roadway at Cadwell Memorial Forest, I finished my second of back-to-back big days. I lamented the lack of trail maps of the forest, but then, it seemed that at the end of November I should have understood that trail map season had run out. Besides, my collection was certainly big enough after all the walking I'd done to that point in the year.

It had been 21 towns in two days. There had been no change with my dad down in Florida. We were at the point of monitoring specific levels of bodily functions; this was up, that was down. Either way, he was still in a coma, and there was absolutely nothing I could do to change that fact.

I focused on the project. I had 22 towns to go, and the whole month of December to do them in.

But November wasn't over yet.

November 30

330. Aquinnah: Gay Head

I awoke on November 30 well before the sun, and I headed south. It was *Vinyid* time.

Parking in the dark I boarded an early cross-sound ferry, then moved west down island, until I could go west no more. I reached Aquinnah, Gay Head, the lighthouse, the cliffs. I was almost blown away by the cold wind.

I stood my ground, with a spotting scope, so I could take a peek at what was offshore. It was, I believe, the best nature sighting stop of the year: northern gannets, gliding over the wavetops; harlequin ducks, hugging the shore; horned grebes, red-breasted mergansers, common eiders and more filling the gaps in between. The seabirds were in constant motion. The surf pounded relentlessly below me.

In the distance I could see Noman's. I could also make out the Elizabeth Islands, where I had walked Gosnold back in August. It was getting to the point where there were few places in Massachusetts I could stand where I could see towns I *hadn't* walked in 2011.

I could afford to be leisurely, as I had just six towns to do on Martha's Vineyard, though I had friends to meet, too. I lingered for a while in Aquinnah to ponder the Wampanoags, beach erosion, shipwrecks, heroes, cranberries and the red flash of the lighthouse, then moved on.

331. Chilmark: Menemsha Hills Reservation

Menemsha Hills came recommended by a friend, so I decided to walk it in its entirety.

I crossed paths with some hunters in a pick-up truck as they trundled down a road I had to pass over to stay on my trail to the sea. I reached one overlook, then another, and unwittingly found a quest box. From atop Prospect Hill - yes, yet another one - I could look back and see Aquinnah.

I wandered down the long path to the beach, noticing the walls closing in on me. A sandy valley formed around my shoulders, in my estimation formed by water runoff down the hill, but what do I know. At the end of that valley, the beach appeared, with its battered lobster traps.

The birdlife continued: two northern flickers, a low-flying turkey vulture, white-winged scoters on the sea. The wind was not letting up.

I retreated up the path, through the moss-covered trees, past the singing Carolina wrens, glad I had taken my friend's advice. Four to go on the island. Twenty to go for the year.

332. Edgartown: Felix Neck Wildlife Sanctuary

I found my friends at the Felix Neck Wildlife Sanctuary, and got my copy of the Martha's Vineyard Land Bank map. The island suddenly looked much different to me.

I headed out toward Sengekontacket Pond, remembering visiting Gus Ben David, the legendary first director of the wildlife sanctuary, on a previous trip. Then we discussed the old landowners, from Felix Kuttashumaquat to one boy named Walter who spent his days skipping school by digging out subterranean houses on the property and playing cards with his friends until sundown.

Hunters were in full, cacophonous force as I walked on this day, letting fly a constant chain of "booms" across the pond. As a friend said, it was getting late in the morning, and there was a good chance some frustrated hunters were simply popping their guns for the sake of it.

I found a dead tadpole on the shore, turned as if ready to find his way back to the water, but it wasn't happening. A flock of mourning doves burst from branches, hidden from my sight as I approached. I followed some small tracks in the sand that reminded me of a mink.

Could have stayed all day. Had to keep moving. Story of my life in 2011.

333. West Tisbury: Long Point Wildlife Sanctuary

Down a long dirt road to find another dirt road. The wind was at its howling best when I started at Long Point, and somewhere in the distance I knew I'd find the ocean churning and crashing.

Immediately I could see buffleheads and white-winged scoters on Tisbury Great Pond, by the hundreds. I had walked quite a distance when I opted to return to the car for a spotting scope. All that proved to do was bring the buffs and coots in closer. It didn't reveal any new species.

Still playing with time, hedging my bets against missing the boat home, I decided to walk the length of the trail toward the beach. I passed an old duck blind, still perfectly situated at about the spot that was closest to the mixed flocks on the big pond. Beyond that point the trail curled around toward Long Cove Pond, where a great blue heron tucked his head down and held fast against the wind.

On the dune, I looked southward for Bermuda, even using the scope and squinting really hard, but the earth was too round. The waves charged up the shore at me, but gave up when their energy ran out. I could also see the Woods Hole Oceanographic Institute's Martha's Vineyard Coastal Observatory tower about a mile offshore, measuring the air, the sea and the sea floor all at once.

I returned the way I came, but swung by the ancient Scrubby Neck Schoolhouse for a peek at the very end. Cute. Quaint. History.

Love it.

334. Oak Bluffs: Pulpit Rock

This locale was a tip-off from a friend and colleague, Suzan, at the Felix Neck Wildlife Sanctuary, and locatable thanks to that trusty Land Bank map I now clutch to my chest, all hunched over, eyes shifting left and right, lest anyone try to steal it from me.

The story of the Pulpit Rock area on Farm Neck, on the opposite side of Sengekontacket Pond from Felix Neck, is one of religion. Some of it is historical, some legendary. John Saunders, an escaped slave, arrived on the island from Virginia and began preaching Methodism. Bringing a new religion to an unsuspecting populace can be risky; Saunders eventually, apparently, lost his life for it.

Before that happened, though, he spread his word liberally. One of the local legends says that he stood on a big rock at the end of Farm Neck and preached to the African-Americans willing to hear his exhortations. I say "legend" only because there is no firm documentation that it was a specific rock on Farm Neck, and other rocks in the area have been identified as "the" rock. There's no doubt he spread the word. It's just a matter of where.

In any case, it's a cool story. The escape from Virginia itself was quite a tale. John and his wife Priscilla were buried in corn aboard a ship headed for "Holmes Hole," the old name for Vineyard Haven, and ended up emerging from that hold to contribute a significant chapter to the fascinating history of African-Americans on Martha's Vineyard.

335. Tisbury: Tashmoo Overlook

Yes, even here on Martha's Vineyard, turkeys have returned. Not only that, this year they've survived Thanksgiving. I found a flock as I pulled up to the Tashmoo Overlook, feeding and scratching in the waning hours of sunlight.

I reached the final stop of the day. I had taken some diversions to see some historic sights, including stops at the East Chop and West Chop Lighthouses, the Martha's Vineyard Historical Society, a cemetery or two, even Edgartown Harbor, to look across the passage to Chappaquiddick Island.

I exercised my legs one more time, but used it more for reflection on the glorious day I'd just spent than anything else. As I understood it, the view I was taking in from the overlook itself, ostensibly of Lake Tashmoo, was supposed to be better than it was. Nature, in its way, had blocked the view by doing what it does, taking advantage of soil, sun and water, and growing. In this case, willow trees were the culprit. The private land owners wanted the trees to stay, others wanted them down. I hoped it would get resolved without too much ill will besmirching the beautiful island.

Time to hit that ferry. Looking to the mainland, I could see the end of the road.

December

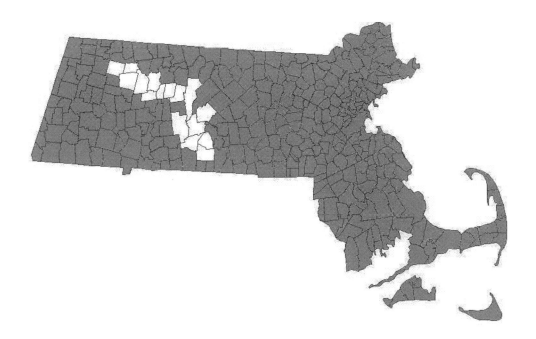

Dad

He woke up in early December. I was at work in Marshfield when the phone rang. My sister had stayed with him throughout, since we all flew down together on November 21. In true dad fashion, he shook out the cobwebs and said, "Did the Patriots beat the Chiefs on Monday Night Football?"

He sounded hollow and frail, weaker than I'd ever imagined he could be. He was a Marine. He had coached hockey players who proceeded directly from his tutelage to the Olympics. He had worked as a landscaper his entire life. I told him I would be there in a few days, as soon as I could get a flight and solidify plans. I would stay for a while as he recovered. We would watch the Patriots kick the Dolphins' asses on Sunday.

By the end of the day, he was back in a coma, and my plans were put back on hold.

I thought again about why I wanted to finish this project. My dad had told me that of all the books I had written - and he read them all, cover-to-cover - he said my first walking book, *Half an Hour a Day on Foot: An Obsessive Exploration of the Nature of the South Shore of Boston*, was by far his favorite. It was the book, he said, he always thought I'd write. I excerpt here from it a section I know he loved:

August 25, 2009 - Off-Trail, North River Wildlife Sanctuary, Marshfield, Massachusetts

It should come as no surprise that there are areas of managed wildlife sanctuaries that are reserved solely for the staff of the organization taking care of them. But know this: there's nothing special about them at all. We're not hording the best wildlife, the rarest plants or the coolest mushrooms. No, they're just utilitarian, the places where we hide the equipment that makes our trails look so good.

From time to time, though, something odd does pop up. Take, for instance, this chicken mushroom at the North River sanctuary. It's been growing on our property for a few years now. It's off-trail, but it's right up my alley.

Oh, that was just wrong.

But true. When I was a kid, my father announced that we were going on a *nasca* hunt. *Nasca*, you say? That's what old Italian families like ours called the chicken mushroom. And as you can guess, we ate it. DISCLAIMER: Don't take my word for it. Mushrooms can be very dangerous, and I don't want anybody making a misidentification and eating a poisonous variety instead. Do not eat any mushrooms unless you are 100% certain of what it is and that it's not poisonous.

That said, we would hunt. The problem was that we were not the only family staking them out. We knew where many mushrooms grew - on oak trees, usually damaged by lightning - and we knew that if we took another family's mushroom, we would hear about it. So we searched.

There were days when my father cancelled work. Our landscaping company would simply shut down and we would head out with pole saws and baskets. We'd locate some *nasca*, add extensions to the pole saw, he would cut, and I would stand beneath the tree with the bucket and wait for the 'shroom to fall. Down it would come and if it was properly wet (we always searched after a rain in mid-September) it would bowl me right over. I would catch it, but would get a smashing blow to the chest in the process.

My dad would then take them home, cook them up, heat up a red sauce and tuck them into a sub roll, eating the *nasca* like a meatball sub, slobbering and moaning as he did so. This became a regular tradition for our family, and probably dates back a century or more with the Galluzzos.

And I don't even like the damn things.

I knew by then why I was walking, as a statement for open space. And I knew why I was *still* walking. I wanted to finish for him.

December 6

336. New Salem: Bear's Den

I kept my cell phone charged and hit the trail, a complete bundle of nerves, but bundled with a purpose.

An old road and a curving stream met me in New Salem, back in bear country, a big switch from my visit to the Vineyard. An old cellar hole right on the banks of that stream told a tale of I don't know what, but would love to know someday.

There was more to the Bear's Den story than what I was seeing, though, through the drizzle of the early morning. I could hear its pages turning.

I followed a trail toward the sound and struck grotto and waterfall. Once again, Massachusetts, you shocked me. It was a moment when, yet again, I wished I was a better photographer. I knew I could never do justice to the spot with my point-and-shoot, but then, nor could I with $5000 worth of gear. It's a poor craftsman who blames his tools. But I had to do something, so in the low level light, I snapped the falls, and wondered if I'd hit the highlight of the day.

337. Shutesbury: Lake Wyola State Park

The mist intensified into a full rain shower as I stepped back to 1987. What was this place?

I can understand old buildings. They're usually economic indicators. Times go bad, people can't afford to build new homes, so the old ones stay.

If they stay long enough and are reasonably maintained, they become part of the local charm, classified as historic and eventually museums.

But this place had not only an old home, but an old barn. Even more of a story there. Barns were, and are, utilitarian. When they fall down, we throw up a new one more easily than we can a home, which requires lighting, insulation, etc. A historic barn is a treasure, like an old shipbuilder's shack or a backyard shoe shop.

And I could understand the golden lion I photographed. The house, a big one right on the lake, probably had a person with some money behind it. A guardian standing outside the door, a bit of sculpture to add to the scenery, was certainly within the realm of plausibility.

But how the hell do you explain the NYNEX phone booth? *NYNEX*? That company was bought by Bell Atlantic in 1987, 24 years in the past. I felt that if I stepped inside and dropped a dime I could call my high school girlfriend and ask her to meet me at the mall for a New Coke.

Oh well, back to the future.

338. Leverett: Metacomet-Monadnock Trail

I walked up the hill, quite a way, dodging tangles of trees that had hit the forest floor. The rain continued.

I heard chickadees, but nothing more.

Trail signs indicated that I had found the M-M, or Metacomet-Monadnock Trail, which runs from the Connecticut-Massachusetts line to Mount Monadnock in New Hampshire. It's supposed to be about 114 miles, but there are problems. More than once, in just that short section of the trail, I ran into signs stating that sections were closed due to private landowners requesting diversions. It must be frustrating trying to not only walk the trail from end to end, but organize and maintain the trail, which the Appalachian Mountain Club does.

As I walked, I found it a bit on the boring side, but let me qualify that statement. Boring in nature to me is still better than exciting on a city street. It was beautiful, but static, bland. But that, I would think, is not the point on a long trail. Not every step can be met with a scenic vista. I'd been lucky as I walked Massachusetts throughout the year, to take in 338 different views to that point. Had I taken one long walk, it might have been different. That walk may be in my future.

But I did, and always do, respect private landowners' wishes.

December 6, and a jogger passed me in shorts. Sheesh.

The rain had let up as I entered the Mt. Toby State Forest, with a lot on my mind. Soon, the sun emerged, to my relief.

I encountered signs along the way and learned of the role that my alma mater - I think that's the first time I've ever used those words publicly, though I've had one for nearly twenty years - plays in the forest. It's a teaching forest, where college students learn about forestry, soil types, injurious insects and more. It was quite a learning experience for me, personally, as I walked.

Raccoon! Sorry. Nature sometimes hits in mid-thought.

The combination of notions of UMASS Amherst, Sunderland and my dad lying in his hospital room brought on another memory. I had a wonderful professor while studying history at the school, R. Dean Ware, a resident of Sunderland, and he had recently passed away. I had nothing but fond recollections of him. He was my mentor as I wound my way into the world of history, a medievalist with a remarkable sense of humor. In between classes, I'd stop by his office and grill him on etymology questions that bugged the hell out of me. "Why do we pronounce 'one' and 'two' the way we do? Why does 'one' have a 'w' sound, and 'two' doesn't?" He loved languages. Once, in class, a student haughtily said he wouldn't be studying anything in Europe, that he would focus solely on the history of the United States. "What's that," Professor Ware asked, "three hundred years? in one language?"

I needed one final credit to graduate after undergoing reconstructive ankle surgery, and he got me over the top by allowing me into a graduate seminar on technical chronology. I focused on "Technical Chronology in the Anglo-Saxon Chronicle during the Danish Invasions under the Reign of King Alfred the Great." Great stuff. Professor Ware and I kept in touch over the years. Every time the history department called and asked me to speak to the undergrads about life with a history degree, I always asked if he'd be around. Every time, he met me for dinner. When we found out we had the same routine of reading the BBC World News website, it was like we had realized we were looking at the same star every night from our different homes.

He was a father figure, there's no doubt about that. I'd lost him, and now I felt like I was losing my own dad.

Ugh. I closed my eyes and let the sun cleanse me a bit.

340. Deerfield: Mt. Sugarloaf State Reservation

Crossing the Connecticut River, I began the long steep ascent up Mt. Sugarloaf. The sun had retreated and fog closed in. I think the wildlife was confused as to what to do. I heard seven species of songbirds, but never saw a single one.

I know now that I didn't fully understand the climb. I saw a trail through the woods that looked too vertical for my tastes - I still had five towns to go for the day - and decided to take the "easy" route up the road, trying to avoid the wet patches of slippery leaves that could easily turn the mountain into a waterslide for me.

Um, yeah...

I actually had to pause a few times. Wearing my winter coat, I was overheating, but didn't want to lose that extra layer and expose my now sweaty self to the cool-but-not-cold air. Decisions, decisions.

But I reached the top, only to find that the tower, at 652 feet, was completely socked in by the fog. If there was a view, I was not to have it. Frustrated, I leaned back into the hill and John Cleese silly-walked my way back down.

341. Conway: Conway Hills Wildlife Sanctuary

Was this it? Had I reached the final Mass Audubon sanctuary? Was I about to walk the last loop in the system? Yes!

I examined the trail map and figured that, if nothing else, I had to find the wolf tree. I had no preconceived notion about finding wolves anywhere nearby, or in that tree's particular past, but wanted to see it just for what it was.

It stood, and stands, for our state's now long-dormant-to-dead agricultural history. We still have farms and agriculture, but nothing to the extent of what once was. The presence of a thick-trunked, wide-crowned tree in the heart of a forest speaks of ancient pasture, and a time when that tree stood alone. The first one I recognized, when I started to really look at individual trees in the forest, was at the Moose Hill Wildlife Sanctuary in Sharon.

I found this one, and it came as advertised, up on a ridge, overlooking the forest. I could see, with my historical eye, cows resting beneath its shade in nineteenth century noontime sunshine. With my other, real eye, I could see a black squirrel. Cool.

342. Buckland: Mary Lyon Church Cemetery

Up yonder by the Deerfield River there lies a little town once known simply as "No Town." There, on a hill, lies a collection of interesting sites, all gathered together in one place.

I walked the Mary Lyon Church cemetery without really making the connection, at first, Then it struck me - "Wait! Mary Lyon! The founder of the Mount Holyoke Female Seminary!" My foray into that realm, now known as Mount Holyoke College, was a single dance in college in which I was too embarrassed to talk to any of the girls. Shyness was once my way of life.

But this arena, what I was seeing on that day, was what my life had become. While old stone after old stone enticed me to draw nearer, I was eventually pulled across the street to the stark and austere memorials to Buckland's fallen military men, on the grounds of the Buckland Historical Society. The building itself had dual entrances, dating back to a time when men and women entered meetinghouses separately.

Fewer than 2000 people lived in Buckland as of the last census, a population that had doubled since 1850, with ebbs and flows. It had incorporated in search of its own church in 1779. The residents felt that rather than move to be nearer to a local church in Charlemont or Ashfield, they should build their own and take on the responsibility of town government.

That was how much they liked the place. I could see why.

343. Hawley: Kenneth M. Dubuque Memorial State Forest

I stood at a back entrance to the Dubuque forest, incredulous. What the hell was taking so long?

For months, while planning my westward forays, I would stare at a warning on the Department of Conservation and Recreation's website. The forest, like the one in Brimfield, was closed due to storm damage. OK, so there were several places across western Mass showing the same issues, but for the most part, they had one-by-one re-opened.

I finally ran out of time, and had to see for myself whether or not the Dubuque forest was open and the website had just not been updated, or the damage was so bad they really hadn't finished cleaning up yet. As far as I could look into the forest, things looked great, but the sign said "Closed." What the heck?

Again, I respected the landowner, even if in this case it was me (and all other Massachusetts taxpayers). After all, if you don't respect yourself...

So I settled for wandering the road leading up to the sign - which was in the same woods anyway, just outside the jurisdiction of the state. By this time, you know me. I found plenty to do.

344. Ashfield: Chapel Brook Reservation

I read a sign on my way to Chapel Brook that stated that since the 1970s, the bear population in this part of Massachusetts had gone from 100 to 3000. If that's not evidence of returning forests, I'll steal a pic-a-nic basket and cause fits for Ranger Smith.

Of course, once I reached the falls, I was speechless. The last smart-alecky remark had slipped from my body as I descended the trail to find not one, not two, but three falls on the same stretch of water. I think I finally beat the Bear's Den for the day, but, in all honestly, who was really counting? Sure, they weren't the Victoria Falls of Zambia or the Birdwoman Falls of Glacier National Park, but they were more than enough for me.

I'm lucky I no longer work in 35 millimeter film, else I'd have run out that day. And I had one stop to go to finish off my trip.

345. Whately: Great Swamp Wildlife Management Area

With the sky still brooding in a steel gray, having forgotten that sunny breakthrough in Sunderland so many hours ago, I meandered down into the Great Swamp Wildlife Management Area, or, should I say, right to its very edge.

A hawk called above, of the red-shouldered variety. I had become an expert on their vocalizations during my atlasing trips into Bristol County during the past few years. But below me, at the level of my feet as I climbed down the slope, I could see smaller birds, moving in and out of the thickety growth.

They were juncos, of the dark-eyed variety, a harbinger of winter if there ever was one, for Massachusetts' lower elevations. It was, after all, December 6.

Six. The number had huge meaning at that moment, for it was the number of towns I had left to conquer.

December 7

346. Warren: Pine Grove Cemetery

This was it, the final day. I was about to make personal history. And, of course, it was raining. Why not? Why break with tradition?

I started in the Pine Grove and St. Paul's Cemeteries in Warren, taking note of the many large branches that had come down across the burial grounds. They were the final vestiges of the storms that had hit western Mass, a theme I'd been running into for months.

I got to thinking about the stones and sometimes columns I was seeing throughout the graveyards. It finally struck me that capitalism never dies. It continues into death, where those who can afford to be are buried under markers taller than the people who were beneath them in economic standing in life.

One final time, during this, the 150th anniversary of the Civil War, I looked for Grand Army men, and found Oliver, Almon and W.L. Switzer. I thanked them, waved goodbye, and rolled on.

347. Brimfield: Brimfield State Forest

I hit Brimfield, and was blown away, no pun intended. I drove down a road into the state forest and finally saw what was taking so long. Holy crap.

There weren't just trees down, there were *forests* down. Entire communities of trees had been mowed asunder by the storms earlier in the year. I had stood in the aftermaths of two major forest fires, one in Montana, one in California, but I had never seen anything like this scene. Perhaps it was a factor of the season. In both previous instances, I had seen the areas at least one spring into the future. Life was greening, the forests were regenerating. But here, in the rain, mist and fog, a few months removed from the damaging winds, all was gray.

I rode out to Dean Pond through another such meteorological battlefield. Hills were bald. A single house stood in the midst of a complete blowdown. How the hell did it survive? Where did the mammals, the amphibians, the birds, the butterflies go?

348. Palmer: Burleigh Park

Onto brighter thoughts, despite the weather. I was the only person at Burleigh Park, unsurprisingly. I'll bet, though, that in the right weather, in the right season, the place rocks with human activity.

There was a baseball field, and there were horseshoe pits. The road at the far end had been completely blocked by downed trees, but I could see juncos and sparrows hopping around inside the new digs. A shelter sported a totem, and from there I wandered up a trail into the woods, along a brook. Blue jays heralded my appearance.

Back by the main entrance, I checked my olfactory senses again. Did I really smell apple cider when I first walked in? I thought, in the tangle, I could see apple trees, so yes, what I was picking up was fermenting apples, like an apple vinegar.

I'd smelled worse, both personally and with my nose.

349and 350. Belchertown and Ware: Quabbin

And so on my final day I finally reached the Quabbin Reservoir. It was funny how it went. I started in the east, finished in the middle. Whodathunkit.

The Quabbin turned out to be a vast playground I wished I had seen before, that whole college days thing again. Oh, in the past, I'd gone birding with a friend through some of the famed gates, but I had never driven the main roads through the reservation. I'd never seen the monuments. Never visited the tower.

I spent more than its share of allotted time, and why the hell not? It was mid-morning, and ambition aside, I had only one town to go when I was done. I could have spent *hours* if I wanted to. It was an interesting, unfamiliar thought.

I walked trails, I stopped at the spillway. I climbed Quabbin Hill to find American tree sparrows. Amazing, on the final day of the project, I was still finding new species of birds for my list. I stood at the Enfield Overlook and thought about what had been lost.

And I realized I had one town left.

Final Interlude: The Towns that Massachusetts Forgot

Before I could get there, I had one stop to make.

Back in the 1930s, Massachusetts gave up on four towns, for the sake of the rest. The Swift River Valley towns - Dana, Enfield, Prescott and Greenwich - were flooded to create a vast drinking water reservoir, purported to hold 412 billion gallons of water. There were villages as well, seen by some historians as parts of the towns, by others as independent communities. Yet, whatever they were, they are no more.

Houses were moved, less important buildings destroyed in place. The flood waters rushed in and took the towns, and their physical history. From a plane, if one looks closely, roadways can still be seen beneath the water's surface.

But the most sacred items of all, the bodies of the residents of the communities who had gone before, were not left behind. I walked among

228

them in their "new" cemetery, on land just outside the main entrance to the reservation.

I wanted to ask them about their hometowns, the four Massachusetts towns (besides Ripton - but that's another story) I could *not* walk on 2011.

351. Hardwick: Patrill Hollow Preserve

And so it came to this: when you start in Dighton, you end in Hardwick. That's just the way it goes.

On the 341st day of the year, I hit the 351st town, and I just let it fly. The rain was coming down in buckets. I got lost on the trails, but I didn't care. At one point, I found my way out of the woods only to find an unfamiliar road, one on which my car was not parked. I ducked back in, laughing. I walked and walked and walked. I eventually found my trusty steed.

Back when I had taken my last steps in my 2009 project, in which I walked every single day of the year for at least a half an hour (save for 5 days with pneumonia in October), I realized that when people said to me, "Do you remember that day back in 2009...?" I could inevitably say, "Sure, I remember it well. I went for a walk that day."

Now, just short of two years later, if someone said to me, "Well, I'm from a little town out in central Massachusetts, you've probably never heard of it," I could honestly say, "I'll bet I have."

The sadness of it all, of course, was that I was reaching this personal goal that I wanted to share with my dad, but he couldn't hear me. I wanted to let him know that I had struck a chord for open space. I'd proven that no matter where you lived in Massachusetts, a nature walk, or a nature experience was not that far away. But he was still clinging to life, and there was still hope. Maybe someday I'd be able to tell him.

I looked south to Rhode Island and wondered. There were only 39 towns in that state, and I had three weeks. I'd already walked New Shoreham. Thirty-eight towns? That was a long weekend for me. But I wanted to be ready to fly to my dad's side at a moment's notice, and decided to hold off.

In the meantime, eight words would ring through my head: "I came, I saw, I kicked its Mass!"

Epilogue

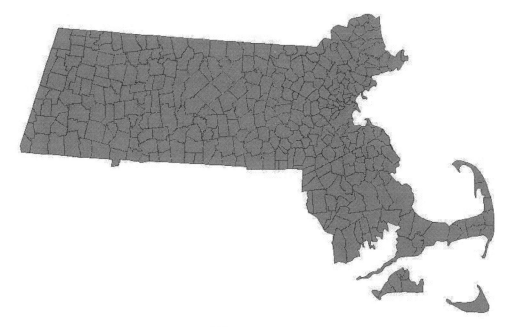

Done

So I proved my mother right. It turned out I was special. I did something nobody had ever done before, or nobody was dumb enough to try. I was the first person ever to visit every town in Massachusetts in one year *and write a book about it*, and that's what made me special. At least that's what the juice box sucking 11-year-old in me wanted to say.

But did the adult me think that I was alone? Not for one second.

The day after I finished the project - remarkably, as I was late on finishing the blogging side of it, with my dad's illness consuming most of my time - I got an email from Bobb. There was a Massachusetts 351 Club forming, meeting in Rutland, in the geographic center of the state. Would I be interested in joining? Hell yeah, I would. There were no prerequisites to membership. One needed only an interest in visiting all 351 towns. Vermont already had a 251 Club by then. I doubted that Rhode Island had a 39 Club, but I couldn't be sure.

Plenty of other people had attempted, or were attempting to visit all 351 Massachusetts towns. My goal was a 30-minute walk on open space and a photograph in each town in one calendar year. Others just wanted the perfect image. I've since met others who want the perfect local story, and others who are after postmarks, or pictures of all the town halls. One acquaintance is attempting to find a Carolina wren in every town in Massachusetts. Once he heard about my project, he sent me his list of towns where he'd struck out. Sadly, though I'd kept bird lists, I couldn't help him. Another friend, Mark, is on a quest to find a Virginia rail in every town - now *that's* dedication to obsession. I hope I never get as crazy as he is.

Yes, I would love to meet the other 351ers, people who, for whatever reason, wanted to touch them all. To date, we haven't gotten together, but we will.

When I see them, I'll tell them the same thing I tell everybody else I meet. Get out and enjoy Massachusetts! Open space surrounds us - for now - and it's there for our use. Bike it. Walk it. Hike it. Bird it. Kayak it. Surf it. Photograph it. Film it. Smell it. Touch it. Hear what it has to say. See it before it's gone.

Break it down into whatever chunks you like - towns, counties, ecoregions, watersheds, whatever - and explore the nature of Massachusetts.

Once you get started, if you have any questions, I'll be here: johnjgalluzzo@hotmail.com.

I want to know your stories.

About the Author

John Galluzzo is the author of thirty-five books, mostly on the local history of the towns south of Boston, Massachusetts. For a fulltime living he designs and leads nature tours for Mass Audubon, both locally and to various destinations in the northeast. He contributes regularly to *South Shore Living*, *Ships Monthly* and other magazines, and has kept a weekly column in his hometown newspaper for more than ten years. In his spare time, he's the Executive Director of the United States Life-Saving Service Heritage Association and editor of their magazine, *Wreck & Rescue Journal*, and serves as the Awards Committee Chairman for the Foundation for Coast Guard History. He lives in Weymouth, Massachusetts with his wife Michelle and the pride and joy of his life (respectfully), Anthony and Benjamin.

Map

Wondering where the heck all these places are? The author has created an online map that can be accessed by emailing him at johnjgalluzzo@hotmail.com.

In Memory

Cpl. Robert Francis Galluzzo

United States Marine Corps
Purple Heart, Vietnam, 1966-67
January 29, 1947 to January 2, 2012
My Dad.

Made in the USA
Charleston, SC
22 September 2012